The sources used included all available and pertinent Russian and American materials—unpublished private papers, interviews with a number of the participants, memoirs, diplomatic documents, newspapers and magazines in both countries and in Europe, including Communist publications.

The author is a member of the department of history at the University of Colorado.

The Origins of
Soviet-American Diplomacy

The Origins of Soviet-American Diplomacy

BY

ROBERT PAUL BROWDER

1953

PRINCETON UNIVERSITY PRESS

PRINCETON, NEW JERSEY

Printed in the United States of America
by Princeton University Press, Princeton, New Jersey

TO MOTHER

PREFACE

THIS is a study of the background, motivations, and actual negotiation of the establishment of diplomatic relations between the Union of Soviet Socialist Republics and the United States in 1933. Chapter 1 deals, by way of introduction, with the years 1917-1929, tracing the most significant events and trends in the unofficial relations between the two nations following the Bolshevik Revolution. In the succeeding chapters, I have attempted to enumerate and evaluate the conditions which prompted the Soviet Union to intensify its campaign for American friendship after 1929 and the United States eventually to reverse its sixteen-year policy of nonrecognition. I have also described the course of the conversations that took place in Washington in November 1933—the first of many controversial Soviet-American sessions—and the agreements which accompanied recognition. Chapters 8 and 9 give an account of the disillusionment that followed, and Chapter 10 is a genuflection to historical hindsight.

Admittedly, the subject matter of this account invites comparison with more recent events. And, although I must agree that much of the story has a familiar ring to modern ears, I would also caution the reader that every situation has its own setting and its own lines even when some of the actors remain the same. The historian knows only too well that the lessons of the past can be but imperfect guides to the present.

In the preparation of this book, I have used both Russian and American materials. Of course, no opportunity was afforded to consult whatever materials may be deposited in the Soviet Archives, but the official Russian documents that have been published as well as the statements and writings of

Soviet leaders and influential spokesmen were of considerable value.

Russian newspapers and other periodicals were used as a source both of information and of government opinion, while Comintern publications and Communist organs both in Russia and abroad served to reveal the opposite face of Soviet foreign policy. A similar investigation was made of American periodicals in an attempt to discover contemporary attitudes on the Russian question.

United States government documents were, of course, used extensively. However, the unpublished records of the State Department were not consulted. Dr. Bernadotte E. Schmitt of the Division of Historical Policy Research of the Department of State, who was familiar with the materials in the archives of the Department, advised me that I would find an investigation of this material unrewarding, for the essential documents concerning the recognition by the United States of the Soviet Union have been published in *Papers Relating to the Foreign Relations of the United States, 1933*, Vol. II. So far as I have been able to discover, the Department of State had little to do with recognition, although several of its officers played important roles in the event, and the decision to recognize Soviet Russia was taken and the subsequent negotiations were conducted by the White House.

Fortunately, I was able to make use of the Roosevelt Papers at Hyde Park, though they too proved to be disappointing, owing to the well-known reluctance of the late president to make memoranda of conversations and conferences.

I am greatly obligated to Professor Schmitt for his aid and advice on several matters pertaining to this study, and to Mr. Herman Kahn, Director of the Franklin D. Roosevelt Library, who carefully collected and microfilmed more than six hundred documents bearing on my subject. I also wish to express my appreciation to the Honorable Herbert Hoover for granting permission to use his private papers in the Hoover Library. Valuable information, for which I am likewise indebted, was supplied by the Honorable William Phillips, former Under Secretary of State; the Honorable William C. Bullitt, former Ambassador to the Soviet Union; Mr. Robert F. Kelley, former Chief of the Division of Eastern European Affairs of the Department of State; and Mr. Louis Fischer, foreign correspondent, author, and expert on Soviet affairs.

I am especially grateful to Professor Michael Karpovich of Harvard University, who acted as advisor during the initial research and writing, for his constructive criticism of the manuscript, wise counsel, and encouragement in the preparation of this work. I also wish to thank Professor Thomas A. Bailey of Stanford University, who read the manuscript with particular care and made many valuable suggestions. It should be unnecessary to add that I alone am responsible for such errors or omissions as may occur in this volume and for the use of the information which was so graciously given me.

Acknowledgment is made to the following publishers for permission to reprint excerpts from copyrighted materials: Harper and Brothers, for the use of *War and Peace, Presidential Messages, Addresses, and Public Papers (1917-1924) by Woodrow Wilson*, edited by Ray Stannard Baker and William E. Dodd (1927); The University of Chicago Press, for the use of Samuel N. Harper, *The Russia I Believe In* (1945); Random House, for the use of Franklin D. Roosevelt, *The Public Papers and Addresses of Franklin D. Roosevelt* (1938-1950); Charles Scribner's Sons, for the use of Benjamin Gitlow, *The Whole of Their Lives* (1948); Duell, Sloan and Pearce, Inc., for the use of Louis Fischer, *Men and Politics* (1941); Simon and Schuster, Inc., for the use of Joseph C. Grew, *Ten Years in Japan* (1944); The Macmillan Company, for the use of Cordell Hull, *The Memoirs of Cordell Hull* (1948); *Foreign Affairs*, for the use of the articles by Karl Radek, "The War in the Far East," x (1932), and "The Basis of Soviet Foreign Policy," xII (1934); *The Nation*, for the use of articles by Louis Fischer in the is-

PREFACE

sues of November 2, 1932, December 28, 1932, and March 29, 1933; *Collier's*, for the use of the article by Henry J. Morgenthau, "The Morgenthau Diaries," in the issue of October 11, 1947; and Mr. Roy W. Howard and the Scripps-Howard Newspapers for the use of Mr. Howard's interview with Joseph Stalin in the *New York World-Telegram*, March 4, 1936. Portions of several chapters first appeared in the *Pacific Historical Review* and the *Russian Review*.

For the most part, my research was carried on at the Hoover Institute and Library, Stanford University, where I held a Rockefeller Foundation Fellowship in Slavic Studies. It is a pleasure to record my appreciation to the Institute for the grant and to the staff of the Library for their never-failing courtesy in helping me to make full use of the unique Russian collection deposited there. Another expression of gratitude is owed to the Council on Research and Creative Work of the University of Colorado for the award of a grant-in-aid. My wife, Rosemary Meininger Browder, typed several drafts of the manuscript, offered invaluable aid in editing, and in innumerable other ways contributed to the successful completion of the volume. My debt to her is incalculable.

Boulder, Colorado   ROBERT PAUL BROWDER
September 1952

CONTENTS

The Origins of
Soviet-American Diplomacy

CHAPTER 1

YEARS OF SILENCE, 1917-1929

Two weeks after the Bolshevik *coup d'état* of November 7, 1917, Commissar of Foreign Affairs Leon Trotsky addressed a communication to the diplomatic corps in Petrograd, announcing the formation of the Soviet Government and requesting its recognition.[1] The American Ambassador David R. Francis, correctly anticipating the policy of his government, ignored the message. His silence marked the beginning of a sixteen-year interruption in diplomatic relations between Russia and the United States.

Washington was not alone in its initial opposition to the new regime. All of the Allied Powers, motivated by diplomatic and military considerations and strongly influenced by an emotional and political antipathy toward Bolshevik doctrines, refused to deal officially with the Soviets. Indeed, their hostility toward the Soviets eventually expressed itself in support of counterrevolutionary forces in Russia and in armed intervention. But tempers cooled in the peaceful and prosperous 1920's. It became increasingly difficult to ignore the existence of the Soviet Union in the conduct of commercial and international relations. One by one the other great powers renewed diplomatic ties with Russia. At the end of the decade, only the United States had declined to explore the path of reconciliation.

During the first months of Communist rule in Russia, Washington adopted a policy of watchful waiting. The American

[1] Iu. V. Kliuchnikov, and Andrei Sabanin (eds.), *Mezhdunarodnaia politika noveishego vremeni v dogovorakh, notakh i deklaratsiiakh* (Moscow. 1925-1928), II, 91-92.

3

government shared the grave concern of its allies over the possibility of a separate peace, and was more disturbed than they by the violent and unconstitutional nature of the Lenin regime. In view of the historic role of the United States as the champion of popular government, such a reaction was not unnatural. Yet the absolutism of the Tsars had never been so repugnant to American ideals as to precipitate a rupture in the relations between the two nations in the years following the welcomed recognition of the young republic by Alexander I in 1809.

The answer to this apparent contradiction lies perhaps in the high hopes generated in America for the establishment of a democratic government in Russia. Tsarism, which had collapsed by virtue of its own ineffectiveness in March 1917, had been replaced by a provisional government, dedicated to the introduction of western political freedoms. It was this government that the Bolsheviks had overthrown before it could put its constructive program into operation. By their betrayal of budding Russian democracy, the Communists put themselves beyond the pale of American friendship.

In addition, the political, economic, and social tenets of Bolshevism, with its avowed goal of universalism through world revolution, appeared to threaten the security of every other nation. Whatever the relative evils of Romanov absolutism and Marxian radicalism, there seemed to be little question that the dynamic ideology of the latter was the more frightening in its international implications.

Still, together with the mounting distrust of Soviet intentions and doctrine, there persisted in Washington a hope that the Russian people would speedily repudiate their new rulers—or at least force them to continue the war against Germany. It was this hope which motivated many of the actions and decisions in American policy toward Russia during the first months of the Soviet regime, and which in turn served to confuse the Communist authorities as to American intentions.

4

Combined with Soviet dissimulation and opportunism, it not unnaturally led to distrust, misunderstanding, and ambivalence of purpose on the part of both nations in their unofficial relations with one another.

On the Soviet side, ominous declarations and decisions were made with alarming rapidity. In vain the Allies, and especially the United States, strove to stem the tide of disaster. On November 8, 1917, the Bolsheviks issued an appeal for a general peace without annexations or indemnities. When the Allies turned a deaf ear to the proposal, the Soviets entered into negotiations with Germany and, on December 15, signed an armistice preparatory to a separate peace. Meantime, Trotsky had begun a propaganda campaign designed to reveal the predatory aims of the Allies, supporting his statements by the publication of the secret treaties in the Foreign Office archives. The Allied governments, uneasy about the effect of these disclosures upon morale in their own ranks, called upon President Wilson to frame an answer to the charges. On January 8, 1918, Wilson went before the American Congress and presented his historic Fourteen Points for a just and lasting peace. Specifically referring to Russia in point six, he demanded that she be given full opportunity to decide her own future without foreign interference. "The treatment accorded to Russia by her sister nations in the months to come," the President declared, "will be the acid test of their goodwill. . . ."[2]

Whatever effect Wilson's words may have had upon the Allied peoples, they did not deter the Soviets from continuing their negotiations with Germany. Although the Russians were appalled at the severity of the German terms, the disintegration of their army and the need for internal consolidation forced the issue. Reluctantly the Soviet leaders concluded that

[2] Ray Stannard Baker and William E. Dodd (eds.), *War and Peace, Presidential Messages, Addresses, and Public Papers (1917-1924) by Woodrow Wilson* (New York, 1927), I, 159-160.

there was no practical alternative to submission and, on March 3, 1918, signed the Treaty of Brest-Litovsk.

The Treaty had still to be ratified by the Congress of Soviets, and its punitive provisions gave the Allies cause to hope that ratification would not be forthcoming. In an effort to demonstrate the good will of America toward the Russian people and at the same time perhaps forestall the final act that would put the treaty into force, Wilson addressed a message to the Soviet on March 11, 1918, stating that despite Washington's inability to render direct aid, the United States would "avail itself of every opportunity to secure for Russia once more complete sovereignty and independence in her own affairs."[3] The reply was reportedly characterized by Grigorii Zinoviev, President of the Petrograd Soviet, as "a slap in the face."[4] It expressed the gratitude of the Congress to "the laboring and exploited classes" of the United States for their message sent by President Wilson and voiced the hope that "the happy time is not far distant when the toiling masses of all bourgeois countries will throw off the yoke of capitalism and establish a socialistic order of society. . . ."[5]

Yet even as this unpleasant communication was being drafted, Trotsky was inquiring of Francis, through Colonel Raymond Robins, the head of the American Red Cross Mission to Russia, what aid Moscow might expect from the United States should the Soviet reject the treaty or repudiate it after ratification because of German rapaciousness. When the Ambassador wired for instructions, Washington responded that the recent pronouncements of the President constituted an adequate answer.[6] The United States refused to commit itself further without concrete evidence of Russia's intention to con-

[3] *Papers Relating to the Foreign Relations of the United States, 1918, Russia* (Washington, 1931), I, 395-396. This series hereafter cited as *Foreign Relations.*

[4] *ibid.*, 486.

[5] Kliuchnikov and Sabanin, *op. cit.*, II, 135.

[6] *Foreign Relations, 1918, Russia,* I, 397-398, 402.

tinue the struggle. It is doubtful that a favorable American answer would have altered the ultimate Soviet decision, but on the other hand, the Bolsheviks were obviously in no position to oppose German might without outside aid.[7] On March 16, 1918, the Soviet Congress voted to accept the onerous terms of Brest-Litovsk.

After Russia's abandonment of the Allied cause, her chances of receiving recognition from the United States were almost nil. Relations with Moscow would have implied cognizance of the Treaty of Brest-Litovsk, an acknowledgment which could prove an embarrassing problem at the general peace settlement of the future. Nor would American public opinion have welcomed any rapprochement at that time. To a people long since confused by the bewildering actions of their one-time ally, the capitulation to Germany seemed the final measure of Russian deceit. The official attitude of the United States in regard to Brest-Litovsk was carefully enunciated by Secretary of State Robert Lansing, who stated that "since the so-called Soviet Government upon which Germany has just forced . . . peace was never recognized by the Government of the United States as even a government *de facto* . . . [n]one of its acts, therefore, need be officially recognized by this government. . . ."[8]

As early as February 1918, the other Allied governments had begun to consider intervention in Russia as a means of re-activating the Eastern front, but until July the United States persistently withheld its sanction, maintaining that such action would play into the hands of the enemy and strengthen the anti-democratic Soviet forces. But the pressure for American approval increased, and on July 2 the Supreme War Council

---

[7] The whole question of whether or not to accept the German terms was the subject of a bitter fight within the Bolshevik party, and a much more complicated issue than the above description can indicate. For an account of this episode, see William Henry Chamberlin, *The Russian Revolution, 1917-1921* (New York, 1935), I, 389-413.

[8] *Foreign Relations, 1918, Russia,* I, 397.

addressed an urgent appeal to Wilson, pointing out the necessity for the formation of an eastern front if victory was to be secured in the western theater by 1919.[9] Faced with that ultimatum, the United States reluctantly agreed to limited participation in a Siberian expedition. But the American government clearly stated that its forces would be used only to guard Allied supplies and for the protection of the Czechoslovak troops, formerly attached to the Russian Army, which were reputedly endangered in their circuitous eastward movement to the French front by attacks from released German and Austrian prisoners of war. The entrance of foreign troops for any other purpose, Washington declared, would "be merely a method of making use of Russia, not a method of serving her."[10]

Although small British and French units were present, American intervention in Siberia was undertaken primarily in conjunction with the Japanese. Each government agreed not to interfere in Russian internal affairs and both renounced territorial ambitions. The agreement, which was susceptible to differing interpretations, also provided for small detachments, roughly equal in size. By the end of the year, however, the Japanese forces were increasing at an alarming rate and Tokyo was openly taking sides in the civil strife in Siberia.[11] The strained relations between Major General William Graves, the commander of the American expeditionary force, and his Japanese colleague clearly testified to the divergent aims of the two governments.[12] Thus, Tokyo showed its hand with

[9] *ibid.*, II, 241-246.

[10] *ibid.*, 287-290. Probably the necessity to watch and restrain the Japanese was the real, albeit unannounced reason for the American decision to participate. See Cordell Hull, *The Memoirs of Cordell Hull* (New York, 1948), I, 299.

[11] *Foreign Relations, 1918, Russia*, I, 434-436, 462-463.

[12] For General Graves' own account of the problems he encountered in his dealings with the Japanese, see William S. Graves, *America's Siberian Adventure* (New York, 1931), *passim*. A recent scholarly account of the intervention is John Albert White, *The Siberian Intervention* (Princeton, 1950).

indecent haste, confirming the suspicions of its professed disinterest.

Until the summer of 1918, the Soviets continued to display a more friendly attitude toward Americans in Russia than to representatives of the other Allies. The appearance of American military and naval units at Archangel and Murmansk in June to aid the British and French in protecting Allied supplies stored there served to produce some enmity. But it was only after the decision of the United States to send troops to Siberia and the withdrawal of Ambassador Francis from Soviet territory, that Moscow definitely placed Washington in the camp of the enemy. The Soviet Government, by that time harassed from within by civil war, was in no mood to draw careful distinctions between the motives of its respective invaders. Moreover, the fine words in the several messages of President Wilson to Russia offered perfect targets for the biting sarcasm of George Chicherin, the new Commissar for Foreign Affairs.

On October 24, 1918, Chicherin addressed a long and bitter communication to President Wilson, asking him how he could reconcile the sixth of the Fourteen Points and the message to the Congress of Soviets with American action in Siberia. The United States, wrote Chicherin, had faced the "acid test" and failed. What did the Allies want, he queried, territory, concessions, exploitation of Russia's natural resources? The refusal of the interventionists to state their aims indicated that the price of peace was too heavy for disclosure. Nor was the Commissar satisfied to speak only of Russia. In the note he diagnosed the Fourteen Points and found numerous inconsistencies. There was no mention, he observed, of freedom for the Philippines, or for India, or Ireland. Unquestionably, the Chicherin message reflected all the hatred of communism for liberal idealism.[13]

---

[13] *Sovetsko-amerikanskie otnosheniia* (Moscow, Narkomindel, 1934), 28-33.

Despite this attack, it was to Wilson that Moscow turned with an offer to negotiate after the signing of the Armistice between the Allies and Germany on November 11, 1918. From Stockholm, Maxim Litvinov, on behalf of his government, called for the participation of Soviet representatives in any discussion of the Russian question at the forthcoming Peace Conference. The plea was addressed to the President, said Litvinov, because of the similarity of the Wilsonian war aims to those of Soviet Russia.[14] Once again the Bolsheviks had expressed their grudging appreciation of the fact that though Wilson might phrase distasteful platitudes, he was their most promising friend among the Allies.

The Soviet proposal was taken under advisement by the Big Five at Paris. After much discussion, and on the suggestion of Wilson, it was decided not to receive any Russian delegation officially at the Conference but to hold a meeting of all Russian factions on some neutral territory. Accordingly, an invitation was dispatched calling for a conference on the Island of Prinkipo in the Sea of Marmora. But the anti-Bolshevik governments on Russian territory categorically refused to sit down at the conference table with the Soviets. Moscow, on the other hand, though it had received no official notification, accepted the invitation with alacrity. Chicherin telegraphed Paris that the Soviet Government was prepared to enter into negotiations immediately for the purpose of securing peace even at the price of heavy sacrifices. To end the Civil War and intervention, the Soviet Government was willing to recognize the debts owed by Russia to the Allies, which had earlier been repudiated; to grant concessions for the exploitation of Russia's natural resources; and was even prepared to discuss the possible cession of territory. The Bolsheviks were also ready to pledge non-interference in the internal affairs of other countries, and on the basis of this and the foregoing terms, to meet with all other political groups in Russia as well as the Allies. Instructions

[14] *ibid.*, 33-35.

were requested as to the time and exact place of the meeting.[15]

The Allies were never to ascertain the sincerity of these far-reaching Soviet concessions. The refusal of the other governments on Russian territory to deal with the Bolsheviks defeated the plan of a meeting. But Wilson continued to hope for a solution to the Russian problem. In order to obtain personal information on the Moscow leaders, he sent an attaché of the American Peace Commission, William C. Bullitt, accompanied by Lincoln Steffens and Captain Walter Pettit, on a secret mission to Russia. Bullitt was impressed by the orderly control Moscow exercised over the areas under its occupation and soon became convinced that Russia would never accept any other than a socialist government.[16] Acting upon that impression, he sat down with the Soviet leaders and together they drafted terms for an agreement between Russia and the Allies.

In this interesting document, which was dated March 12, 1919, the Soviet authorities again expressed their willingness to meet with the Allies as well as with their Russian opponents to negotiate peace. The following conditions were laid down as acceptable bases for such a conference: withdrawal of all foreign troops from Russian territory; removal of the economic blockade against Russia; mutual recognition by all governments on the territory of the old Russian Empire; and acknowledgment by these states of their obligation to pay part of the Russian debt owed the Allies, the details of payment to be decided at the conference with reference to the financial situation of Russia. Included also was a proposal for reciprocal pledges of noninterference in the internal affairs of other states. The acceptance by Moscow of these terms was made dependent upon Allied approval by April 10.[17]

In the course of these discussions, Litvinov evolved a plan

[15] Kliuchnikov and Sabanin, *op. cit.*, II, 221-223.
[16] *Foreign Relations, 1919, Russia*, 85-89.
[17] *Sovetsko-amerikanskie otnosheniia*, 37-39.

calling for the United States to take over all Allied claims against Russia and to cancel in return a corresponding amount of the Allied debts to Washington. Litvinov felt that it would be to the advantage of the Soviet Government to have only one creditor, and was hopeful that the United States would offer better terms than its associates. With the approval of Lenin, the proposal was made orally to Bullitt for the consideration of President Wilson.[18]

Bullitt returned to Paris highly enthusiastic about the prospects for peace on the strength of the agreement he carried with him. But by then Wilson had turned to other problems of the general European settlement, and Bullitt received no encouragement in his Russian endeavors. The recent victories of the anti-Bolshevik armies under Admiral Kolchak in Siberia no doubt contributed to the cold reception. Embittered by the failure of his mission, Bullitt resigned from the American Peace Delegation and returned to the United States, where he later caused the President considerable embarrassment by disclosing the nature of his trip.

Any rapprochement with the Bolsheviks at this time would undoubtedly have met with strong opposition in America. As more information and misinformation concerning Communist rule filtered across the sea, American dislike and fear of the Russian regime reached new proportions. The period of the "Great Red Scare" was well under way.[19] The press was filled with tales of Bolshevik atrocities, with little effort being made either to sift the true from the false or to evaluate the conditions in Russia which prompted such measures. The founding of the Third (Communist) International in March 1919, followed in September by the establishment of an affiliated

---

[18] Louis Fischer, *Why Recognize Russia?* (New York, 1931), 51.

[19] For descriptions of this period, see Foster Rhea Dulles, *The Road to Teheran* (Princeton, 1945), Chapter 10; Frederick Lewis Schuman, *American Policy Toward Russia Since 1917* (New York, 1928), 151-156; and Lovenstein, *American Opinion of Soviet Russia* (Washington, 1941), 49-50.

American party, confirmed the world revolutionary aims of the Bolsheviks, while the announcements emanating from the new organization served to increase American suspicion and hatred of all things Communist. In spite of the unfertile ground that America offered for Communist doctrine, the public saw the Bolshevik spectre in every outbreak of industrial strife that arose from the maladjustments of postwar economy.

Nor were the dangers of communism proclaimed only by the public and the press. The State Department published information on the activities of the Bolsheviks which did nothing to lessen the general apprehension.[20] Simultaneously, the Department of Justice under the direction of Attorney-General A. Mitchell Palmer began a campaign of deportations and mass arrests which continued through 1921. By the summer of 1919, even Wilson had abandoned his verbal neutrality towards Russia. In the course of his nationwide tour to rally support for the Treaty of Versailles and the League of Nations, he spoke of the Moscow regime as "the negation of everything that is American." "And do you honestly think . . . ," he asked an audience in Des Moines, "that none of that poison [of Bolshevism] has gotten into the veins of this free people? Do you not know that the world is now one single whispering-gallery?"[21] Although the President was arguing primarily for a prompt ratification of the Treaty to prevent the spread of chaos in Europe, the implication of his words was unmistakable.

It was an inauspicious moment indeed for the Soviet Government again to solicit friendly relations with Washington. But on March 22, 1919, the State Department received a communication from Ludwig C. A. K. Martens, a resident of New York, enclosing credentials signed by George Chicherin, ap-

[20] The Department of State, *Memorandum on Certain Aspects of the Bolshevik Movement in Russia* (Washington, 1919), *passim.*
[21] Baker and Dodd, *War and Peace*, II, 15.

pointing him Soviet envoy to the United States.[22] Martens was an engineer by profession, who had come to the United States from England in 1916 as the representative of a Russian munitions concern. Although born in Russia, his parents were German, and he had apparently never become a subject of the Tsar. Nevertheless, he had been active in the Russian revolutionary movement and as a result was forced to flee to England in 1906.

In his letter to the Department, Martens emphasized the particular desire of Moscow to enter into commercial relations with the United States, and promised large orders should trade be resumed between the two countries.[23] No official cognizance was taken of Martens' communication. The United States recognized only the Ambassador of the Provisional Government, Boris Bakhmetev, as the representative of Russia in the United States. But the activities of Martens in placing tentative orders among American concerns eventually forced the Department to issue public statements in April and May warning that agreements and concessions with the then rulers of Russia would probably not be considered binding by future regimes in Moscow, and reminding American businessmen that their government did not recognize the Soviet authorities. "Extreme caution should be exercised as to representations made by anyone purporting to represent the Bolshevik Government," stated one release.[24]

In June 1919, New York State law enforcement agencies raided the office of Martens in New York to search for subversive documents. The raid was violently protested by Chicherin, who was under the impression that Martens had been arrested. Before the New York authorities could make further moves against the "Soviet envoy," Martens removed himself

[22] Ten months earlier Moscow had nominated Maxim Litvinov, then in London, to the same post, but there had been no response from Washington. *Foreign Relations, 1918, Russia*, ɪ, 551.

[23] *ibid., 1919, Russia*, 133-141.

[24] *ibid.*, 144.

to Washington. But his position there proved equally insecure.
The Department of Labor instituted deportation proceedings,
with the blessings of the State Department, and on December
16, 1920, the deportation order was issued. Martens was declared an undesirable alien who advocated the overthrow of
the American government by force and violence. This opinion
was based on his position as the representative of the Soviet
Government, which was controlled by the Russian Communist
party, which in turn was a member of the Third International.[25]

On receipt of this information, Chicherin made public his
instructions to Martens to return to Russia with his staff and to
cancel all the orders he had placed in the United States. Chicherin expressed his confidence that the action of the American
government in no way reflected the opinion of the American
people, especially the working classes, toward the Soviet Republic.[26] There was, apparently, some criticism by the Russian
Communist party of Martens' acquiescence in the deportation
order without recourse to the courts, for Chicherin went before
the Bolshevik members of the Eighth Congress of Soviets to
explain why he had not instructed Martens to contest the decision. He admitted that as long as the Labor Department ruling remained in force, no representative of the Soviet Union
could be recognized by the United States. But he directed the
attention of his audience to the fact that the incoming Republican Administration in the United States represented the
business interests of America and, as such, could be expected
to promote trade relations with Russia. The new Secretary of
Labor might, therefore, rescind the deportation ruling. If, on
the other hand, the order were taken before the Supreme
Court, which had a majority of Democratic members, it would
probably be upheld, thus making its cancellation less likely.
For that reason, Chicherin explained, it was desirable to have
Martens leave the United States rather than aggravate a situa-

[25] *ibid.*, 148-149; *ibid.*, *1920*, iii, 480.
[26] *Sovetsko-amerikanskie otnosheniia*, 44-45.

tion that had every possibility of improving in the near future.[27] The State Department allowed Martens to depart voluntarily both because of his willingness to do so and also, no doubt, because of a realization that deportation would be an unpleasant precedent should a future rapprochement occur with the Soviets.

As has been noted above, the United States based its earliest refusals to grant recognition to the Soviet Government upon the doubtful prospects of its continuation in power. A second and equally important consideration was the unconstitutional form of Bolshevik rule. The latter reason was not in accord with the traditional recognition policy of the United States which had, until the Administration of President Wilson, followed the principle of recognizing any government no matter what its character so long as it in fact exercised control over the area of the state. Wilson's most conspicuous earlier deviation from that principle had been in relation to Mexico and the new policy was carried over to the Russian problem. The most comprehensive exposition of the attitude of the Wilson Administration toward Russia was formulated by Secretary of State Bainbridge Colby, the successor of Lansing. In answer to an inquiry by the Italian Ambassador as to the position of the Washington government in regard to the Soviet-Polish War, Colby wrote on August 10, 1920, that the United States considered it impossible to "recognize the present rulers of Russia as a government with which the relations common to friendly governments can be maintained." Reaffirming the friendship of the American people for the people of Russia and the desire of the United States to see Russia's territorial integrity maintained, the Secretary pointed out that the Soviet regime was not based on popular support, but had come to power through "force and cunning," and continued to maintain its position by "savage oppression" of all opposition. The

[27] *Vestnik narodnogo komissariata inostrannykh del*, No. 1-2 (1921), 7-8.

Soviet Government, he averred, had refused to fulfill its international obligations and was wholeheartedly pledged to world revolution. "They have made it quite plain," he said, "that they intend to use every means, including, of course, diplomatic agencies, to promote such revolutionary movements in other countries."[28]

George Chicherin did not permit these assertions to go unanswered. In a circular letter to all Russian representatives abroad, he described the Colby note as "a polemical attack without precedent in diplomatic practice." "Soviet Russia," he protested, "cannot ignore it." The circular was to be used as a basis for explaining "to the public in general, and to the toiling masses in particular, the falseness and unfairness of the American Government." With his customarily forthright pen, Chicherin dealt with the Colby charges one by one. The opposition of Washington to the Soviet system he ascribed to the desire of American financial interests to dominate Russia and the world. To the accusation of oppression, he countered with the declaration that "crude force . . . rules supreme and despotic everywhere a parliamentary regime exists, yet according to Mr. Colby, that is the only regime worthy of recognition." Only in Russia was it possible to find a people really free "from exploitation by the privileged minority." He defied the United States to prove that the Soviet Government had ever violated a pledge to abstain from propaganda activities in a foreign country. Although Chicherin readily admitted that Moscow was sympathetic to the universal struggle of the masses for freedom, he affirmed that "the Soviet Government believes that the Communist regime cannot be forced upon another people, and that the struggle for it must be conducted by the toiling masses themselves in each country."

But Chicherin ended his letter on a conciliatory note. Despite the attitude of the incumbent American Administration, the Russian government felt sure that friendly relations could

[28] *Foreign Relations, 1920,* III, 466-467.

be established, and that more far-sighted business leaders would see the advantage of commercial and diplomatic relations with Russia.[29]

Moscow did in fact entertain the hope that a Republican victory in the United States would bring a change in American policy toward Russia.[30] Consequently, soon after the inauguration of President Warren G. Harding in 1921, an appeal for the resumption of relations was transmitted to Washington. The message referred to the hostility of President Wilson toward the Soviet Government and suggested that the new Administration might pursue a more friendly policy. The desirability of regularized trade relations was emphasized and the pledge of noninterference in American internal affairs was reiterated.[31] But the answer of Secretary of State Charles E. Hughes made it clear that the position of the United States was unaltered. Trade, said Hughes, was an empty promise as long as the basis of production in Russia continued on an unsound foundation. If the Bolsheviks planned measures which guaranteed life and property in Russia, then the United States would be interested in hearing of them.[32]

It is possible that the Republican party would have reversed the policy toward Russia had it not been for the Communist tenets of confiscation of private property, repudiation of debts, and world revolution, all of which were even more distasteful to Republican conservatism than to Democratic liberalism. The new Administration did discard the arguments of instability and unconstitutionality as reasons for nonrecognition, but new emphasis was put upon the unorthodox economic policies of the Bolsheviks.

On December 6, 1923, President Calvin Coolidge listed in a message to Congress the prerequisites to any reconsideration

[29] Kliuchnikov and Sabanin, *op. cit.*, III, 56-60.
[30] Mikhail Pavlovich, *Sovetskaia Rossiia i kapitalisticheskaia Amerika* (Moscow, 1922), 48ff.
[31] *Sovetsko-amerikanskie otnosheniia*, 46.
[32] *Foreign Relations, 1921*, II, 768.

of America's Russian policy: "Whenever there appears any disposition to compensate our citizens who were despoiled, and to recognize that debt contracted with our government, not by the Czar, but by the newly formed Republic of Russia; whenever the active spirit of enmity to our institutions is abated; whenever appear words meet for repentance, our country ought to be the first to go to the economic and moral aid of Russia."[33]

Encouraged by this statement, Chicherin telegraphed the President, expressing the "complete readiness" of the Soviet Government "to discuss all problems mentioned in your message."[34] The response was a brief, cold rebuff from Hughes, who informed the Commissar that the United States was "not proposing to barter away its principles."[35]

In the years following until 1933, no change took place in official American policy toward the Soviet Union. The expeditionary force to Siberia was withdrawn in 1920, after the Czechs had been successfully evacuated and the Russian counterrevolutionary forces in that area had collapsed. Intervention had been a mistake.[36] Nothing constructive had been accomplished, and the Soviets were antagonized in a manner that was to affect their attitude toward the participating powers for many years to come. The United States had entered the campaign with reluctance and had attempted to maintain a neutral position vis-à-vis Russia's internal strife. But the task proved almost impossible in view of the conditions in Siberia. Russia, though bitter about America's partnership in the ex-

---

[33] *Congressional Record*, 68th Congress, 1st Sess., 1923.

[34] *Sovetsko-amerikanskie otnosheniia*, 58.

[35] *Foreign Relations, 1923*, II, 787.

[36] In a letter to the President of the Council of the League of Nations in January 1921, Wilson wrote: ". . . armed invasion is not the way to bring peace to the people of Russia. . . . attempts at military coercion can but end in disorder." *Foreign Relations, 1921*, II, 924-927.

pedition, to some extent recognized the special position of the United States and its efforts to restrain the Japanese.[37]

A mission of mercy from the United States in the following year served in some measure to temper the antagonism of the Soviets. In July 1921, Moscow was finally forced to acknowledge publicly that famine, the consequence of seven years of war and revolution followed by drought, gripped a large part of the territory under its control. An appeal for foreign aid was issued by Maxim Gorky. Herbert Hoover, the new Secretary of Commerce in the Harding Cabinet and Director of European Relief during the war, offered the desired help on behalf of the American Relief Administration. Russia accepted and an agreement on the terms under which assistance would be granted was signed by Walter L. Brown, for the American Relief Administration, and Maxim Litvinov, for Moscow, in Riga, on August 20, 1921.

For two years the ARA labored in Russia, supplying not only food for the starving, but enough seed grain to make future harvests possible. Over sixty million dollars was expended in aid to the famine areas. The United States Congress approved an appropriation of twenty million dollars, and the War Department turned over to the Relief Administration nearly four million dollars worth of surplus medical supplies. Of the remaining funds, twelve million came from the Soviet Government and the balance from various social, philanthropic, religious, and service organizations in the United States.[38] There was skepticism among the Bolsheviks as to American motives and many hindrances were thrown in the path of the Relief Administration. The inherently suspicious nature of the

[37] Pavlovich, *op. cit.*, 36. Today, however, Soviet historians have re-evaluated the part of the United States in the intervention with the result that now America is seen as the leader of the movement and the most dangerous and insidious of the participants. See A. Girshfeld, "O roli SShA v organizatsii antisovetskoi interventsii v Sibiri i na Dalnem Vostoke," *Voprosy Istorii*, No. 8 (August, 1948), 3-22.

[38] Harold H. Fisher, *The Famine in Soviet Russia, 1919-1923* (Stanford University, California, 1935), 138-167, 553.

Communists amplified the difficulties. But there was also much sincere appreciation of the work of the Administration. Mikhail Pavlovich, a Bolshevik scholar high in Party councils, wrote in 1922 that: "The aid rendered Russia by the United States in relief to the starving was grandiose, even unprecedented. . . . The Soviet Government and the worker-peasant masses will never forget that great assistance which the Transatlantic Republic afforded to the Russian people. . . ."[39]

Whatever the degree of friendly feeling generated by this episode, it had no appreciable influence on official relations between the two nations. In the United States during the 1920's some voices spoke out for a reconciliation with the Soviet Union, but the pro-recognition movement was weak and unorganized. One of the outstanding exponents of such a course was Republican Senator William Borah of Idaho. He was joined periodically by a few other members of Congress, although party lines appear to have played little part in the alignment.[40] There was a growing interest in the Russian experiment by liberals and artists in the United States and many representatives of these groups traveled to the Soviet land to see for themselves. But in general the attitude of America was one of latent hostility or of apathy.

The opponents of recognition, more numerous and better

[39] Pavlovich, *op. cit.*, 99-101. See also Fisher, *op. cit.*, 133-137, 395-401. Compare these statements with a recent evaluation of the ARA in a lecture by the Soviet historian N. L. Rubinshtein at Moscow in 1947. Rubinshtein declared that "the aim of this diplomacy of 'condensed milk' was clear. . . . The American imperialists wanted to create 'relief' committees made up of counter-revolutionaries, anti-Soviet elements, to send to Soviet Russia a whole army of spies and undercover agents. . . ." N. L. Rubinshtein, *Sovetskaia diplomatiia v bor'be protiv izoliatsii SSSR i ustanovlenie diplomaticheskikh otnoshenii s kapitalisticheskimi stranami* (Moscow, 1947), 10-11.

[40] Fischer, *Why Recognize Russia?*, 139; George Samuel Moyer, *Attitude of the United States Toward the Recognition of Soviet Russia* (Philadelphia, 1926), 148-149, 150, 158; Schuman, *American Policy Toward Russia Since 1917*, 234-239. For an account of Borah's fight for recognition, see also Claudius O. Johnson, *Borah of Idaho* (New York, 1936), 354-368.

organized than their adversaries, continued to point up the dangers in any rapprochement with Russia. In the forefront of this group stood the American Federation of Labor, which understandably opposed Communist labor doctrines. The Roman Catholic church proved an equally relentless foe of any dealings with atheist Bolshevism, while patriotic societies joined in the chorus of those who feared that Americanism would be undermined by any contact with the Soviets. But the American people were too engrossed in their own prosperity and too confident of their national security to be greatly concerned about nondomestic problems. The basic antagonism to Russia was still strong though not as vocal as it had been in the first years after the Revolution. No single issue was responsible for the continuing aversion, but rather the whole complex of Soviet acts which the American public, with few exceptions, listed under the heading "communism."

Moscow was aware of American apathy toward the problem of recognition,[41] and after 1923 made no more direct appeals to Washington. In public and private statements, however, the Soviets continued to make known their desire for normal relations with the transatlantic republic. Litvinov, as Vice-Commissar for Foreign Affairs, informed the Central Executive Committee of the USSR in April 1926 that he was sure direct negotiations with the United States would lead to a satisfactory solution of the questions outstanding between the two countries.[42] Again in 1928, in an address to the same body, he expressed the hope that direct contact with America might soon be a reality. He emphasized the friendly feeling in Russia for the United States, recalling the aid given in the famine of 1921-1923 by the ARA.[43] The signing of the Kellogg-Briand Pact by both the Soviet Union and the United States raised

[41] Kedrosta (pseud.), "Vybory v Amerikanskikh Soedinennykh Shtatakh," *Mezhdunarodnaia Zhizn*, No. 1 (1925), 53-55; see also Louis Fischer, *The Soviets in World Affairs* (London, 1930), II, 761-762.

[42] *Pravda*, April 27, 1926.

[43] Maxim Litvinov, *Vneshniaia politika SSSR* (Moscow, 1935), 17-19.

Moscow's hopes for a rapprochement,[44] but the opinion voiced by some in America that this act in itself constituted recognition was rejected by Litvinov.[45]

In December 1929, there was an exchange of notes between Secretary of State Henry L. Stimson and Litvinov which did nothing to improve the feeling between the two states. Stimson directed the attention of both Russia and China to their obligations under the Kellogg Pact to solve by peaceful means their difficulties in connection with the Sino-Russian dispute over the Chinese Eastern Railway.[46] The note was sent with the best of intentions; indeed, Washington was apparently inclined to sympathize with the Soviet side of the disagreement.[47] But Moscow was extremely displeased with the interference. Replying to Stimson's communication, Litvinov expressed his surprise that the United States, "which at its own desire does not have any official relations with the Government of the Soviet Union, finds it possible to apply to it with advice and instruction."[48] The Russian press hastened to comment on the statement of Litvinov, pointing out that the Stimson message had come at a time when negotiations toward an amicable settlement were almost concluded.[49] In fact, an agreement was signed shortly after the exchange of communications.

There was one point of contact with the United States which the Russians hoped would lead to eventual recognition. In 1920, Washington had rescinded the interdiction against commercial relations with the Soviet Union, and this had been followed by a gradual development of commercial intercourse. The Kremlin believed that normal relations would be estab-

[44] Fischer, *Why Recognize Russia?*, 73-78; Fischer, *The Soviets in World Affairs*, II, 761-762.

[45] Litvinov, *op. cit.*, 19.

[46] *Foreign Relations, 1929*, II, 367-368.

[47] Pauline Tompkins, *American-Russian Relations in the Far East* (New York, 1949), 223-224, 231.

[48] *Sovetsko-kitaiskii konflikt, 1929 g.: sbornik dokumentov* (Moscow, Narkomindel, 1930), 78-80.

[49] See *Izvestia*, December 12, 1929.

lished when the need for formalizing trade became evident to business leaders in America. There was, however, a "vicious circle" inherent in that reasoning, for commerce was restricted by the very absence of diplomatic relations. Consequently, it became necessary to convince American financial circles that diplomatic intercourse would lead to the establishment of Russia as a dependable economic partner of the United States.[50]

To this end a number of reassuring statements were made by Soviet leaders in the 1920's. Joseph Stalin told the American Labor Delegation to Russia, in September 1927, that the co-existence of socialist and capitalist systems, advocating opposing theories of economics and government, in no way precluded agreements between them. "Exports and imports," he said, "are the most suitable ground for such agreements," pointing out the need of each country for the products of the other.[51] In 1928, Litvinov called the attention of the Central Executive Committee to the need for a legal basis for Russian trade with the United States, expressing his conviction that commercial development would eventually break the political barrier.[52]

The prediction of Litvinov was based on more than optimism. The Soviet Union was about to embark on a gigantic program of industrial expansion, the first of the Five Year Plans. In order to meet the goals set for that plan, Russia would have to import on a gigantic scale. It was the ideal opportunity to test the trade-to-recognition theory, for technically-advanced America was the logical place for Russia to turn for her import needs. What Litvinov could not foresee was that a great depression would strike the world in the next year and affect not only the economic relations of Russia with the capitalist world, but also the Five Year Plan itself.

[50] D. Val'ter, "Russkii vopros v Amerike," *Mezhdunarodnaia Zhizn,* No. 4-5 (1925), 52-54.

[51] *Pravda*, September 15, 1927.

[52] Litvinov, *op. cit.*, 17-19.

CHAPTER 2

THE LURE OF TRADE

ONCE the doors were opened to Soviet purchasing in the United States, the volume of trade between the two countries increased with unexpected rapidity. The adoption of the New Economic Policy in 1921 stimulated the restoration of Russia's war-torn economy, and the revival of production was reflected in the orders placed abroad for goods and new equipment. America, as one of the chief sources for the needed materials, was soon sending more to the Soviets than she had sent to Tsarist Russia before the war. In 1924-1925, the United States occupied first place among the nations supplying Soviet imports, and, although she dropped to second position behind Germany in the following four years, her exports to Russia remained at a high level.[1]

The development of trade took place without the benefit of the facilities and protections usually afforded by the Government of the United States for trade with foreign countries. But the Soviets had in some measure lessened the risks and inconveniences by the creation of trading organizations in the United States. In 1919, the Products Exchange Corporation was established in New York and, with the lifting of the economic embargo against Russia, it began to place orders with American firms. The increase in trade during the next few years led the Soviet trading company in London, Arcos, to open a New York branch in 1924, known as Arcos-America.

[1] Nauchno-issledovatel'skii institut monopolii vneshnei torgovli, *Vneshniaia torgovlia SSSR za 20 let, 1918-1937 gg.: statisticheskii spravochnik*, S. N. Bakulin and D. D. Mishustin, compilers (Moscow, 1939), 29. Hereafter cited as *Vnesh. torg. 20 let*. See Appendix A, Tables I and III.

Later, in May of the same year, the two organizations combined to form Amtorg, which became the principal Soviet-American commercial agency in the United States. Amtorg was chartered as a joint stock company under the laws of New York State, and at the same time concluded a concession agreement with the Council of People's Commissars.[2]

As an American corporation, Amtorg was able to conduct its business protected by and subject to the laws of New York and therefore to command more confidence from the companies with which it dealt. It purchased goods from Russian trusts and other organizations for resale in the United States, and acted as agent for those concerns in placing orders with American firms. With the growth of Amtorg, the various Soviet trusts which had maintained independent representatives in America put their affairs in the hands of the larger organization. By 1929, the major portion of Soviet commercial activity in the United States was channeled through Amtorg.[3]

Although the United States no longer forbade trade with the Soviet Union, certain obstacles besides the absence of diplomatic relations remained to hinder free intercourse. Not the least important of these was the continued prohibition against importation of gold from Russia. Basing its decision upon the fact that all gold in the Soviet Union was confiscated from its rightful owners by the usurping Bolshevik government, which therefore had no right to dispose of it, the American State Department ruled that the metal would not be accepted by the U.S. Mint or assay offices without a sworn affidavit attesting it to be of non-Soviet origin.[4] Russia was in the process of recovering from the economic chaos of the War and Civil War years and her need for imports was in no way matched by her availability of exports to pay for them. She

[2] Nauchno-issledovatel'skii institut monopolii vneshnei torgovli, *Torgovye otnosheniia SSSR s kapitalisticheskimi stranami* (Moscow, 1938), 58-59. Hereafter cited as *Torg. otno.*
[3] *ibid.*
[4] *Foreign Relations, 1920*, III, 725.

therefore hoped to use her gold reserves and the gold extracted from her mines to pay for part of her purchases abroad. But in the country where her trade balance was particularly unfavorable, Russian gold could not be accepted in payment.[5]

The same domestic economic situation also made Russia most desirous of obtaining credits, preferably long-term financial credits, for her foreign purchases. Officially, there were no obstacles offered to the granting of such credits by American firms. But the uncertainty inherent in the absence of political relations acted as a brake upon such transactions. True, some of the larger American firms—notably General Electric, General Motors, Standard Oil, and International Harvester, were able to grant sizable commercial credits to Russia for relatively long terms. But the smaller companies equally interested in the Soviet market were unable to finance such agreements. The great companies were also able to apply successfully to banking houses for loans to cover term credits, a facility which their smaller competitors did not enjoy. Direct financial loans for long terms by American banking houses were not available to the Soviets, although the Chase National Bank and Equitable Trust Company did finance short-term loans for the purchase of cotton in the United States.[6]

Despite these handicaps, the Soviets continued to trade extensively with America. In the years up to 1929, the chief items of import from the United States were cotton, rubber, nonferrous metals, semi-finished goods, equipment, automobiles, tractors, and agricultural machinery.[7] The United States, on the other hand, took little from Russia. The Soviet Union was far

[5] M. Landa, "Etapy, itogi i perspektivy vneshne-torgovykh otnoshenii mezhdu SSSR i SASSh," *XV let bor'by za monopoliiu vneshnei torgovli,* Institut mirovogo khoziaistva i mirovoi politiki komakademii i nauchno-issledovatel'skii institut monopolii vneshnei torgovli (Moscow, 1932), 200-201.

[6] E. C. Ropes, "American-Soviet Trade Relations," *The Russian Review,* III, No. 1 (1943), 91; Louis Fischer, *The Soviets in World Affairs* (London, 1930), II, 762-768.

[7] *Vnesh. torg. 20 let,* 246-247.

down on the American import list,[8] a fact which served to increase the difficulties of Russia in establishing a satisfactory commercial relationship with the United States.

The year 1929 was in many respects a significant turning point in Russian-American relations. The inauguration of the First Five Year Plan in 1928-1929 ushered in a new era of commercial activity between the two countries and set in motion political currents which were to affect profoundly the policy of each nation toward the other. In considering this development, almost equal consideration must be given to the contemporaneous descent of the world economy into a great depression. The interaction of these two events multiplied the impact either one might have produced on Russian-American relations.

The objectives of the First Five Year Plan were largely in the field of heavy industrial expansion and agricultural collectivization. The first called for the import of great quantities of machinery for the establishment of basic industrial enterprises and the assistance of experts in the operation of the new factories. The drive toward collectivization was accompanied by a program for the mechanization of agricultural work. Until Soviet industry was able to produce under its program the required tractors, trucks, and farm machinery, Russia had to turn to foreign producers. The nation best prepared to meet the mushrooming demand was the United States, with its advanced industrial development and superior technical skills.

There is also sufficient evidence to suggest that the Soviets were aware of the possible influence on American recognition of a sharp increase in the volume of their purchases in the United States. As has been noted previously, the connection

---

[8] *Foreign Commerce and Navigation of the United States for the Calendar Years 1920-1929* (Washington, 1921-1930), *passim.* Hereafter cited as *Foreign Commerce* followed by respective calendar year.

between trade and recognition had long been clear to the Russian government.[9] The imports necessary for the industrialization and mechanization of Russia offered a tremendous opportunity to intensify that campaign. In December 1929, Maxim Litvinov noted the expanding relations of Russia with American business circles, and directed attention to the especial fitness of American industry to aid in Soviet expansion. "Under the proper conditions," he concluded, "it might be possible to take steps of the most far reaching importance in the direction of an economic rapprochement between the two countries."[10] It is safe to assume that the conditions referred to were political. In general, however, Moscow did not force the issue, but rather waited for the impact of its buying on the American market to produce the desired effect and then encouraged the resulting trend toward diplomatic relations with persuasive statements.

The sharp rise in American exports to Russia in 1929 and 1930 was certainly sufficient to arouse the interest of many businessmen in the United States. Orders by Amtorg in 1929 were almost three times those of 1928.[11] In 1930, the total export to Russia reached the sum of $114,399,000 as compared with $74,091,000 in 1928.[12] That year the United States wrested first place from Germany as the chief source of imports for the USSR, supplying 25 per cent of the total.[13] In 1930 and 1931, Russia was the largest purchaser of American agricultural and industrial equipment.[14] There was also a great demand by

[9] See D. Val'ter, "Russkii vopros v Amerike," *Mezhdunarodnaia Zhizn,* No. 4-5 (1925), 52-54.

[10] Maxim Litvinov, *Vneshniaia politika SSSR* (Moscow, 1935), 49-50.

[11] *Economic Review of the Soviet Union,* v (1930), 26-27.

[12] *Foreign Commerce 1930,* xi-xii. It should be noted that the figures of Amtorg do not correspond with those of the United States Department of Commerce for a given year, as Amtorg listed the orders placed in the United States whereas the Commerce Department listed actual exports during the year.

[13] *Torg. otno.,* 57; *Economic Review of the Soviet Union,* ix (1934), 133-134.

[14] *ibid.*

Russia for technical aid from American experts in various fields of industry and agriculture. Many of the firms that sold equipment also contracted to send their representatives to assist in the establishment of new plants in the Soviet Union and to instruct Russian engineers on the use of the imported machinery.[15] In 1930, Amtorg published a list of American companies which had concluded technical aid agreements with the Soviets or were doing contract work for them. Forty-three firms were listed, including such important concerns as Du Pont de Nemours, Electric Auto-lite, Ford Motors, International General Electric, Radio Corporation of America, Seiberling Rubber, and Sperry Gyroscope.[16]

Even under normal conditions, such a rapid increase in exports to any one country would have directed attention to the possibilities of the new market. But the New York stock exchange disaster of October 1929 had marked the beginning of a world depression. In the United States, banks closed their doors, investment values shrank, millions of men joined the ranks of the unemployed, and trade dwindled. The expanded commerce of Russia had, therefore, an added importance to market-hungry American producers. The attractiveness of Amtorg's orders brought strong competition among firms both large and small. The former were better able to meet the Russian terms for the reasons already mentioned,[17] but their less powerful rivals were willing to take sizable risks to get the orders. When it is realized that during those years Russia was the only large customer for many American manufacturers, the interest in and competition for Soviet orders is not difficult to understand.[18]

[15] *Torg. otno.*, 59; see also *Za Industrializatsiiu*, November 21, 1933.
[16] *Economic Review of the Soviet Union*, v (1930), 131-132.
[17] Ropes, *loc. cit.*
[18] Professor Otto Hoetzsch points out the paradox that during the years 1928-1932 America, which represented the opposite pole from socialism as exemplified by Russia, collaborated most actively on a private basis in assisting the construction of socialism in the USSR under the Five Year

The sudden expansion of trade with the Soviet Union in 1929 and 1930 had a noticeable effect upon American attitudes toward Russia. Those concerns which were most aided by the new market were the first to urge that reconsideration be given to the thirteen-year government policy of nonrecognition. For example, Mr. James D. Mooney, Vice President of General Motors, told the American Automobile Club of Paris, in October 1930, that diplomatic relations were absolutely necessary if full advantage were to be derived from the commercial possibilities of Russia. The stability of the Communist regime, the need of Russia for American goods, and the excellent credit rating of Moscow were in his opinion sufficient reasons for the United States to extend recognition.[19] In the spring of 1931, a press survey showed a significantly large minority of newspapers interested in a trade agreement, if not in outright diplomatic relations with Russia.[20] The *Brooklyn Eagle* called for recognition in the name of trade, pointing out that the step would in no way constitute a sanction of the Bolshevik form of government.[21]

At the same time, members of Congress urged a change in American policy. Senator Wheeler of Montana, in a series of newspaper articles, warned that unless the United States revised its antagonistic attitude toward Russia, Germany and Great Britain would procure the major part of Soviet trade.[22] In an address before the Republican Club of New York in February of 1931, Senator Cutting of New Mexico seconded the plea of his Democratic colleague for a new approach to

---

Plan. Otto Hoetzsch, *Le caractère et la situation internationale de l'Union des Soviets* (Genève, 1932), 98.

[19] *New York Times*, October 8, 1930.

[20] "Stimson Study of Russia," Editorial Analysis of the Republican National Committee, Herbert Hoover Archives, Hoover Library, Stanford University, California.

[21] *Brooklyn Eagle*, December 7, 1930, as quoted in the *Congressional Record*, 71st Congress, 3rd Sess., 314.

[22] *Washington Herald*, September 21, 28, October 5, 1930, as quoted in *ibid.*, 4671-4674.

Moscow, minimizing the danger of communism and noting that the Russian debt to the United States was too small to warrant it standing in the way of a reconciliation.[23]

The rising tide of interest in a commercial and even political rapprochement with the Soviet Union was carefully fostered by Moscow. In an interview given to Thomas D. Campbell, a Montana wheat magnate, in 1929, Stalin asked the American why Russia was not able to place her trade on a firmer basis with the United States. Campbell answered that it was largely the fear that Communist propaganda and agitation would come with a closer relationship. Stalin countered with the observation that other countries with the same unfounded fear shrewdly continued to take advantage of Russia's commercial opportunities. As evidence, Stalin told Campbell in confidence that the British were at that very moment working on a deal to give Russia a loan for further buying in England. But the Soviet leader emphasized that it was to America that Russia would prefer to turn for most of the materials needed for her new industrial offensive.[24] In November 1930, Stalin asked Walter Duranty how the United States could withhold formal recognition because it opposed strengthening Communist rule, and simultaneously continue to supply the machines and goods to be used in the economic expansion of the regime. Rather than trying to undermine the American system, Stalin argued, the Soviet Union could be accused of supporting capitalism by giving it a market for its products during the depression.[25]

The introduction of the Five Year Plan also had a certain psychological effect on American attitudes toward Russia, representing as it did to many a dynamic experiment in the midst

[23] *ibid.*, 4006-4007.
[24] The stenographic record of this interview appeared in I. Stalin, "Gospodin Kempbell priviraet," *Bol'shevik*, November 30, 1932, 10-16. Stalin published the record with a personal introduction in order to refute certain statements concerning his ideological differences with Trotsky, attributed to him by Campbell in Thomas D. Campbell, *Russia, Market or Menace?* (New York, 1932), 15-18.
[25] *New York Times*, December 1, 1930.

of a discouraged depression world. Although it was a return to Bolshevik principles after the N. E. P., which had given some people in the United States hope for a rejection of communism, the hysteria on the subject had subsided enough to allow a more objective observation of this attempt at planned economy. There certainly was much criticism of the plan on the basis both of the brutal disregard for human life and of the poor quality of the goods that were being produced, but American interest was attested by the number of volumes that appeared on Russia during that period.[26] Many tourists from the United States journeyed to the Soviet Union to see the "great experiment" with their own eyes. Intourist, the official Russian travel agency, reported that twice as many foreigners visited Russia in 1930 as in 1929 and that sixty per cent of them were Americans.[27] Louis Fischer wrote that: "For thousands of intellectuals and intelligent people a trip to Russia had become a compulsory summer course with credit."[28]

But there was another side to the Soviet trade program which was not so appealing to foreign producers. In order to pay for the increasing volume of her imports, Russia had embarked on a forced export schedule.[29] Although the United States was less affected than some other countries by the influx of Soviet goods, the cry of dumping soon rose from those few manufacturers in America whose products were in competition with Russian exports. Charges of dumping in connection with Soviet safety matches and asbestos were brought before the Treasury Department, and in 1930 and 1931 orders were issued by the Secretary finding that both items were being sold in the United States at less than a fair price. Special levies

[26] Meno Lovenstein, *American Opinion of Soviet Russia* (Washington, 1941), 148-149.

[27] *Soviet Union Review*, IX (1931), 225.

[28] Louis Fischer, *Men and Politics, An Autobiography* (New York, 1941), 190.

[29] M. M. Zhirmunskii, *Organizatsiia i tekhnika sovetskogo eksporta*, Nauchno-issledovatel'skii institut monopolii vneshnei torgovli (Moscow, 1935), 39-42.

were placed on Soviet matches and a bond was required for asbestos pending further investigation.[30] Those two decisions were paralleled by a third, banning the entry of lumber and pulpwood from four European areas of the Soviet Union on the grounds that they were the products of forced labor.[31]

To what extent were the charges justified? The Soviets unquestionably increased their exports to the farthest limits possible. But did that constitute dumping? Technically, the term refers to the practice of selling surpluses abroad at a price below that which can be commanded on the domestic market. On the basis of that definition, the charge was not warranted, for there was no surplus of the materials in question within the Soviet Union. They could all have been used in Russia. But the object was to sell all the goods possible abroad, even at the expense of the internal demand, in order to get foreign exchange to pay for imports.[32] If, in the pursuit of that objective, it was necessary to lower the price of products to obtain a large market, that device was accepted as a necessary sacrifice.[33] Obviously, the effect of the practice was much the same as dumping, for goods were sold abroad at prices below the prevailing level. But two fears expressed by foreign critics in connection with the export flow were unfounded: namely, its permanence and the suspicion that it was a device to capture control of the international economy for the purpose of furthering world revolutionary aims.[34]

Restrictions against Russian dumping were not limited to the

[30] *Treasury Decisions*, LVII (1930), 774; *ibid.*, LX (1931), 334.

[31] *ibid.*, LIX (1931), 348. The regions specified were the Kola Peninsula (including the Murman coast), Karelian ASSR, the Komi ASSR, and the Northern Area (a geographical region south of the White Sea bounded on the East by the Urals, on the West by the Karelian ASSR, and reaching south of Vologda).

[32] A. Stoupnitzky, *Statut international de l'URSS, état commerçant* (Paris, 1936), 151-162; Max Beloff, *The Foreign Policy of Soviet Russia, 1929-1941* (London, 1947), I, 31.

[33] S. P. Turin, "Foreign Trade of the USSR," *Slavonic (and East European) Review*, X (1931-1932), 342.

[34] *ibid.*; Beloff, *op. cit.*

United States. France, Belgium, Rumania, Canada, and Yugo-slavia enacted much more stringent measures in 1930 and 1931.[35] Needless to say, the Soviet Government was exercised by such actions not only as handicaps to the continuance of the needed export trade, but also as slights to its highly sensitive national honor. In retaliation, the Council of People's Commissars authorized the Commissariat of Foreign Trade to forbid purchases in countries which established discriminatory measures against Russian commerce. Action was taken against France, but apparently not against any other country, at least not officially.[36]

The concern of Moscow about the extension of discriminations against Soviet trade was reflected in the proposal of Litvinov for an universal economic nonagression pact. Addressing the League Commission for European Union at Geneva in May 1931, Litvinov expressed the desire of Russia for an international agreement on this subject. In answer to the charges of dumping, he admitted that Soviet prices were lower, but attributed that fact to the elimination of the middleman in Communist economy. He denied that there was any difference between domestic and foreign prices of Soviet products. Russia needed export receipts, he said, and therefore had no reason for causing a price slump in the world market.[37]

Thus the Soviets readily acknowledged the forced increase in their export designed to meet import payments. But they argued that in the American trade especially, there was no other method as long as satisfactory credit arrangements were not available. If there was objection to Russian products entering the United States, the obvious solution, advantageous to

[35] *Documentation Relating to the Foreign Economic Relations of the USSR,* Prepared for the Monetary and Economic Conference in London June 1933 (Moscow, 1933), 17.

[36] *ibid.,* 17-19.

[37] Litvinov, *Vneshniaia politika SSSR,* 224-228. The League requested American participation on the commission established by it to study the question of an economic nonaggression pact. The United States declined to participate. *Foreign Relations, 1931,* I, 607.

both countries, lay in the extension of credit, not the imposition of discriminatory legislation. Credits and above all the establishment of normal diplomatic relations were offered as common sense alternatives to "dumping." The continued absence of these necessary conditions, Moscow warned, combined with anti-Soviet measures reacted only to the detriment of American industry and commerce.[38]

The charge of forced labor particularly infuriated the Soviets. Perhaps it was the truth of the accusation that made it so painful to them, for the use of convict labor in Bolshevik Russia at that time was substantiated by evidence from a number of sources.[39] Government and press joined in the chorus of protest and denial. Even *Bor'ba Klassov*, the leading historical journal, entered the list, publishing an article calling upon the United States to look at its own history and clean its own house before casting aspersions upon other nations. The discussion centered, of course, upon slavery in the South before 1865, with the further insinuation that the present plight of the negro was little better.[40] Whether the author intended a refutation or a justification presents an interesting subject for thought.

Following deceptively close upon the American discriminations and the answering threats of the Soviets came the beginning of a noticeable drop in Russian orders in the United States. The reasons for the decline in trade will be dealt with later in the chapter. In this case, as is so often true in his-

[38] See *International Press Correspondence*, August 21, 1930, 775-776. See also *Izvestia*, February 14, 1931.

[39] See Sir Alan Pim and Edward Bateson, *Report on Russian Timber Camps* (London, 1931), for the report of the investigation by the British Anti-Slavery Society. A description of the forced labor camps in the period under discussion can be found in Vladimir Tchernavin, *I Speak for the Silent Prisoners of the Soviets* (Boston, 1935), see especially 251-253.

[40] E. Serebrianskii, "Prinuditel'nyi trud v istorii SASSh," *Bor'ba Klassov*, No. 2 (1931), 90-95.

torical events, the misconceptions of the moment proved to be more influential than the true facts.

American customs figures show that export to Russia fell to $103,717,000 in 1931 as compared to the high of $114,399,000 in 1930.[41] Soviet statistics, although varying slightly, tell approximately the same story.[42] At first inspection the decline did not appear alarming, but investigation of the actual orders placed by Amtorg in 1931 told a different story and should have prepared the United States for the drop of 89 per cent in exports to Russia disclosed by the 1932 figures. Although the actual shipments in 1931 were only 8 per cent less than those for 1930, Amtorg purchased over 60 per cent less in the second year than in the first.[43] Much of the trade shown for 1931 was, therefore, delayed export of orders placed in the previous year. The full impact upon American thinking did not come until 1932, but the firms which depended upon Russian orders began to feel the pinch some time before that.

As long as trade continued to increase without the aid of a formal agreement, the agitation in the United States for a rapprochement with Russia had achieved only moderate importance. It was when Russian orders shrank that the tempo for a reevaluation of American policy began to accelerate. The Soviets had taken their business elsewhere, the advocates of recognition said, because of the absence of normal relations between the two governments. With the additional handicap of administrative restrictions on Russian imports and the continued lack of credit facilities, Russia had finally turned away from the American market. Business leaders who had a vital interest in the growth of sales to the Soviet Union spoke to their associates of the need for some sort of arrangement with Russia. Ralph Budd, President of the Chicago, Burlington and Quincy Railroad, told the American-Russian Chamber of Commerce of the great possibilities for American industry in the

---

[41] *Foreign Commerce, 1931,* s 4.   [42] *Torg. otno.,* 57.
[43] *Economic Review of the Soviet Union,* vii (1932), 89.

Russian trade should the proper conditions prevail.[44] In an address to the businessmen of the south coastal states, Thomas A. Morgan, President of Curtis Wright and the Sperry Gyroscope Company, reiterated Mr. Budd's remarks.[45] Colonel Hugh Cooper, an American engineer who was serving as technical advisor to the Soviet Government on the Dnieper hydroelectric project, contrasted the fall in United States export to Russia with the increase in German-Soviet commerce, and suggested a trade delegation be sent to Russia to make an on-the-spot study of her potentialities as a market.[46] This idea became an actuality in June 1932, when the formation of an investigating commission composed of eight businessmen was announced.[47] In San Francisco, the Commonwealth Club, an organization of businessmen, voted for recognition of the Soviet Union, after over a year of study and a series of lectures by Russian scholars in the west.[48]

Members of the House and Senate also advocated a re-examination of Russian-American relations in the interest of trade. In April 1932, Representative Sabath introduced a resolution calling on the President to instruct the Secretary of State to enter into negotiations with Russia looking toward the establishment of commercial and political relations.[49] Senator Johnson of California joined the movement with a statement which neatly summed up the attitude of those who favored recognition. "There are," he said, "billions of dollars' worth of future orders in Russia for American workers to fill, and in these times it is simply economic idiocy for America, by its policies, to preclude Americans from trade and commerce which so readily could be obtained."[50] With similar

[44] *ibid.*, 175-176.   [45] *ibid.*, 158-159.
[46] *ibid.*, viii (1932), 54-55.
[47] *Business Week*, June 15, 1932, 9.
[48] "Should the United States Recognize Soviet Russia?," *The Commonwealth*, viii (1932), 99-100.
[49] *Congressional Record*, 72nd Congress, 1st Sess., 8741.
[50] *New York Times*, April 24, 1932.

words, Senators Pittman of Nevada and Robinson of Arkansas took their places beside the ever persistent Senator Borah in urging a rapprochement with Russia.[51]

However, other spokesmen continued to see grave dangers in any change in American policy. Father Edmund A. Walsh, prominent Catholic educator and Vice-President of Georgetown University, led the fight of the Roman Catholic church against a resumption of American relations with Russia. In his book, *The Last Stand*, published in 1931, Dr. Walsh argued that it was not a question of debts or of Soviet stability which kept the two nations apart, but rather the irreconcilability of two radically different ideologies of government and ethics.[52] The American Federation of Labor, defending "free workers against competition with unfree labor," stoutly refused to alter its position on Russia,[53] although at least two other labor organizations favored some sort of conditional recognition.[54] Also in the forefront of opposition at an early date was Representative Hamilton Fish of New York, who headed a committee of Congress formed in 1930 to investigate and report on the subversive activities of the Bolsheviks in the United States.[55]

Any decision to extend a friendly hand to Russia had, however, to be made by the Chief Executive of the United States Government, and there was little hope for the pro-recognition faction in that quarter. President Herbert Hoover, despite his

[51] *ibid.*, April 23, 1932.

[52] Edmund A. Walsh, *The Last Stand, An Interpretation of the Soviet Five Year Plan* (Boston, 1931), 273-307.

[53] *American Federationist*, September 1930, 1048.

[54] The Amalgamated Clothing Workers took a more liberal stand, see Lovenstein, *American Opinion of Soviet Russia*, 104-105, as did also the United Mine Workers, who passed a resolution on February 1, 1932, recommending recognition and a commercial treaty if Russia would discontinue her propaganda activities in the United States and "fulfill her government's honorable obligations." *New York Times*, February 2, 1932.

[55] "Investigation of Communist Propaganda," *House Reports*, No. 2290, 71st Congress, 3rd Sess., January 17, 1931. The report of this committee painted a lurid picture of Communist activity in the United States. Fish became the symbol of anti-Sovietism to Moscow.

leadership in the Relief Mission to Russia, had for many years made clear his deep-seated antagonism to all that the leaders of the Soviet Union represented. Recognition by America would, in his opinion, lend respectability to a regime characterized by brutal oppression and, at the same time, clear the way for an influx of Communist agitators and Communist propaganda into America.[56]

During his entire term in office, Mr. Hoover received letters of information and advice on the Russian question from interested and oftentimes influential citizens. Some of these communications relayed Russian suggestions for a settlement of the issues blocking a rapprochement. Professor Jerome Davis of Yale wrote the President, in the summer of 1929, that during his recent trip to Russia he had been advised by Stalin of Bolshevik willingness to meet all the financial claims of the United States.[57] A year later S. L. Bertron, a New York financier and a member of the Root Mission in 1917, informed Mr. Hoover that the "highest Russian authorities" would welcome a small committee from the President to discuss a resumption of relations based on the cessation of Communist propaganda, the restoration of confiscated American property, and an adjustment of the American debt. In answer, Mr. Hoover wrote that: "It does not appear to us that any change should be made in our policies at the present time." The State Department, in a separate acknowledgment, reaffirmed the President's declaration.[58]

Toward the end of his Administration, the Chief Executive

[56] Exchange of letters between Herbert Hoover and Stanley Washburn, October 10, 1930, October 11, 1930, "Russia, 1929-1932," The Herbert Hoover Archives, Hoover Library, Stanford University, California; see also William Starr Myers, *The Foreign Policies of Herbert Hoover, 1929-1933* (New York, 1940), 24-26.

[57] Exchange of letters between Herbert Hoover and Jerome Davis, June 28, 1929, June 29, 1929, July 1, 1929, "Russia, 1929-1932," The Herbert Hoover Archives, Hoover Library, Stanford University, California.

[58] Exchange of letters between Herbert Hoover and S. L. Bertron, August 8, 1930, August 11, 1930; W. R. Castle, Acting Secretary of State, to Mr. Bertron, August 25, 1930, *ibid.*

indicated that the increasing demand for trade relations had in no way altered his stand. "There are many reasons pro and con for the policies you suggest," he replied to a letter from William O. Thompson, a prominent Chicago and New York attorney, who urged recognition in the interests of trade," [but] I have felt that the reasons against it are of such dominant order as not to warrant our taking the responsibility."[59]

Meanwhile, Moscow had indicated through other channels as well that it was willing to reach an agreement on the American debt. Speaking to the Sixteenth Party Congress on July 27, 1930, Joseph Stalin declared that, on the condition of the extension of credit to Russia, his government was prepared to pay "a small part of our pre-war debts" by means of extra interest on the credits granted. That was all that the Soviets could concede, said Stalin, pointing out that the creditors were hardly in a position to speak of international morality and obligations after their intervention in 1918.[60] Later in that year, Stalin reiterated this proposal in an interview granted Walter Duranty. "We have done what we could," he said, "but we won't hang on their [Americans'] necks. . . . We are still willing to do what I said before: get the debt question settled . . . and resume normal relations, as we have done with the rest of the great powers."[61] The reference to financial settlement with the other powers was hardly supported by the facts. Although recognition had been granted by both France and Great Britain in the middle 1920's, no debt agreement was ever reached despite long and tortuous negotiations.[62]

Moscow observed the growth of pro-recognition sentiment

[59] Exchange of letters between Herbert Hoover and William O. Thompson, May 25, 1932, May 27, 1932, *ibid.*

[60] *Pravda*, July 29, 1930.

[61] *New York Times*, December 1, 1930.

[62] For the French-Soviet debt negotiations, see Fischer, *The Soviets in World Affairs*, II, 617-622, 708-711; and P. Milioukov, *La politique extérieure des soviets* (Paris, 1936), 188-204. The British-Soviet debt discussions are described in W. P. and Zelda K. Coates, *A History of Anglo-Soviet Relations* (London, 1945), 154-181.

in America with evident satisfaction. Soviet publications noted every favorable or promising statement by an American leader. In March, April, and May 1932, scarcely a day passed without some allusion in the press to the encouraging developments in the United States. American articles favoring closer ties with the Soviets were often quoted at some length. In four-page papers, where space must be carefully allocated on the basis of propaganda value and general interest, the large number of dispatches from the United States was significant. *Izvestia*, in a discussion on trade with the United States, laid the blame for the decrease on restrictive measures and credit conditions, but emphasized that "the betterment of the situation, both as regards Soviet exports into America and as regards credits, in large measure rests on the question of the regularization of political relations between the two countries."[63]

In the United States, the official publication of Amtorg, the *Economic Review of the Soviet Union*, was best fitted to impress American business circles with the potentialities of Russian trade under favorable conditions. The magazine emphasized the harmful influence of the Treasury Department orders not only in connection with the actual articles affected, but also in creating an atmosphere of insecurity which deterred Russia from purchasing in the United States.[64] More subtle methods were also used by the *Review*, which was circulated to financial and industrial concerns in the United States. For example, the issue of March 1, 1932 employed a device which was used rather extensively throughout that period. On one side of a double page was an article headlined in heavy type: "Amtorg Purchases in the U. S. Decline 55 Per Cent in 1931," while the opposite page featured an article titled: "Record Soviet Purchases in Germany." In the discussion on German trade, it was pointed out that the recent credit agreement with Russia had vastly increased export to the Soviet Union at a

[63] *Izvestia*, January 14, 1932.
[64] *Economic Review of the Soviet Union*, VII (1932), 27-29.

time when German industry was particularly in need of new orders.[65]

The October 1932 issue of the same magazine published a statement outlining the financial arrangements which Amtorg considered essential to a revival of Russian-American trade. Firms in the United States were advised to honor Amtorg notes without any cash payment until at least a year after delivery, and to establish the full time limit of credits at 15 months to two years, preferably longer. Only under these conditions could American industry hope to compete with German and British firms which offered comparable or even better terms. Amtorg further suggested that a new commercial policy toward Moscow be undertaken soon, as import planning for the Second Five Year Plan was already under way. If the United States wished to take advantage of the great opportunities offered by the new Plan, speed of decision was essential.[66]

In the previous month, Peter Bogdanov, Chairman of the Board of Directors of Amtorg, had reiterated the second point in the Soviet explanation for the downward trend of trade between the two countries. "If business on a really large scale is to be established, corresponding to the actual possibilities of our market, this must be preceded by the establishment of normal relations between our two countries. Only when we shall have a definite commercial and political status in this country shall we be able to make plans for increasing our trade here without the fear that unexpected obstacles may suddenly put an end to such a development."[67]

Raise the restrictions on Soviet imports, grant long term credits, and establish political relations with Russia, and America would be able to exploit a tremendous market for her surplus goods in the midst of the depression. Thus ran the

[65] *ibid.*, 100-101.
[66] *ibid.*, 19-20.
[67] As quoted in the American Foundation, Committee on American-Russian Relations, *The United States and the Soviet Union* (New York, 1933), 90. Hereafter cited as *The United States and the Soviet Union.*

argument of American advocates of a rapprochement. Soviet spokesmen confirmed the analysis.[68]

Yet there were other factors involved in the trade decline about which Moscow said little in its remarks for foreign consumption. To be sure, credits had been granted with very favorable conditions by Germany in 1931, and England had gradually improved the facilities for credit to the Russians after 1929. The Piatakov Agreement with Germany, in April 1931, had extended credit to the sum of Rm 300,000,000 to the Soviet Union for the purchase of industrial equipment. The terms of the notes under the agreement varied from 14 to 29 months, and the Reich Government guaranteed payment up to 75 per cent.[69] In 1929, the British Government had extended its legislation regarding government guarantees of credit to include Russia. By the autumn of 1931, the time on Soviet credits had been extended to an average of 22 months, with the government guaranteeing the creditor up to 60 per cent of the loan. The British system was extremely complicated, however, involving careful official scrutiny of each transaction, while the interest rates remained high. As a result, the exporters did not realize as much Russian business as might have been expected.[70]

The upswing in German trade with Russia ran almost parallel to the decline in Russian orders in the United States. There is every reason to believe that Russia did turn away from the United States because of the more favorable conditions offered her elsewhere.[71] But Russian trade as a whole continued to rise only through 1931. Therefore, for only one year did American trade with Russia decrease while overall Soviet imports increased. Total Russian imports, in fact, dropped almost

[68] Landa, *op. cit.* (see note 5 *supra*), 209-211; *Torg. otno.*, 54-55; J. D. Yanson, *Foreign Trade in the USSR* (London, 1934), 119, 121-122.
[69] W. Höffding, "German Trade with the Soviet Union," *The Slavonic (and East European) Review*, xiv (1935-1936), 480-482.
[70] Stoupnitzky, *Statut international de l'URSS*, 443-447.
[71] See USSR Chamber of Commerce, *Quarterly Review*, No. 4 (Oct.-Dec.), 1932, 40.

30 per cent in 1932. Imports from Germany stayed above the 1930 level through 1932 or as long as the credits were available, but, in 1933, they dropped to less than half the figure of the previous year. The entire import of Russia for 1933 was one-half of that for 1932 and about 30 per cent of the 1930 figure.[72] In evaluating Russian-American commerce, therefore, it is clear that factors other than those advanced by Moscow must be taken into account in order to explain the decline during these years.

The drastic reduction of imports effected by Soviet Russia in the years 1932 and 1933—which continued until 1935—was not emphasized abroad, or at least not in the United States. When reference to it was made by Soviet representatives, it was generally minimized and the impression given that it was due either to the lack of foreign credits or to the increased production under the Five Year Plan or a combination of both. An obvious effort was made in all discussion to emphasize the potentialities of trade with Russia should the hindering obstacles be removed. In the United States, Soviet spokesmen played suggestively upon the temporary rise in German and British exports to the Soviet Union.[73]

Within Russia, official publications explained the import curtailment in terms of industrial growth during the Five Year Plan. As early as 1932, the Soviet sources stated, the growth of internal production made it possible to decrease imports, and to buy abroad only if the conditions offered were favorable to the USSR.[74] According to the reports of the Foreign Trade Commissariat, it had been possible to put this program into operation ahead of schedule because of the exceptionally rapid ad-

[72] See Appendix A, Tables I and II.

[73] See *Economic Review of the Soviet Union*, VII (1932), 271; *Soviet Union Review*, XI (1933), 50-52.

[74] Nauchno-issledovatel'skii institut monopolii vneshnei torgovli, *Vneshniaia torgovlia sovetskogo soiuza*, D. D. Mishustin, ed. (Moscow, 1938), 91. Hereafter cited as *Vnesh. torg.* See also Landa, *op. cit.*, 109; A. Rozenholtz, *Foreign Trade and Economic Independence of the USSR* (Moscow, 1935), 5-7.

vances in the first years of the Plan.[75] Assuming that that explanation for the decline in purchases abroad was the only one, it is still difficult to justify the promises of increased trade held out to the United States.

But it appears most likely that another development was of paramount importance in the decision to curtail imports— namely, the effect of the world economic crisis on the Soviet Union. In fact, the constantly reiterated denials by Moscow that the depression had affected Soviet trade only served to verify that explanation. It was absolutely necessary for the Soviet Union to maintain a high export level plus the best credit conditions possible in order to continue the import requirements of the Five Year Plan. The cost of foreign purchasing had to be paid out of current export or deferred by means of credits. However, unhappily for Russia, an international economic collapse occurred during the first year of the Plan. International markets shrunk. Prices fell and, as is usual in depression conditions, the drop was faster for raw materials and unfinished goods than for machinery and equipment. The Soviets depended on the former for receipts to pay for the latter, with the result that, as the crisis deepened, it became more and more difficult for them to obtain sufficient foreign exchange to pay for imports.[76]

Meanwhile, the desired long-term credits did not materialize, and the Russians were forced to take short-term credits. The cumulative effect upon their commercial indebtedness was a more telling influence upon the reduction of imports than was the increase of domestic production. Further evidence to support that theory can be found in the fact that imports began to increase again in 1935, although by that time production in the Soviet Union certainly was far above the 1932-1933 level.[77] As late as May 1931, a trained foreign

[75] *Vnesh. torg.*, 91.

[76] *Torg. otno.*, 11, shows the greater decline in rubles received per ton exported than in rubles paid out per ton for imported goods.

[77] See Appendix A, Table II. Alexander Baykov, *Soviet Foreign Trade*

economic attaché in Russia characterized the need for manu-
factured goods as acute, which makes it difficult to believe
that within a year the situation had so improved as to justify
any drastic curtailment of import on the basis of adequate
supply within the country.[78]

It does not seem unwarranted, therefore, to assume that
Soviet orders in the United States would have declined during
these years regardless of the existence of specific legal and financial handicaps. Yet it is also probable that long-term credits
would have kept the trade level somewhat higher. The sharp
decline in Soviet trade with Germany in 1933 and 1934, despite a further loan of Rm 140,000,000,[79] makes it doubtful,
however, that Russia could have sustained a high import level
even with long-term credits. In any case, there was little justification for the extremely optimistic promises of trade held out
to the United States by Moscow.

All the factors mentioned by Russia as hindrances to her
purchasing in the United States undoubtedly played a part in
the decision to reduce imports from America. The gold ban
made it impossible to make up the unfavorable trade balance
in bullion payments; the discriminatory measures acted as a
material as well as a psychological barrier; and the absence of
credits was a decided handicap. But all those conditions, with
the possible exception of the discriminatory measures, had
existed in 1930 when the United States held first place among
the exporters to Russia. In that year, when her own economic

(Princeton, 1946), 60, also suggests this explanation for the reduction
of imports. In December 1931, Soviet foreign indebtedness reached its
peak of 1,400 million gold rubles, almost three times the figures of 1928
and 1933. Walter Duranty's interview with Stalin, *Izvestia*, January 4,
1934; and A. Rozenholtz, "SSSR-samaia kreditosposobniia strana,"
Pravda, November 7, 1935.

[78] G. P. Paton, *The Organization of Foreign Trade of the Union of
Soviet Socialist Republics* (London, His Majesty's Stationery Office,
1931), 20. Paton was Commercial Counsellor to the British Embassy
in Moscow.

[79] Baykov, *op.cit.*, 57n.

position made it possible for Russia to buy in America, the political estrangement apparently did not hinder her buying.

It is not suggested that Moscow deliberately reduced Soviet import from the United States in order to exert pressure for recognition, but rather that it made full use of the opportunity forced upon it by basic economic considerations to encourage the belief in American business circles that a political rapprochement would bring with it an upswing in Russian orders.

An examination of the influence of economic factors on Soviet-American relations from 1929-1933 reveals two opposing curves of interest. In the earlier period, the Russians were primarily in search of an economic *modus vivendi* with the United States in order to facilitate their purchasing there. Political relations were desirable and would probably follow, but they were not the primary objective. America, on the other hand, though interested in the Soviet market during the first years of the Five Year Plan, did not reach the peak of her interest in economic relations until the end of the period, when the depression deepened and Soviet orders declined. By that time, the Soviet Union had a greater desire for political than for economic intercourse and was fundamentally concerned with recognition by the United States, though it continued to use the trade argument as a weapon in its campaign. International developments, especially in the Far East, injected a new urgency in the appeals of Moscow for a diplomatic rapprochement.

CHAPTER 3

THE FAR EASTERN CATALYST

PEACE was essential to the Soviet Union during the First Five Year Plan. War not only would have prevented the accomplishment of the economic expansion the Plan envisaged, it would have endangered the very existence of the socialist state as yet militarily unprepared. It is not surprising, therefore, to find that the struggle for peace went hand in hand with the struggle for industrial advancement and agricultural consolidation. During these years, Russian diplomacy had the primary task of protecting Soviet Russia from the alarms of war, at least until she was strong enough to meet an enemy with hope of victory. This responsibility fell upon the shoulders of Maxim Litvinov, who replaced the ailing George Chicherin as Commissar for Foreign Affairs in July 1930.[1]

Less dramatic and less caustically brilliant than his predecessor, Litvinov was nevertheless a person of intelligence and the possessor of a physical vitality which contrasted with Chicherin's chronic ill-health. There had long been a basic antagonism between the two men both on the personal and on the policy level. To Chicherin, the Middle East had been the area of paramount importance to Soviet diplomacy, while relations with the western nations, toward which, excepting Germany, he had a distinct antipathy, were of secondary importance. Litvinov, on the other hand, saw that the safety of Russia both in the east and the west could never be secured without

---

[1] At the time of his appointment, Litvinov declared that: "The important task of Soviet diplomacy is the security of peaceful conditions and freedom from external blows for our socialist construction." N. Kornev, *Litvinov* (Moscow, 1936), 39.

friendly or at least normal relations with the Great Powers, which in the last instance directed the movements of world diplomacy. The new Commissar was a realist, ready to sacrifice impractical theoretical goals for material improvements in the international position of the Soviet Union.[2]

The first prolonged threat to Russian security after Litvinov assumed the directorship of Soviet foreign policy began in September 1931, when the Japanese army in Manchuria seized upon the terrorist act of a Chinese nationalist as cause for reprisal and conquest. Within a few days the Japanese occupied Mukden, and in the next months their control was rapidly extended over a wide area. The historical ambitions of Japan on the Asiatic mainland gave Moscow every reason to be concerned about the security of its Far Eastern provinces contiguous to Manchuria. Yet, in the early stages of the occupation, the Soviet Union followed a policy of cautious restraint in its relations with Tokyo. Apparently the Kremlin was suspicious that the Manchurian incident was the beginning of a widely supported anti-Soviet crusade.[3] Undoubtedly it wished to avoid offering Japan any excuse for an attack on Siberia. In any case, Russian protests were more frequently directed at the League for its ineffective peace machinery than at the foreign office in Tokyo.[4]

Significant of the Russian attitude was the Litvinov proposal of December 1931, for a nonaggression pact with Japan.[5] Moscow was greatly disturbed by the Japanese danger, but for the sake of continued peace it was willing not to contest the ac-

[2] This brief evaluation of Litvinov is based largely on a conversation with Mr. Louis Fischer, who probably knew the Soviet statesman as well as did any foreigner, and upon Fischer's *Men and Politics, An Autobiography* (New York, 1941), 128-130. See also Arthur Upham Pope, *Maxim Litvinoff* (New York, 1943). Kornev, *op. cit.*, is strictly a panegyric.

[3] *Izvestia*, September 21, 1931.

[4] Max Beloff, *The Foreign Policy of Soviet Russia, 1929-1941* (London, 1947), I, 178.

[5] Harriet Moore, *Soviet Far Eastern Policy, 1931-1945* (Princeton, 1945), 11.

tivities of Japan as long as no attack was made on Soviet territory. The Japanese, however, vouchsafed no answer to the Litvinov suggestion, at least not until December 1932,[6] thus increasing Russian apprehension. In the meantime, tension developed over the use of the Chinese and Eastern Railway in Manchuria, and Soviet ire was aroused by the reported recruiting of Japanese auxiliaries from the White Russian colonies in Mukden and Harbin. By December 1931, V. M. Molotov, the Chairman of the Council of People's Commissars, was able to characterize the Manchurian situation as the "most important problem of our foreign policy."[7]

In March 1932, the Soviet Government stiffened its attitude and gave Japan warning that anti-Russian acts and statements would no longer be ignored. The change was heralded by an editorial in *Izvestia* on March 4, which was reprinted the following day in all the leading newspapers. Since September, the paper declared, Russia had done all in her power to continue proper relations with Japan despite the direct interest Russia must have in any activities in Manchuria. But the Japanese had chosen to continue anti-Soviet acts and accusations to the point where Russia was now forced to take cognizance of them, and in return to inform Tokyo that she was aware of the underlying plans of the Japanese for aggression against the Soviet Union. To support these charges, *Izvestia* quoted from several documents of purported Japanese origin which appeared to substantiate the aggressive aims of Tokyo.[8]

The shift from appeasement to intransigence played an important role in Russian-American relations, for from that time on Russia displayed a heightened interest in a rapprochement with the United States. Three factors contributed to this new awareness of America's importance to the Soviet Union. First,

[6] When the Japanese did at last reply to the proposal, it was to declare that such an agreement was impossible until the questions at issue between the two governments were first settled, *ibid.*
[7] *Pravda*, December 24, 1931.
[8] *Izvestia*, March 4, 1932.

51

of course, was the necessity for peace during the period of forced economic expansion. The second element had a longer history in Soviet thought.

Among the basic tenets of Soviet foreign policy and Communist theory was the belief in an ever-present antagonism and an inevitable conflict between Japan and the United States. Although in the long-term view, this rivalry was placed second in importance to the Anglo-American antagonism, in 1932 its culmination in hostilities was considered more imminent, with England perhaps joining Japan against the United States. Lenin, in an early exposition of this thesis, told the Eighth Congress of Soviets in 1920 that all the facts, economic, diplomatic, and commercial, in the history of Japanese-American relations pointed to the inevitability of a conflict over the hegemony of the Pacific Ocean and its surrounding areas.[9] A year later, in a four line summary of his views on the future of international alignments, he wrote:

> Entente versus Germany
> America versus Japan (and England)
> America versus Europe
> Imperialist world versus "Asia"[10]

Thus, according to Lenin, the United States was not only the prime enemy of Japan, but it stood also in opposition to France and England, both of which were regarded with suspicion by Russia as possible instigators of a future war against Soviet rule, and both of which she suspected in 1931 and 1932 of tacitly approving the actions of Japan in Manchuria.

Lenin's views were shared by Leon Trotsky, who in 1920 suggested to John Reed, an American Communist correspondent, that Wilson's anti-Soviet policy was scarcely the wisest one for America in view of the relations between Tokyo and Washington.[11] Mikhail Pavlovich, in his little book on Russia

---

[9] V. I. Lenin, *Sochineniia*, 2nd ed. (Moscow, 1930), xxvi 7.

[10] *ibid.*, 313.

[11] L. Trotsky, *Kak vooruzhalas revoliutsiia* (Moscow, 1924), ii, Part 2, 283-284.

and America, published in 1922, pointed out that the constant possibility of war with Japan should influence the United States toward a rapprochement with the Soviet Union.[12] And, finally, it is possible to find a statement by Stalin suggesting a desire to give the theory life by artificial means. Grigory Bessedovsky, in his somewhat lurid exposé of Soviet diplomacy, relates that in 1927 Stalin wanted to sell the Chinese and Eastern Railway to Japan in order to increase the antagonism between the two countries.[13] With due allowance for the errors of memory, the episode does reveal the persistence of the idea in official Soviet thought.

The third source of Russian hope for American support, and one which served to confirm the long-held theory, was the obvious opposition of the United States to Japanese activities in Manchuria. Although Washington showed no intention of engaging in hostilities or of taking any material measures, neither did it conceal its dislike of Japanese action. The forthright statements of American policy were in decided contrast to European pronouncements. Secretary of State Henry L. Stimson had cooperated with the League of Nations from the beginning in an effort to investigate the Manchurian affair. And when it became apparent that the League was in no hurry to assign the responsibility, Stimson moved unilaterally to declare the Japanese action an infraction of the Nine Power Agreement. In January 1932, he announced that the United States would not recognize any situation resulting from a negation of the principles of the Pact of Paris—a clear and direct reference to the puppet regime in Manchuria which the Japanese were in the process of establishing. In the same month, it was reported that the United States fleet would conduct extensive maneuvers in the Pacific. Moscow interpreted the

[12] Mikhail Pavlovich, *Sovetskaia Rossiia i kapitalisticheskaia Amerika* (Moscow, 1922), 54-55.

[13] Grigory Bessedovsky, *Revelations of a Soviet Diplomat* (London, 1931), 176.

news as another expression of American enmity toward Japan.[14]

These moves were encouraging to Russia, but the Soviet Government did not consider them in any way adequate to meet the Japanese threat. In fact, Russian suspicions of European hypocrisy, in connection with the half-hearted moves to censure Japan, extended to the United States as well. The Soviet leaders feared that an actual attack on them by the Japanese might take the form of an anti-Communist movement and be condoned, if not joined, by the western powers—nor did they exclude the possibility of American participation in such a campaign.[15]

Nevertheless the United States had acted more forcefully than the other powers, and the fundamental differences between Tokyo and Washington gave hope that the future might bring stronger reactions to Japanese aggression. Russia and the United States were both working for peace in the Far East and had few points of conflict at the moment in that area. Moscow recalled with new interest the role of America in the Siberian intervention of 1918-1920, and was inclined to give greater credence to American claims that her primary purpose had been to restrain the Japanese.[16] General William Graves' account of the intervention was translated into Russian and given an extensive review in the pages of *Pravda*. According to the reviewer, Graves' book made it clear that the United States went into Eastern Russia not to dismember it, but to keep Japan from carrying out her plans of aggrandizement. The timeliness of the book's publication was pointedly emphasized by the reviewer. It was, he observed, a propitious indication that American military circles had abandoned any plan of intervention against Russia and were directing all their

[14] *Izvestia*, January 6, 1932.

[15] *Pravda*, August 1, 1932; G. Voitinskii, E. Iolk, N. Nasonov, "Sobytiia na Dal'nem Vostoke i opasnost voiny," *Bol'shevik*, March 31, 1932, 42-55; editorial in *Pravda*, December 1, 1931.

[16] A. Kantorovich, *Amerika v bor'be za Kitai* (Moscow, 1935), 585-588.

hostility at Japan.[17] When, early in 1933, the State Department published the volumes of *Foreign Relations* covering the period of intervention, the Soviet press found these conclusions strengthened.[18] In both cases, however, it was carefully noted that the Red Army, not the American forces, had thrown Japan out of Siberia, and that the entire policy of the United States, whatever its result, was based on imperialistic rivalry with Japan rather than sympathy for Russia.

For a variety of reasons, therefore, all related to the international situation, a political rapprochement with America was sought by Russia with an urgency that the exigencies of trade had not produced in the previous years. There were many evidences of this new emphasis in the winter and spring of 1931-1932. Late in 1931, M. A. Karskii, the Soviet envoy to Lithuania, told the American Chargé there of Russian disappointment that the absence of relations prevented cooperation in damming the Japanese advance. It was clear to the Soviets, he said, that Japan would never be content with her present conquests, but would in time engulf the whole East, moving first to seize the Philippines. And he significantly pointed out that America was handicapped by the lack of any bases from which to prosecute a war against Japan effectively.[19] Karskii spoke again, in February 1932, of the potentialities of joint Russian-American action in the Pacific, stating that "the most salutary thing that could happen in the Far East right now was for Russia and the United States to join in a common pressure upon Japan, if necessary breaking that country as between the two arms of a nut cracker."[20]

Meanwhile, Litvinov was voicing the same opinion in Geneva. Speaking to a committee made up of representatives

[17] *Pravda*, September 8, 1932.
[18] *ibid.*, February 24, 1933.
[19] Pauline Tompkins, *American-Russian Relations in the Far East* (New York, 1949), 256.
[20] Fullerton to Stimson, February 26, 1932 (760N.00/23), United States Department of State Archives, as cited in *ibid.*, 256.

of American peace organizations and civic groups, Litvinov diverged somewhat from his discussion of disarmament to touch on events in the Far East. He rejected the theory that one cause of the ineffectiveness of measures for peace was the nonmembership of some states in the League, and advanced the argument that a more important factor was the "economic and political estrangement between several states . . . and the Soviet Union." For evidence he chose the situation in the Pacific area, where the states most concerned, namely, the United States, the Soviet Union, and China, had no formal relations.

Enlarging on that theme, he continued: "It seems to me that not much imagination and political perspicacity are required to understand the extent to which this circumstance influenced, if it did not actually cause, present events in the Far East, or to understand that but for this circumstance these unfortunate occurrences might not have arisen or might have appeared quite different."[21] The importance that the Soviet Government attached to the remarks of Litvinov was suggested by the publication of the complete text on the front pages of the leading Moscow newspapers.

In fact, in the absence of official documents, probably no better evidence of Russian interest in a rapprochement with the United States in 1932 can be found than the pages of *Izvestia* and *Pravda*. Stimson's notification to Japan and China of the doctrine of nonrecognition, and the letter of Stimson to Senator Borah, released on February 24, which amplified the same principle, both received extensive though not entirely uncritical coverage in the Soviet press.[22] *Izvestia* had several news items in February from the Tass correspondent in New York, testifying to the growing warlike mood in the United

[21] *Izvestia*, February 22, 1932.

[22] The United States Minister to Switzerland reported to Washington that Karl Radek, the influential Soviet publicist, had sent a long analysis of the Stimson letter to Moscow from Geneva with the comment that "it was the most effective step yet taken to exert pressure on Japan and at the same time to reduce the risk of war." *Foreign Relations*, 1932, III, 449.

States, and the aroused anti-Japanese feeling.[23] Simultaneously, however, appeared articles describing the horrors of unemployment in the United States and the continued well-being of such capitalist monsters as Morgan in the midst of general starvation.[24]

Thus, the press reports did not whitewash the United States nor make its internal policies attractive. But they did tend, in a manifestation of wishful thinking, to exaggerate American alarm over Japanese activities. A Tass dispatch from New York in March suggested that the United States was pursuing a two-faced policy, namely, pretending to work with the League for a peaceful settlement, and at the same time making only token efforts to control the agitation within the country for a blockade of Japan. In other words, opined the correspondent, Washington actually approved of a more aggressive policy toward Japan. In support of his theory, the Tass man noted that as prominent a person as Newton D. Baker, the former Secretary of War, was a leader in the anti-Japanese campaign.[25] This report illustrated a recurring Soviet fallacy in evaluating American actions, a fallacy which has on more than one occasion led Moscow astray in its appraisal of the objectives of the United States. Moscow has never been convinced that any sizable element of the American public and press would be permitted to voice its opinions if they were not at least tacitly approved by the government. As a result, there is a tendency to overemphasize the importance of private opinion, especially when enunciated by well-known individuals, or even to give undue weight to official pronouncements that are not representative of the prevailing public opinion.

Following the strong editorial in *Izvestia* on March 4, 1932, in regard to continued Japanese provocations, there was a noticeable upswing in speculative articles and news items in the

[23] See, for example, *Izvestia*, February 28, 1932.
[24] *ibid.*, February 29, 1932.
[25] *Pravda*, March 3, 1932; see also *ibid.*, February 28, 1932.

Soviet press on the possibility of a change in the American attitude on Russia. When John Bromley, Chairman of the General Council of Trade Unions in England, made the statement that a rapprochement between Russia and the United States would create a great force for peace in the Far East, *Izvestia* quoted his remarks in some detail.[26] Then, on March 14, came a report from Shanghai that diplomatic circles in China were discussing the possibility of a resumption of relations.[27] Four days later, both *Pravda* and *Izvestia* came out with front page stories stating that informed British sources believed Washington to be considering an about-face toward Russia. These "sources" disclosed that the United States was not too disturbed about a satisfactory settlement of the debt problem, but felt that the propaganda issue was the greatest hindrance to a closer relationship. The informants also observed that Washington was noting the more friendly attitude of the Soviet press toward the United States in recent weeks and felt that it reflected Kremlin opinion.[28] The fact that the latter statement was printed by the Russian press without comment was perhaps significant.

Moscow apparently made no effort to capitalize on this report and to approach the American government. If it had any intention of doing so, its hand was no doubt stayed by the prompt disavowal of the rumor by the State Department on March 18, 1932.[29] But that rebuff did not stop the further publication of encouraging reports from abroad. Ten days later, the Soviet press printed extensive excerpts from the *New Republic*, which urged collaboration between the two nations to keep the peace in the Far East.[30] And in May, articles by Oswald G. Villard and Frederick L. Schuman in the *Nation*, on the same subject, were quoted at length.[31] The remarks of

[26] *Izvestia*, March 11, 1932. [27] *Pravda*, March 14, 1932.
[28] *ibid.*; *Izvestia*, March 18, 1932.
[29] *New York Times*, March 19, 1932.
[30] *Pravda* and *Izvestia*, March 28, 1932.
[31] *ibid.*, May 28, 1932.

American senators and representatives advocating a revaluation of the Russian question were also faithfully reported.[32] After May the coverage was somewhat less extensive, possibly because of the temporary betterment in Soviet-Japanese relations from that date through the summer.[33] But scarcely a week passed without some allusion to the problem.

The month of June 1932 gave the Soviet Government the opportunity to point up in another area its friendlier attitude toward the United States. At Geneva, where the World Disarmament Conference was in session, Hugh Gibson, the American delegate, presented, on June 22, the Hoover plan for a sharp quantitative reduction in all armaments. In the discussion which followed, Litvinov rose to speak for the Soviet Union. He expressed Moscow's dissatisfaction with the lack of progress made by the Conference and reminded the delegates that his government was for complete disarmament, but he emphasized Russia's willingness to support any positive steps toward that goal. As to the Hoover proposals, he saw in them an attempt to break the deadlock and move forward, and for that reason and "because to some extent they proceeded along the same lines as the Soviet proposals which were not accepted," he was very glad that they had been laid before the Conference.[34]

Though this was faint praise, it was nonetheless suggestive, for Moscow had found little to commend in the proceedings of the Conference to that date. The United States along with the other powers had been accused of hypocrisy and no real in-

[32] See, for examples, *ibid.*, March 7, April 23, 24, 25, 27, 28, and July 26, 1932.

[33] Beloff, *The Foreign Policy of Soviet Russia, 1929-1941*, I, 81, explains that the tension decreased because of the mutually satisfactory revision of the fisheries agreement which had been a point of contention between the two governments. Apparently, the stiffened Soviet attitude, as indicated by troop concentrations upon the Russo-Japanese border, also had an alleviating effect.

[34] Wilbur Lee Mahaney, *The Soviet Union, The League of Nations and Disarmament, 1917-1935* (University of Pennsylvania, 1940), 135-139.

tention of disarming. Earlier in the year, the Soviets had referred with particular sarcasm to the American pacifistic statements at the Conference. They declared that the United States was anxious for other nations to disarm, but unwilling to take effective steps in that direction itself.[35] In fact, America was accused of carrying out a gigantic fleet building program at the very moment she was advocating arms reduction at Geneva[36]—a palpable untruth.

But the Hoover proposal was printed in full on the first page of the leading Soviet newspapers,[37] and the editorial comment which followed was not as unfriendly as previous coverage of American proposals. There was tacit admission that the United States desired disarmament, but on the other hand there was no attempt to attribute its action to altruistic motives. America had only wished to answer the charge of her European debtors that she gave them no opportunity to pay. If they spent less on armaments, Hoover implied, they could pay their debts. It was also suggested that domestic politics on the eve of the presidential election played their part. The United States did not expect the plan to be adopted: it merely wanted to bring European hypocrisy into the open.[38] Still it was a little "spark" lighting up the dark corners of a world preparing for war.[39]

This appraisal, an admixture of approval for the particular policy and distrust or suspicion of the motives which prompted it, was characteristic of Soviet diplomacy. Other examples, previously discussed, come to mind immediately. The fact that Moscow supported the stand taken by another government in no way indicated that it shared the long term objectives of that government. Collaboration was always in the name of expediency. And it is in that light that the Russian attempt to

[35] See *Pravda*, February 11, 12, 27, 1932.
[36] Maxim Litvinov, *The Soviets Fight for Disarmament* (New York, 1932), Introduction by M. Lunacharsky, 9-10.
[37] *Pravda* and *Izvestia*, June 24, 1932.
[38] *Pravda*, June 24, 1932; see also *ibid.*, July 2, 1932.
[39] *ibid.*, August 1, 1932.

gain the cooperation of the United States against Japan must be viewed. This is an important point and is basic to any approach to Soviet-American relations. One will look in vain for admissions that the United States opposed Japanese aggression because it valued peace as such or entertained an unselfish sympathy for the Chinese people. Those motives, for the purposes of the moment, were the exclusive property of the Soviet Union, and to award any of them to the capitalist nations would have narrowed the carefully maintained ideological gap between the two systems, between the good and the bad.

To some extent, of course, this element can be found in the foreign policy of every nation. But in Russian diplomacy a new ingredient had been added—communism, which gave Moscow a priority on righteousness. Yet until the new utopia spread over the rest of the world, Russia was forced to work with representatives of the old order. It was this basic contradiction which explained much of the ambivalence in Soviet foreign policy and statement. As Communists it was necessary to say one thing, as members of the Government of the Soviet Union it was often necessary to say something quite different. The operating theories were generally based on Communist precept, but their implementation usually had to be given a less frightening explanation abroad if they were to succeed.

Thus the Communists believed that the United States would not stand idly by while Japan gained more territory and influence in China. It would eventually move to stop that advance. But it was only her interest in Eastern markets and raw materials that prevented America from condoning the action of Japan. She would not have been as disturbed if Japan had turned northward into Russian Siberia. Although Japan and the United States were thought to be engaged in a death struggle for hegemony in the Far East, there was an underlying fear that America would be willing to postpone the contest if Japan would turn her forces on the Soviet Union.[40] It

[40] Voitinskii, Iolk, Nasonov, *loc. cit.* (see note 15 *supra*).

was even suggested that possibly some sort of agreement along these lines was in existence between the Japanese and the most powerful business groups in the United States.[41]

In general, however, the emphasis was on the increasing Japanese-American friction in China. The growing importance of that area of conflict was repeatedly discussed in Communist publications as the strongest manifestation of the desire of capitalism to seek war as a way out of the depression. As to the opposing line-up in that conflict, the Communists anticipated England joining Japan against the United States in view of the basic irreconcilability of British and American imperialism.[42] France was a less well-known quantity, sometimes considered as a partner of Great Britain, sometimes as a possible ally of the United States.[43] Germany was, of course, still a weak nation militarily and her role was not considered of much importance in non-European affairs. In the final analysis, therefore, the United States remained the most promising temporary collaborator with the Soviet Union in any effort to curb Japan, with the constant reservation that America, like any of the other imperialist nations, was interested only in her material gain.

Such was the Communist line of 1932. But the idea of working with America was implied rather than stated by Communist organs, as opposed to Soviet. Although the Soviet Union might seek allies, the Comintern was still fighting all capitalists, including the ruling classes of a possible ally. This division of purpose had been true since 1917. It was, in fact, a precept clearly enunciated by Lenin on numerous occasions. The Russian Communist party, as the party in actual power

---

[41] *Pravda*, May 30, 31, 1932.

[42] "Krizis kapitalizma i opasnost voiny," leading article in *Bol'shevik*, February 29, 1932, 8-10; see also a series of articles by O. Kuusinen, "Mezhdunarodnoe polozhenie i zadachi sektsii Kominterna," *Bol'shevik*, November 1, 15, and December 31, 1932.

[43] Compare O. Kuusinen's speech in xii *plenum* ikki: *stenograficheskii otchet* (Moscow, 1933), iii, 19, with Karl Radek, "Mezhdunarodnye protivorechiia v 1932 godu," *Bol'shevik*, November 30, 1932, 50-64.

in a national state, had to make agreements with capitalists in order to protect the only established proletarian state. But the other sections of the International and the Comintern itself had the function of revolutionary propaganda and agitation even in those countries with which Russia at the moment was working in harmony.

In the period under discussion, however, this doctrine was in the process of modification. Russian nationalism under the dictatorial guidance of Stalin was constantly strengthening the role of the Russian party in the International, a development accelerated both by the entrenchment of Stalin's power within the Soviet Union and the International and by the purportedly greater dangers of attack upon the Soviet Union from without. By 1935, the defense of Russia rather than the spread of communism was to become the primary purpose of the Comintern.[44]

An episode at the XII Plenum of the Central Executive Committee of the Third International illustrated the double-pronged policy of the Comintern towards the United States in 1932. In April, Karl Radek, the outstanding Soviet publicist on foreign affairs and generally considered the mouthpiece of Stalin, had written that if Russia were "provoked into battle, she will have the right to seek temporary allies among those capitalist powers which at that moment do not infringe on her borders or interests." But Radek added that the workers of the world must

[44] F. Borkenau, *The Communist International* (London, 1938), 340-343, 375ff. For an interesting discussion of this development by an American Communist who was expelled from the Comintern in 1929, see Jay Lovestone, *Soviet Foreign Policy and the World Revolution* (New York, 1935), *passim.* An especially frank admission of the subordination of the Comintern to the Russian party after 1932 can be found in the testimony of the notorious Russian spy, Dr. Richard Sorge, before Japanese interrogators after his capture in 1942. He gave as evidence his own career, pointing out that he began his work under the Comintern and later received instructions directly from the Soviet government. "This activity," he said, "has worked for the economic and political stability. . . . and the defense of the Soviet Union. . . . from attack." *The Sorge Spy Ring, A Case Study in International Espionage in the Far East,* U. S. Department of the Army [?] (Washington, 1948 [?]), 4.

not presume that such an alliance would indicate Russian partnership in the aims of her temporary allies.[45]

The leading Communist newspaper in the United States,
the New York *Daily Worker*, interpreted this statement as referring to America, and editorialized that it offered "new possibilities for the mobilization of the masses in the United
States, directly in support of the [Soviet] peace policy. . . ."[46]
But at the XII Plenum that summer, the American Communist
party was severely criticized for its statement. The primary
task of the American party was not agitation against the Japanese, but against the imperialists in its own country who continued to supply arms to the Japanese. The article in the *Daily
Worker* was a betrayal of Communist principles.[47] Accordingly,
the representative from the United States admitted the error
of his party in suggesting the United States as a "natural ally"
of Russia. The mistakes of the American party lay in the assumptions that the Soviet Union could ever have a "natural
ally" among the capitalist nations, and that the ruling classes
of the United States were less dangerous than the Japanese
imperialists.[48]

Yet at the same Plenum the American party was given the
task of popularizing "among the workers the demand for the
recognition of the Soviet Union."[49] Although the instructions
of the Central Committee ordered the American party to engage in a fight against capitalism and imperialism in its own
country, the over-all emphasis was decidedly on the defense
of the Soviet Union, not on any revolutionary activity in the
United States.

Back in America, it was possible to see the reflection of this
policy not only in the *Daily Worker*, which was to be expected, but in a new magazine, *Soviet Russia Today*, published
by the Friends of the Soviet Union, a presumably non-party

---

[45] *Izvestia*, April 10, 1932. [46] *Daily Worker*, April 12, 1932.
[47] XII *plenum* IKKI, *op. cit.*, I, 24.
[48] *ibid.*, III, 74. [49] *ibid.*, III, 13.

organization which religiously followed the Communist line. The aims of this journal were to "fight the enemies of the Soviet Union" and to foster "mass campaigns" for recognition.[50] Filled with photographs illustrating the prosperity and well-being of the Soviet citizen, and the gigantic industrial development of Russia, it held out the promise of increased employment in the United States through normal trade relations.[51] But it was in its preoccupation with the defense of Russia against attack that the magazine best disclosed its backers. Many articles dealt with the need for recognition if Japan were to be stopped on the road to conquest. In September 1932, Corliss Lamont stated that the best test of American sincerity in the struggle for peace was the attitude displayed toward the USSR. No other step would more clearly show that the United States really desired to strengthen the peaceful world than a resumption of relations with Soviet Russia.[52] The issues of this magazine were, however, chiefly interesting as reflecting the fight for recognition by the Communist party and its friends in America. Their actual influence was extremely limited, a fact which was eloquently testified to by the constant appeal for subscriptions, and by the uncertainty of publication owing to lack of funds.

The end of 1932 brought a Soviet diplomatic achievement which illustrated the Janus-like quality of Communism in power. Moreover, it provided Moscow with a new argument for a Russo-American rapprochement. On December 12, Russia and China resumed diplomatic relations. The event was hailed by Moscow as a great step forward in the task of preserving peace in the Far East, but it modified only slightly if at all the attacks on the Nanking government by the Comintern, which naturally supported the Chinese Communists.

[50] *Soviet Russia Today*, I, No. 1 (February, 1932), 2.
[51] *ibid.*, I, No. 5 (June, 1932), 3, 13.
[52] *ibid.*, I, No. 8 (September, 1932), 3.

Throughout the negotiations between China and Russia and especially following their successful conclusion, the Russians and the Chinese sought to convince the United States that it should follow the example set and recognize the Soviet Union.

The Sino-Russian conversations began at the Disarmament Conference in Geneva. As early as October 12, 1932, the United States Minister to Switzerland reported a conversation with Dr. W. W. Yen, the Chinese representative at the Conference, in which he had been apprised of Litvinov's desire to see the United States also enter into relations with Moscow. Dr. Yen told the American Minister that Litvinov considered a pre-recognition settlement of the American private and public debt impossible and if that were the criterion then relations might be delayed for fifty years.[53]

Nevertheless, on December 12, Litvinov made a statement, the import of which could hardly have been missed by Washington. Remarking that the resumption of normal relations between China and Russia was of such obvious benefit to both nations that it required no explanation, he went on to say: "What does require explanation is the rupture of relations between states or the refusal of relations. . . . [I]t is beyond doubt . . . that the commencement of the present troubles in the Far East is in no small degree due to the fact that not all of the states situated on the shores of the Pacific Ocean have been maintaining diplomatic relations with one another. . . . Only when all states maintain relations with one another will it be possible to speak seriously of international cooperation in the cause of peace. . . ."[54]

Four days later, Dr. Lo, the Chinese Foreign Minister, told Nelson Johnson, the American Minister in Nanking, that he was sure Russia desired American recognition, and asked what chance there might be for a change in Washington's policy.

[53] *Foreign Relations, 1932*, IV, 297.
[54] *Pravda*, December 13, 1932.

Johnson replied that he did not anticipate any change, at least under the present Administration.[55]

On December 20, 1932, Mr. Stanley Hornbeck, Chief of the State Department's Division of Far Eastern Affairs, had a conversation on the same subject with Dr. Chinglun Lee, former Chinese Vice-Minister of Foreign Affairs, who was on a special mission to the United States. Dr. Lee was particularly interested in the reaction of Washington to the recent rapprochement of his country with the Soviet Union, and wished to make it clear that the step in no way implied the return of China to the 1924-1927 period, when she had relied on Communist leadership. Hornbeck replied that the United States realized the difference in the two situations and was always pleased to see the nations of the Far East "on good terms with one another." Taking advantage of this opening, Dr. Lee asked what he termed an "indiscreet question": was there any chance of American recognition of Russia in the near future? Hornbeck's answer, paralleling that of Johnson, gave no evidence that Washington was contemplating a change in its fifteen-year-old policy.[56]

The Soviet press, however, reported from both Washington and Tokyo that the Sino-Russian rapprochement and the developing situation in the Far East were causing Washington quietly to revaluate its policy.[57] And, although the Russians undoubtedly overestimated the importance of the rumors, Washington was in fact giving the subject consideration. The reports from Japan of Ambassador Joseph C. Grew indicated that the Japanese military were in a dangerous mood. In a dispatch dated August 13, 1932, Grew warned that the Nipponese "military machine . . . . has been built for war, feels prepared for war, and would welcome war." "I am not an alarmist," the Ambassador wrote, "but I believe that we should have our eyes open to all possible future contingencies. The facts

[55] *Foreign Relations, 1932*, iv, 436. [56] *ibid.*, 446.
[57] *Pravda* and *Izvestia*, December 15, 1932.

of history would render it criminal to close them."[58] Later, in February 1933, Grew cautioned the Department: "We must bear in mind that a considerable section of the public and the army, influenced by military propaganda, believes that eventual war between either the United States or Russia, or both, and Japan is inevitable."[59] Meanwhile, from China, Minister Johnson, as early as January 1932, expressed the belief that no effective solution to the Sino-Japanese problem could be achieved without regard to the importance of the Russian role in the situation,[60] an opinion in which the Chinese Government concurred.[61]

In the spring of 1932, Secretary Stimson had traveled to Europe and attended the Disarmament Conference, and there the subject of Russian recognition had been discussed with him by other members of the American Delegation. On his return to the United States, Stimson asked the Far Eastern Division of the Department to draft a memorandum for him, stating the advantages and disadvantages of recognition in terms of the Far Eastern situation. Throughout the summer, Stimson gave the problem his "close attention." But by September, he had decided against the step. In a letter to Senator Borah, he explained his reasons. The position of the United States in regard to the Far East, the Secretary pointed out, was based on moral principles, namely, the sanctity of international obligations, and was expressed "through pacific means calculated to avoid anything which approached force or political alliance."

With these tenets in view, he continued: "If under these circumstances and in this emergency we recognized Russia in disregard of her very bad reputation respecting international obligations and in disregard of our previous emphasis upon that aspect of her history, the whole world, and particularly Japan, would jump to the conclusion that our action had been

[58] Joseph C. Grew, *Ten Years in Japan* (New York, 1944), 64-65.
[59] *ibid.*, 77.   [60] *Foreign Relations, 1932*, III, 26-27.
[61] *ibid.*, 21.

dictated solely by political expediency and as a maneuver to bring forceful pressure upon Japan. . . . I felt that the loss of moral standing would be so important that we could not afford to take the risk of it. However innocent our motives might be, they would certainly be misunderstood by the world at large and particularly by Japan. . . ."[62]

But there is some reason to believe that the letter reflected more the views of President Hoover than those of his Secretary of State. During the last two years of Mr. Stimson's tenure, the deepening international crises brought to the fore a latent conflict between the policies of the two men. Mr. Hoover felt that the United States should remain aloof from the events which threatened the peace of the world, exerting only moral influence on the side of justice. The Secretary, on the other hand, believed that America was obligated to take an active role in the fight against aggression.[63] One possible step in that direction would have been closer cooperation with the Soviet Union. Certainly, that move would have met with the President's disapproval, running counter not only to his views on the overall foreign policy of the United States, but also to his great and long-standing distrust of the Soviet regime.

In any case, Louis Fischer came away from an interview with Stimson, in February 1933, with the firm impression that the Secretary had personally favored the recognition of Russia. On the same day, Fischer also saw Senator Borah, who told him that Stimson would have recognized Russia the previous summer had it not been for the opposition of the President. Borah's remarks were based on a conversation he had had with the Secretary, apparently about the time of the above-quoted letter.[64] In January 1933, Stimson gave still another indication that he was not averse to friendlier relations with

[62] *ibid., 1933*, ɪɪ, 778.
[63] Henry L. Stimson and McGeorge Bundy, *On Active Service in Peace and War* (New York, 1947), 199-200.
[64] Fischer, *Men and Politics*, 213.

Russia. Ambassador Grew in Japan had refused to sign an Address to the Emperor drafted by the new Dean of the Diplomatic Corps in Tokyo, Soviet Ambassador Alexander A. Troyanovsky. This was fully in accordance with the American practice of not recognizing any representative of the Russian government. But, at the insistence of other members of the Corps in Tokyo, Grew perfunctorily wired Washington for confirmation of his action. Much to his surprise, he received a reply instructing him to sign the Address and, further, to carry out all the social functions necessary between a member of the Corps and the Dean. It was quite permissible for him to call on and receive Troyanovsky as long as the exchanges clearly indicated that he was not entering into relations with him as a representative of Russia.[65] In the realm of protocol it was a step of some importance.

The Japanese were undoubtedly aware of Russian attempts to convince America that recognition was desirable, and probably aware that the Department of State had given some attention to that demand in view of its concern over further aggression by Japan. Mr. Stimson recorded a conversation with the Japanese Ambassador to the United States, in May 1932, in which the Ambassador refuted the reports that Tokyo had any hostile designs against Russia. Such rumors, the Ambassador asserted, were of Russian origin and intended to frighten the United States into recognizing Russia.[66] After Litvinov's remarks on December 12, regretting the absence of relations between certain Far Eastern powers, the Foreign Office in Tokyo denied the validity of the Commissar's words. The Manchurian affair, the Japanese officials claimed, had absolutely no connection with the nonrecognition of the Soviet Union by the United States.[67]

[65] Grew, *op. cit.*, 58-59.
[66] *Foreign Relations, 1932*, IV, 42.
[67] *ibid.*, 440-441. It is interesting to note, however, that the Japanese were using the nonmembership of Russia and the United States in the League of Nations as a reason why they need not be bound by League

But the fears of the Tokyo government were revealed else-where in the conjecture of Toshio Shiratori, Director of Information at the Foreign Office, that there was a secret under-standing between China, the United States, and Russia.[68] This concern was also substantiated by a survey of Japanese-American and Japanese-Russian relations received at the United States Embassy in Japan from a "Soviet source," the findings of which tended to confirm the Embassy's own evaluation. According to the Russian analysis, the Japanese were very apprehensive of a rapprochement between America and the Soviet Union. In the meantime they were arming on a vast scale. Since little resistance could be expected from the Chinese, it was logical to assume that the Japanese were preparing to turn against Russia. The document concluded with the frank admission that Moscow "badly needs the resumption of diplomatic relations with the United States." Although the Soviet Union could not agree to pay the debts owed America because of the resulting complications in its relations with other countries, it was prepared, according to the writer, to grant attractive economic favors in lieu of payment.[69]

Meanwhile, Soviet contentions were gaining support in the United States. Senators Joseph Robinson and Key Pittman considered the Far East equal to trade in importance as an argument for recognition. A resumption of relations, they declared, would open the way to fruitful cooperation in stemming the Japanese advance in China.[70] Similarly, Senator Hiram Johnson stated that "some move in the direction of normal relationships with Russia at this time would do more to remove the perils from the Far East, and therefore from the world in general, than any other single act."[71] From Moscow, Louis Fischer, writing as an American but speaking for the Russians,

---

decisions. "Records of the Special Session of the Assembly," *League of Nations Official Journal* (Geneva, 1933), III, 71.

[68] *Foreign Relations, 1933*, III, 182.   [69] *ibid.*, 228-230.
[70] *New York Times*, April 23, 1932.   [71] *ibid.*, April 24, 1932.

pointed out that "any real understanding is possible only between friends or between nations with common goals, common
interests or common enemies. Russia and Japan have no common enemies. If there were any real statesmen in Washington,
they would know how to take advantage of this situation."[72]

In general, however, trade remained the primary incentive
for recognition in the United States. Even those Americans
who saw the diplomatic advantages of a closer relationship
with Russia believed that their goal would have a greater appeal through commercial arguments than by emphasis on
foreign affairs. Newspaper publisher Roy Howard, during the
spring of 1932, began a campaign in the Scripps-Howard press
for a resumption of relations with the Soviet Union. But in a
letter to President Hoover, he explained that despite his belief
that the Far Eastern crisis was the all-important reason for
such a step, he was aware that isolationist America must be
persuaded by economic factors and not frightened by international complications.[73]

The Kremlin, for its part, made every effort to keep the
recognition issue alive. Seeking to influence American opinion,
Karl Radek wrote, in an article for *Foreign Affairs*, chiding the
United States on its Russian policy: "The attitude of the
United States toward the Soviet Union, which entails sacrific-
ing the advantages of an economic and political *rapprochement* to the considerations of parochial politicians in search of
thrillers for home consumption, is an example of the complete
lack of vision and determination in the foreign policy of the
United States. The Japanese laugh at the threats of the American press. They point out that the United States is incapable
even of making a decision to resume normal relations with the
Soviet Union. . . ."

[72] *Nation*, November 2, 1932, 420.
[73] Roy Howard to Herbert Hoover, August 2, 1932, "Russia 1929-1932,"
Herbert Hoover Archives, Hoover Library, Stanford University, California.
The Soviet press noted this newspaper campaign, but significantly emphasized its references to the Far Eastern situation. *Izvestia*, April 7, 1932.

In conclusion, Radek added, with unmistakable implication, that Moscow was ready to "collaborate with any power which desires the peaceful development of the Far East."[74]

Vyacheslav Molotov also employed the technique of derision in his report to the Central Executive Committee of the USSR in January 1933. Taking note of the rumors that Washington was considering the question of recognition, and that some "wise acres" still thought a special study should be made of the Soviet regime before any action was taken, Molotov suggested that the time for inquests was long since past. In any case, he inquired, how could an investigation be conducted without the existence of normal diplomatic intercourse?[75] In an editorial on the Molotov address, *Izvestia* deplored the American "hide and seek" attitude toward Russia which served only to hinder trade and make more difficult the cause of peace. But the newspaper also noted with pleasure the strengthened trend toward recognition which had developed in the United States during 1932.[76]

A month later, in Tokyo, the Russian Military Attaché drew the American Attaché aside at a social function to impress upon him the interest of Russia in a "friendly understanding" with the United States. It would be a mutually advantageous move, he asserted, and, in order to facilitate it, Russia would be willing to make an arrangement "equivalent" to the paying of her war debt. The propaganda problem, he admitted, would be harder to settle, because of the difficulties experienced by Moscow in controlling the Communists.[77]

The incumbent American Administration remained adamant. But 1932 was an election year, and in November the American people had repudiated the Republican party and swept into the Presidential office the Democratic Governor of New

[74] Karl Radek, "The War in the Far East, A Soviet View," *Foreign Affairs*, x (1932), 556.

[75] *Izvestia*, January 24, 1933.

[76] *ibid.*, January 25, 1933.

[77] *Foreign Relations, 1933*, ii, 779-780.

York, Franklin D. Roosevelt. Roosevelt's statements on Russian relations had been few, but there was reason to believe that he did not exclude the possibility of a rapprochement. Moscow awaited developments under the new Administration with interest.[78]

[78] *Izvestia*, January 8, 1933.

C H A P T E R   4

HARBINGERS OF RECOGNITION

THE recognition issue played little part in the American Presidential election of 1932. In fact, it was not brought forward for public consideration by either candidate. Nevertheless, an attempt was made by those individuals and organizations which felt strongly on the subject to force the two major parties to take a stand. They did not succeed, but as a result of their endeavors, the Russian question hovered around the edges of the campaign with enough persistency to give some indication of the undisclosed views of the candidates.

The Republicans met in convention in Chicago on June 14 and renominated Herbert Hoover. Thirteen days later, the Democrats met in the same city and chose Governor Franklin D. Roosevelt of New York as their standard bearer. Although shortly before the conventions it was rumored that certain leading Democrats, including Senator Joseph Robinson, favored advancing recognition "as an essential item for general recovery,"[1] neither party included any reference to the subject in its platform. President Hoover's previous statements left little doubt as to his convictions. Roosevelt's views were unknown, but his liberal approach to many national issues encouraged recognition advocates.

Considerable significance was attached to Roosevelt's conference of July 25, 1932, with Walter Duranty.[2] Duranty later wrote that Roosevelt displayed a keen interest in Russian affairs and exhibited an unprejudiced approach to the issues involved.[3] But following the interview, the Democratic nom-

---

[1] *New York Times*, June 4, 1932.   [2] *ibid.*, July 26, 1932.
[3] Walter Duranty, *I Write as I Please* (New York, 1935), 320-321.

75

inee maintained a discreet silence concerning the Russian question. Two months later the editors of *Soviet Russia Today*, endeavoring to force a statement from all the presidential candidates, addressed to them letters inquiring what action they intended in the event of their election.[4] William Foster, the Communist nominee, and Norman Thomas of the Socialist party replied that they favored recognition. President Hoover curtly responded through his secretary that he had no comment.[5] But Franklin Roosevelt, while not committing himself to any course, answered that he would give the matter his impartial consideration and attempt to reach the best decision within his power—words which gave Russia some reason to hope for a change in American policy under Democratic leadership.[6]

On November 8, the people of the United States cast their ballots. The Roosevelt victory was a landslide and the Democrats captured an overwhelming majority in both Houses of Congress. Although the election was waged almost entirely on domestic issues and primarily on the problems confronting the country as a result of the rapidly deteriorating economic sit-

[4] For the answers of the candidates, see *Soviet Russia Today*, I, No. 9 (October, 1932), 4.

[5] In October, it was suggested privately to Mr. Hoover that he announce himself in favor of recognition in order to gain badly needed votes in the east and midwest from industrialists and the unemployed. The idea was rejected by his eastern campaign manager, Senator Felix Herbert, who called the suggestion "dynamite." There is no record of Mr. Hoover's reaction to the scheme. Letter from Sidney Saperston to Theodore G. Joslin, President Hoover's Secretary, October 16, 1932; letter from Joslin to Senator Felix Herbert, October 17, 1932; letter from William H. Hamilton to Joslin, October 20, 1932, "Russia, 1929-1932," The Herbert Hoover Archives, Hoover Library, Stanford University, California.

[6] At the same time Roosevelt was apparently careful not to antagonize anti-Soviet Russians in the United States. In fact, there is evidence that he assured a representative of one émigré organization that he had no intention of recognizing the Moscow government. Consequently, the organization urged its members to give him their support. Prince Paul Chavchavadze to Governor Roosevelt, November 3, 1932, The Papers of Franklin D. Roosevelt, The Franklin D. Roosevelt Library, Hyde Park, New York. Hereafter cited as Roosevelt Papers.

uation, private and public spokesmen who interested themselves in foreign affairs saw the Roosevelt victory as a step toward better relations with the Soviet Union. A new wave of demands for recognition developed.

Those who believed that recognition would aid in the search for prosperity were far more numerous than those who looked to the international scene for their reasons. Businessmen, pointing out that Germany and even Persia sold more to Russia than did the United States, noted that the Soviets had always paid their commercial obligations promptly, and urged Roosevelt to facilitate commercial relations with Russia.[7] In February 1933, the United States Chamber of Commerce took cognizance of its members' concern with the issue, and appointed a committee to travel to the Soviet Union and report on economic conditions there.[8]

Prominent Americans on the periphery of national politics contributed to the "hue and cry" for recognition. Alfred E. Smith, speaking before the Senate Finance Committee, said he did "not know any reason for not doing it." "There is no use trading with them under cover. . . ." he explained, "we might just as well be represented there and let them be represented here at Washington, and let us do business with them in the open."[9] Another New York Democrat, Samuel Untermeyer, took the same stand,[10] while Republican Governor Gifford Pinchot of Pennsylvania expressed his conviction that recognition would be in "the best interests of our own country."[11] William Allen White indicated his support for a reconciliation, emphasizing the value of the Russian market.[12] Petitions for recognition from educators and clergymen were forwarded to the President elect.[13]

The outlook for a serious investigation of Russian-American

[7] *Business Week*, February 1, 1933.
[8] *New York Times*, February 14, 1933.
[9] *ibid.*, March 1, 1933.　　　　　[10] *ibid.*, February 28, 1933.
[11] *ibid.*, January 23, 1933.　　　　[12] *ibid.*, October 1, 2, 1933.
[13] *ibid.*, January 30, February 13, 1933.

relations by the new Administration was, in fact, growing more favorable. Senator Claude A. Swanson of Virginia, who was slated for the chairmanship of the Senate Committee on Foreign Relations in the new Congress, predicted that Roosevelt would give his attention to recognition early in his Administration.[14] Senator Borah, who had deserted the Republican ranks during the campaign and thrown his support to the Democratic ticket, restated his position, declaring Russia the "greatest undeveloped market in the world," and concluding that diplomatically the United States "cannot avoid taking her into consideration."[15] In January 1933, a *New York Times* poll of the Senate showed that twenty-two of the members who would continue in office after March favored recognition. Although Democrats predominated in the ranks of those favoring the step, the opposition contained enough members from the same party to minimize the influence of party *per se* on the question.[16]

As was to be expected, the left-wing groups also intensified their campaign. The Friends of the Soviet Union urged its members to set up committees in every community and to inaugurate a petition drive, gaining the cooperation if possible of fraternal and trade union organizations. In this manner it hoped to bring the Russian question forcibly to the attention of the new national leaders.[17]

The opposition continued to defend its case with equal vigor. Father Walsh told a meeting of the National Civic Federation, a stout foe of Soviet Russia, that "you cannot make a treaty with that evil trinity of negations (anti-social, anti-Christian, anti-American)." To receive an ambassador from

---

[14] *ibid.*, December 4, 1932. Claude Swanson was appointed Secretary of the Navy in President Roosevelt's first Cabinet.

[15] *New York Herald-Tribune*, December 15, 1932, as quoted in *Congressional Digest*, October, 1933, 238, 240.

[16] *New York Times*, January 10, 1933.

[17] *Soviet Russia Today*, I, No. 11 (January, 1933), 3; *ibid.*, No. 12 (February, 1933), 5.

Moscow, he stated, would be "a canonization of impudence."[18]
President William Green of the American Federation of Labor
referred ominously to the consequences of American competition with Russian wages and working conditions.[19] And out
of the past another voice spoke to caution the American people
against recognition. Bainbridge Colby, in answer to an inquiry from the A.F. of L., indicated that his views had not
changed in the years since he drafted the State Department
note of 1920. Russia, he wrote, was still an "enemy state," determined "to undermine and overthrow our institutions," and,
therefore, it was unthinkable for her to be accepted by the
United States as a sister nation. Such an act would, Colby believed, "repudiate one of the historic achievements of the
Democratic Party," namely, the enunciation of the policy of
nonrecognition.[20]

If appearances seemed to indicate that the leaders of the
Democratic party did not share Colby's views, there was on
the other hand no doubt that the outgoing Republican Administration did. Something in the nature of a parting statement on the subject was made by Under-Secretary of State
Castle, on March 3, 1933, in a letter to Mr. Fred Eberhardt of
New Jersey, an industrial advocate of commercial relations
with Russia. Castle wrote that though the Hoover Administration had always been in favor of sound trade relations with
the Soviet Union, it could not support recognition as long as
Russia refused to honor her international obligations. Pointing
out that the absence of credits was the serious obstacle, Castle
justifiably declared that the "mere act of recognition" would
in any case do little toward facilitating Soviet purchases in
America. The Under-Secretary noted the significant over-all
drop in Soviet imports, though he admitted that Germany,
England, and Italy were continuing to receive more Russian
orders than the United States because of government under-

18 *New York Times*, February 21, 1933.
19 *ibid.*, January 30, 1933.   20 *ibid.*, February 22, March 2, 1933.

writing of Soviet credits. Castle, however, did not suggest that the United States adopt similar measures in an effort to capture its share of the Russian trade.[21]

Moscow watched the Presidential election in America with considerable interest, paying particular attention to the foreign policy statements of the two parties and their candidates. In August 1932, *Izvestia* published a series of articles on the campaign written by P. Lapinskii (Pavel Mikhailskii or Lewinson), a Soviet journalist who had spent a good deal of time in the United States and was familiar with the American scene.[22] Lapinskii reported that, despite the absence of any reference to Russia in the party platforms, a revaluation of the entire question was taking place in the United States. He observed that the economic argument was most frequently heard. But he insisted that a more realistic view of the problem would show Americans that it was in fact the Far Eastern situation which made the question of recognition one of "Byzantine etiquette." Time would tell, Lapinskii concluded, whether "stupid class interest" or a sober approach to reality would prevail in future American foreign policy.[23]

During the autumn and winter of 1932 and 1933, the Soviets became aware of Roosevelt's unspoken but widely rumored sympathy for a new policy toward Russia. The Duranty interview was taken as an encouraging sign,[24] and after the Democratic victory, which Moscow had anticipated,[25] the Soviet press published a large number of dispatches from its American correspondents, reporting the hopeful predictions by Democratic leaders of favorable action by Roosevelt.[26] The petitions to Roosevelt were duly noted,[27] and significant articles

[21] *Foreign Relations, 1933*, II, 780-782.
[22] *Izvestia*, August 6, 8, 16, 1932. [23] *ibid.*, August 16, 1932.
[24] *ibid.*, August 17, 1932. [25] *ibid.*, November 5, 1932.
[26] See, for example, *ibid.*, August 23, November 20, December 6, 1932; *Pravda*, February 2, 1933.
[27] *Izvestia*, January 30, 1933.

on recognition in American journals were reprinted in the newspapers.

In February, *Pravda* devoted four large columns to a translation of Raymond L. Buell's discussion in the *New York Times* on America's stake in the Far East. Buell listed the preservation of China's territorial integrity, the protection of the Philippines, and the maintenance of naval equality in the Pacific as the fundamental objectives of the United States. And he called attention to the active diplomatic role America had played in opposing Japanese aggression.[28]

The publication of this article reflected Moscow's preoccupation with the Far Eastern policy of Washington as did the translation a few weeks later of an article by Louis Fischer. Mr. Fischer wrote: "The Russian issue . . . must be faced immediately. The only two great powers which really object to Japanese expansion are the United States and the Soviet Union. . . . Now America needs Russia's aid in the Pacific. The longer it takes Mr. Roosevelt to see this fact and act upon it, the more Japan will bite off. . . ."[29]

But when Franklin D. Roosevelt took the oath of office, the United States was on the verge of complete economic collapse. His first efforts as President were concerned with emergency measures to forestall the impending disaster. Speaking to the expectant and anxious people of the United States at the inaugural, Roosevelt made clear what his immediate task was to be. "Our international trade relations," he said, "though vastly important, are in point of time and necessity, secondary to the establishment of a sound national economy. I favor as a practical policy the putting of first things first."[30] It is not surprising, therefore, that there was no change in the Russian policy of the United States in the first days of the new Administration. Secondary problems had to take second place.

[28] *Pravda*, February 17, 1933.
[29] *Nation*, December 28, 1932, 633; *Izvestia*, January 9, 1933.
[30] Franklin D. Roosevelt, *The Public Papers and Addresses of Franklin D. Roosevelt* (New York, 1938), II, 14.

The American advocates and opponents of recognition were not misled by the official silence. Anticipating the time when Roosevelt would turn his attention to Russian relations, they kept the issue before the government and the public.[31] On March 24, 1933, the American Women's Committee for the Recognition of Russia presented petitions at the White House and the State Department urging immediate recognition in the "interests of trade and peace."[32] At the other end of Pennsylvania Avenue, the Senate received a similar request in the form of a memorial from the State Senate of New Mexico.[33]

Financial interests were active in Washington, "devising credit schemes" and "creating atmosphere."[34] Reversing its previous position, the American-Russian Chamber of Commerce passed a resolution recommending diplomatic relations with Russia,[35] following a similar action by the United States Board of Trade.[36] The commercial enthusiasts for recognition, spurred on by Russian statements, envisioned fantastic sales to the Soviet Union as the result of a rapprochement. One economist predicted that the United States would sell five billion dollars worth of goods to Russia in three and one half years after recognition and that the effect would be to put at least one million men back to work.[37]

In early April, the Senate discussed the subject for the first time in the new session. Senator Arthur Robinson of Indiana brought up the question of propaganda and warned that the Soviet embassy would become a center for Communist activity in America. But Senator Borah rose to declare that never

[31] Secretary of State Cordell Hull wrote that from his first days in office he began "to receive petitions asking that our government recognize Soviet Russia. . . ." Cordell Hull, *The Memoirs of Cordell Hull* (New York, 1948), I, 172.

[32] *New York Times*, March 25, 1933.

[33] *Congressional Record*, 73rd Congress, 1st Sess., 113.

[34] *Business Week*, April 5, 1933, 24.

[35] *Soviet Union Review*, XI (1933), 172.

[36] *New York Times*, June 25, 1933.

[37] David Ostrinsky, "A Five Billion Dollar Customer," *Forum* XC (1933), 131-136; *New York Times*, September 15, 1933.

"since Mr. Stalin became dictator of the Russian government [has there been] any attempt to interfere with the Governmental affairs of the United States." The fear of propaganda, he continued, was "based upon the suggestion that the intelligence, character and patriotism of the people are matters of grave doubt."[38] In June, Senator George Norris of Nebraska came out for recognition, emphasizing the trade advantages and submitting as his opinion that religion and morals in Russia were no barrier to a friendly relation with her.[39]

All these statements underlined the influence of certain intangible factors upon the attitude of Americans toward the Soviet Union. The Kremlin, seeking tranquillity during its economic and political retrenchment, had studiously cultivated an aura of respectability. The statements of Litvinov and Stalin as well as other Russian spokesmen, which stressed the peaceful purposes of Russia, had not been without their effect. Stalin's purported abandonment of world revolution for "socialism in one country" had lulled American fears of the Communist menace, while Moscow's insistence upon the practicability of the "peaceful co-existence" of the two systems, capitalist and socialist, led to hopes that Russia might be dealt with in the same manner as other countries. Even the debt problem had become less of a handicap to proper relations with the Soviets. As Samuel Untermeyer pointed out: "If we were to sever our relations with every nation that has treated us with ingratitude or repudiated its obligations, we would be 'on' the outs' with most of the important nations of the world."[40] By 1933, repudiation had become the order of the day. As a result of these developments, Americans were more willing to discount or disregard the risks involved in closer ties with Soviet Russia.

The trend was by no means universal, however. The Brooklyn *Tablet*, the official organ of the Catholic diocese of Brook-

---

[38] *Congressional Record*, 73rd Congress, 1st Sess., 1538-1546.
[39] *New York Times*, June 25, 1933.   [40] *ibid.*, January 28, 1933.

lyn, charged that recognition would be "treason" and claimed that the "authenticated" atrocities in Soviet Russia made the "reported" cruelties of Chancellor Adolph Hitler in Germany "read like the hazing indulged in by high school fraternities."[41] In an effort to fight the alleged Communist threat to America, a patriotic organization was formed called the Paul Reveres, the immediate task of which was to wage a campaign against recognition. Many of the members were leaders in the American Legion and the Daughters of the American Revolution,[42] both of which were on record as opponents of any rapprochement with Soviet Russia.[43] Perhaps the high point of the opposition's spring campaign was a rally held in Washington, on April 18, to "arouse public sentiment" against any reconciliation with the Communist regime. Sponsored by the American Legion, the American Federation of Labor, the Daughters of the American Revolution, and several fraternal organizations, the demonstration featured addresses by Dr. Walsh, William Green, Hamilton Fish, and Louis A. Johnson, National Commander of the Legion.[44] All the speakers, and especially Hamilton Fish, painted a fearful picture of the possible results of diplomatic intercourse with Russia.[45]

The *National Republic*, "A Magazine of Fundamental Americanism," well represented the super-patriotic emotional opposition to any dealings with Russia.[46] Making no attempt to evaluate the actual considerations pro and con in the problem

[41] As quoted in *ibid.*, March 25, 1933.

[42] *ibid.*, April 9, 1933.

[43] The D. A. R. National Convention voted to send a letter to the Senate opposing recognition. *Congressional Record*, 73rd Congress, 1st Sess., 1860. The American Legion formalized their opposition in their National Convention in October. *New York Times*, October 5, 6, 1933. Roosevelt was, however, assured by Representative Wright Patman that not more than five per cent of the Legion membership would be antagonized by recognition. Representative Wright Patman to Franklin D. Roosevelt, October 26, 1933, Roosevelt Papers.

[44] *New York Times*, April 19, 1933.

[45] *Congressional Record*, 73rd Congress, 1st Sess., 2189.

[46] See any issue of the *National Republic* during the spring and summer of 1933.

of recognition, the journal fed American fears of Communist activities within the country. The *Chicago Tribune* adopted the same technique, editorializing that "soon we shall have them [Soviet sympathizers] demanding . . . [that the] government shall clasp hands with Stalin, welcome his emissaries, and salute the bloody banner of the world's greatest despotism with the guns of our republic."[47] The *Columbus Dispatch* warned that recognition meant "opening the way for Soviet consular offices in all our cities, which would be used here as elsewhere, as cover for Communistic missionary agitation."[48]

More reasoned doubts were expressed by the *New York Times*, which questioned the efficacy of recognition alone as a panacea for Soviet-American trade. Recalling to its readers the fact that trade with Russia was at a high point in 1930-1931 when the United States had no relations with Moscow, it suggested that tariff revisions, the lifting of import restrictions, and the granting of government credits would have to accompany recognition if it were to accomplish all that its advocates claimed.[49]

A significant indication of American public opinion on recognition during this period of waiting was the newspaper poll conducted by the Committee on Russian-American Relations of the American Foundation. A questionnaire sent to newspapers throughout the country asked each journal whether it favored recognition of Russia followed by negotiations to adjust outstanding questions. The Foundation received replies from 1,139 newspapers. Of this number, 718 or 63 per cent favored recognition as defined; 29 or 2.6 per cent favored recognition but with qualifications; 306 or 26.9 per cent opposed recognition; and 86 or 7.5 per cent expressed no real preference. A breakdown of the results by circulation produced sub-

---

[47] As quoted in the *National Republic*, May, 1933, 26.
[48] As quoted in the *National Republic*, June, 1933, 25.
[49] *New York Times*, March 21, 1933.

stantially the same percentage figures.[50] Although the poll certainly indicated a decided swing toward recognition, the method of polling was open to considerable error as a public opinion gauge and, therefore, must be accepted with reservations.

Another mirror of American opinion and comment was the Soviet press. On occasion adding their own interpretation of the reports they printed, but more often letting the items speak for themselves, the Russian newspapers reflected the keen interest of Moscow in the trend toward recognition. Some disappointment was shown when President Roosevelt made no mention of the issue in his inaugural address and, in fact, devoted very little time to any aspect of foreign affairs.[51] But Russian hopes appeared undimmed, for the following months saw no lessening of press preoccupation with the subject.

Beginning in May, certain specific acts of the Roosevelt Administration gave great impetus to both Russian and American anticipations, and likewise served to engender a belief in Moscow that Washington was determined to take a more active part in the international arena. On May 16, 1933, President Roosevelt telegraphed a direct appeal to the heads of fifty-four governments asking their cooperation in the coming World Economic Conference to be held in London, and urging that a definite effort be made to salvage the Disarmament Conference. Specifically, the President recommended the abolition of all offensive weapons, and the signing by all powers of a pact of nonaggression. Included among the addressees was President Mikhail Kalinin of the Soviet Union.[52] This was the first direct communication between the United States Government and the Kremlin since the Revolution, and, as such, was

[50] Meno Lovenstein, *American Opinion of Soviet Russia* (Washington, 1941), 139-146, gives a detailed analysis of the Foundation's findings and his own breakdown of the results of the poll.

[51] *Izvestia*, March 6, 1933.

[52] Roosevelt, *Public Papers and Addresses*, ii, 185-191.

hailed as a practical step toward a Russo-American reconciliation. Although the President denied the implication,[53] it is very possible that the thought was present in his mind.

In any case, the Soviets were greatly pleased by the message. It was given a tremendous spread on the front pages of *Pravda* and *Izvestia*, with extensive coverage of the foreign reactions, all of which commented on the President's reference to the Far Eastern situation as well as to Europe.[54] Highlighted also was the significance of Russia's inclusion among the governments addressed. Soviet editorial comment, however, waited upon the dispatch of Kalinin's answer from which it took its cue. Kalinin wired Roosevelt that the peaceful aims outlined in the message were precisely those of the Soviet Union, and particularly directed the President's attention to Russia's efforts in the past for disarmament and collective security.[55]

Izvestia declared that despite the "acid-sweet" reactions to the President's note in European capitals, little material response to the suggested measures could be expected outside of the Soviet Union. Although the Soviet Government was well aware that the United States was concerned primarily with the salvation of the capitalist system, which in its weakened state might collapse in the event of war, still Roosevelt's efforts to keep the peace would gain the "decided support" of Russia. "This will show," concluded *Izvestia*, "that the wise proposals of a representative of the capitalistic powers can find support only in a proletarian state."[56] *Pravda's* remarks largely paralleled those of its sister publication, but further evaluated Roosevelt's move as a sign that "the U.S.A. is proceeding toward a more vigorous foreign policy, being forced to that step

[53] *New York Times*, May 17, 1933.

[54] *Izvestia* and *Pravda*, May 17, 18, 20, 1933. Secretary Hull later wrote that he and the President "wanted to leave no doubt that we had Japan in mind as well [as Germany]." Hull, *Memoirs*, I, 273.

[55] Roosevelt, *op. cit.*, I, 200-201.

[56] *Izvestia*, May 21, 1933.

by circumstances," particularly those in the Far East.[57] The next day, an article in the same newspaper went a step farther, declaring that the message signified a "marked change in the traditional foreign policy of the U.S.A.," the renunciation of isolationism. The writer, I. Erukhimovich, asserted that it had taken three years of international crisis for the United States finally to decide on action of some sort against aggression.[58]

Nor was the economic aspect of the President's message ignored. *Za Industrializatsiiu*, in discussing this factor, made a frank bid for recognition. Referring to rumors that Roosevelt was in favor of economic as well as military disarmament, i.e. the lowering of the barriers to world trade, the newspaper contended that America would certainly receive Russian co-operation in that area. The first step would be the facilitation of economic intercourse between the two countries. And the United States could no longer depend on halfway measures to achieve that end. It must come through full diplomatic recognition. Only then could America and Russia move forward together in the campaign for peace and world economic recovery, goals sought by both.[59]

Soviet estimates of a transformation in United States foreign policy were strengthened almost immediately by Norman Davis' amplification of the President's message in an address to the Disarmament Conference. Davis explained that America was prepared not only to reduce her armaments, but also to consult with other states if peace were threatened and to abide by any collective measures agreed upon, provided the United States concurred that an act of aggression had taken place.[60]

This was a bold statement from isolationist America, although it is doubtful if it was supported by public opinion. Moscow, however, pounced on it as further proof of greater participation by Washington in world affairs. In an article

[57] *Pravda*, May 21, 1933.   [58] *ibid.*, May 22, 1933.
[59] *Za Industrializatsiiu*, May 21, 1933.
[60] The Department of State, *Press Releases*, VIII (January-July, 1933), 387-392. Hereafter cited as *Press Releases*.

entitled "Columbus Returns to Europe," Karl Radek noted that Roosevelt had enunciated the principles of a new foreign policy, while Davis had actually enumerated the steps America was willing to take. But the Soviet publicist cautioned his readers against assuming that the United States would go to war. All that had been promised was cooperation in economic or political sanctions. That fact notwithstanding, Radek pronounced the address a radical step forward for Washington.

The reasons for the change in American policy were obvious, Radek declared. During the twenties, the United States had depended on its financial power for influence abroad and had made large investments in Germany and the Far East, but with the depression the economic club had lost its force. Thus America found herself militarily unprepared and economically helpless when aggression threatened her interests. As a result, she was compelled to renounce isolationism in order to protect her investments.

Seeing the potentialities of this event for the Soviet Union, Radek concluded: "Columbus returns to Europe not only to look after his dollars, but also to enlist partners for a possible campaign in the Far East. The address of Norman Davis is not only proof of a change in the relations between the imperialist powers but is also pregnant with many-sided consequences for the relations of the imperialist powers with the USSR."[61]

Writing from New York, Tass correspondent Lapinskii confirmed Radek's analysis that America was discarding isolationism in both the economic and political fields.[62] It was surprising with what lack of caution and reservation the Soviet spokesmen interpreted these moves by the United States, with almost complete disregard for the fact that the American public was in no way prepared to take forthright steps abroad. Perhaps Radek could be excused, though he was an astute observer, but Lapinskii, in America and familiar with Ameri-

[61] *Izvestia*, May 24, 1933.   [62] *ibid.*

can thought, should have seen that Roosevelt's actions were far ahead of public opinion.

The convening in June of the World Economic Conference at London offered another opportunity for the United States and Russia to draw closer together. The Soviets believed that Washington, as part of its more vigorous foreign policy, was seeking support in connection with its strained economic relations with Western Europe, especially England.[63] The Conference gave Moscow a platform from which to appeal to the United States for a reconciliation along economic lines, and also provided a meeting place for the representatives of the two countries. And at least one of the American delegates might be expected to lend a sympathetic ear to the Soviets— William Bullitt, who had been appointed a Special Assistant to the Secretary of State in April.

The initial address of the Soviet delegate, Maxim Litvinov, on June 14, 1933, although couched in general terms, was undoubtedly aimed primarily at the United States. Litvinov reiterated the oft-repeated Soviet boast that Russia, because of her unique economic system, had been unaffected, directly at least, by the world depression. The rise of economic nationalism in other nations and the levying of special restrictions upon the import of Soviet goods had, however, forced Russia to reduce her trade schedules drastically. The Soviet Delegation believed that the purpose of the Conference should be to find ways and means of absorbing the surplus goods which were stocked in the capitalist countries for lack of a market and, thereby, to stimulate world trade and increase industrial production. Having made this point, Litvinov then proceeded to suggest what aid the Soviet Union could give in achieving the desired goal. If long term credits were offered and discriminatory measures removed, said Litvinov, his government might reconsider its trade schedules and thus exert a most beneficial influence upon world economic conditions. "According to the

[63] *Pravda*, May 12, 1933.

calculations of the Soviet Delegation," announced the Commissar, "the Soviet Government under the above mentioned conditions might place abroad in the near future orders to the sum of about one billion dollars."

Litvinov broke down his over-all figure into categories, every one containing commodities which the United States was singularly well-equipped to supply. Included were nonferrous metals, leather, textiles, machinery, agricultural goods, consumer goods, and new ships. In view of this offer, the Commissar suggested the reconsideration of his proposal for an economic nonaggression pact. And, finally, Litvinov pointed out that a basic factor which created unrest in the world was the relations of some capitalist countries to the one hundred and seventy million people of Russia. The establishment of cordial relations between these countries and the USSR would do much to ease the existing tensions. "For its part," said Litvinov, "the Soviet Government has steadfastly and consistently supported the principle of peaceful co-existence and refrained from any aggressive measures in all areas of international life, except on those occasions when it has been forced to make reprisals."[64] Here indeed was a speech calculated to whet the appetites of market-hungry Americans, and at the same time lull their fears of Soviet radicalism.

As a matter of fact, conversations between Russia and the United States for the purpose of negotiating a government guaranteed loan for Soviet purchases were already under way before the convening of the Conference in London. Around the first of June, Amtorg approached the Reconstruction Finance Corporation in an effort to finance the purchase of seventy thousand bales of surplus American cotton. When questioned, officials of the R.F.C. admitted that discussions were in progress, but denied that the transaction, if completed, would have any effect upon relations between Moscow and

[64] Maxim Litvinov, *Vneshniaia politika SSSR* (Moscow, 1935), 231-237.

Washington. At the White House all inquiries went un-answered.[65]

During the Conference, both Bullitt and Assistant Secretary of State Raymond Moley, Roosevelt's special emissary to the London meeting, met with Litvinov. On July 2, Moley and the Commissar discussed the pending loan to Amtorg, and the following day the Reconstruction Finance Corporation announced that it had extended a four million dollar credit to Amtorg for the purchase of sixty to eighty thousand bales of American cotton on the open market.[66] The loan was for one year at five per cent and was to cover seventy per cent of the Soviet purchases.[67] Although it was not for a long term, the credit opened a breach in the economic barriers between the two countries, and was significant as having been granted by a government agency.

In the United States, reaction to the news was varied. Hamilton Fish labeled the deal "inexcusable, improper, and probably illegal," while Senator Kenneth McKellar of Tennessee hailed it as an "excellent way to move surplus cotton."[68] The *Philadelphia Public Ledger* saw "no reason why we should not seek to sell our goods if satisfactory arrangements for payment can be made." But the *Nashville Banner* viewed Russia as the "same outlaw nation that it has been from the day Bolshevism banished the autocracy of a Czar and substituted a reign even more devastating and ruthless." On the other hand, the *Providence News-Tribune* suggested that closer connections between Russia and the rest of the world might hasten the deterioration of the Soviet system. "Wild blood is not tamed nor taught," it editorialized, "by being left to roam or rave through its native jungle."[69] Apparently, business circles were inter-

[65] *New York Times*, June 14, 1933.

[66] *ibid.*, July 3, 1933; Edgar S. Furniss, "Soviet Diplomatic Successes," *Current History* xxxviii (1933), 758.

[67] Jesse Jones, Chairman of the Reconstruction Finance Corporation, to Franklin D. Roosevelt, June 24, 1933, Roosevelt Papers.

[68] *New York Times*, July 4, 1933.

[69] As quoted in *Literary Digest*, July 15, 1933, 8.

ested in the possibilities of the new arrangement, however, for the R.F.C. received some forty requests for similar loans to enable American manufacturers to sell to Russia on credit.[70]

Soviet industrial and economic organs greeted the loan as a most encouraging indication of closer relations with the United States. Despite the smallness of the loan, it was considered an important forward step for the American government, and a reflection of the more friendly attitude of Washington toward the Soviets since the advent of the new Administration. In view of the apparent evolution in American policy, the question was raised whether Russian export-import planners for the Second Five Year Plan should depend more upon the United States in their buying schedules. *Za Industrializatsiiu* warned against any dangerous overestimate of the future development of Russian-American trade. Not until a legal base existed upon which commerce could operate would a real growth occur. Only after Washington had decided to grant the Soviet Government *de jure* recognition could any real optimism for the future of reciprocal trade be justified.

But the newspaper hastened to add that when a diplomatic reconciliation did take place, Russia would be prepared to purchase extensively in the United States. There were some Americans, claimed *Za Industrializatsiiu*, who distorted the Soviet aim of economic independence by arguing that it meant a decrease in buying abroad, with the result that Soviet orders would never again reach their 1931 peak. On the contrary, the editors asserted, Russian industry would increase its demands and require even broader economic relations with other countries.[71]

Despite this cautious appraisal, Moscow considered the R.F.C. loan one of the few successes of the otherwise unproductive Economic Conference. The promises of a fruitful market in Russia held out by Litvinov had not only speeded

[70] *New York Times*, August 21, 1933.
[71] *Za Industrializatsiiu*, July 14, 1933.

the loan negotiations, but also aroused the interest of private business in the United States, as indicated by the prorecognition resolution of the American-Russian Chamber of Commerce.[72] The Soviet Delegation at London sensed that the attitude of the American representatives indicated a trend in Washington toward a rapprochement with Russia, a fact which was believed to have contributed to the failure of Germany to create a bloc of anti-Soviet countries at the Conference.[73] Soviet disappointment in the results of the Conference in general was, however, expressed by Litvinov in an interview in Paris on July 7. Characterizing the London meeting as another "half-moribund" world conference, he prescribed, as an increasingly necessary alternative, closer direct relations between those countries which were sincerely interested in peace. "We wish," he said, "to maintain the best relations with all states which have no designs against the interests of our nation and whose peaceful policies coincide with our own policy."[74] Moscow was making every effort to inform the world of its harmlessness and its preoccupation with world tranquillity.

Indeed the situation in the Far East and the advent of a new danger to the Soviet Union in the west were making Russia more and more desirous of establishing herself as a respected member of the international community. In her period of military weakness, which stemmed from the all-out economic effort and its accompanying dislocations as well as from the reorganization of the party and government under Stalin, Russia needed to seek support from outside her borders. This policy had been gaining momentum ever since the inauguration of the First Five Year Plan, and by 1933 was fully recognizable. Two of its facets were the emphasis on

[72] *Izvestia,* July 15, 1933.
[73] *New York Times,* July 5, 1933; L. Mad'iar, "SSSR i kapitalisticheskie strany na ekonomicheskoi konferentsii," *Kommunisticheskii Internatsional,* July 10, 1933, 39; E. Varga, "Chem ob'iasniaetsia neudachnyi iskhod londonskoi konferentsii," *Bol'shevik,* August 16, 1933, 97-105.
[74] Litvinov, *op. cit.,* 256.

collective security and the establishment of normal and if possible friendly relations with the peace-seeking nations. In the pursuit of these goals, it was necessary to minimize the Communist world revolutionary aspect of the Soviet Government and to emphasize Russian willingness to work side by side with other nations for the guarantee of mutual safety. The many examples already noted testify to the application of the policy.

In the spring of 1933, the tension between Japan and Russia was greatly increased by the breakdown of agreements over the operation of the Chinese and Eastern Railway. Moscow addressed a note to Tokyo listing the many Russian grievances, and then, in May, made the bold move of offering to sell the railroad to Japan.[75] This was significant evidence of Russia's need for peace, and, in fact, with the opening of negotiations on the sale, there was a noticeable easement in the strained relations between the two countries.[76] But the relief was short-lived. By midsummer, new complications arose over the price offered by the Japanese and over Russian suspicions that Tokyo was not bargaining in good faith.[77] Although sober observers felt that war was not imminent, they also admitted that an incident might well set off the unpredictable Japanese war machine.[78] In October, relations were further worsened when Moscow newspapers began the publication of purported Japanese documents which disclosed plans to seize the Chinese and Eastern Railway.[79]

The second menace to the Soviet Union which took form in 1933 was the rise to power of Nazism in Germany. Although

[75] Harriet Moore, *Soviet Far Eastern Policy, 1931-1945* (Princeton, 1945), 26-31.

[76] Max Beloff, *The Foreign Policy of Soviet Russia, 1929-1941* (London, 1947), I, 167-168.

[77] Moore, *Soviet Far Eastern Policy, 1931-1945*, 32-33.

[78] Joseph C. Grew, *Ten Years in Japan* (New York, 1944), 95; *Foreign Relations, 1933*, III, 421-424.

[79] *Izvestia*, October 9, 1933.

for the first year after the Hitler victory Soviet publications were surprisingly careful in their analysis of the German developments, an undertone of apprehension was nevertheless evident.[80] The trial of the Bulgarian Communist, Gregorii Dmitrov, for the Reichstag fire, the frankly hostile proposals of the German Minister of Economics, Alfred Hugenberg, at the London Conference, the violent anti-Communist pronouncements of the Nazi leaders, all clearly showed the danger to Russia of Hitler Germany.

Communist organs, both Russian and international, began to pay greater attention to the fight against Fascism.[81] Fear of a rapprochement between Great Britain and Germany was also expressed. When the Four Power Pact was signed by England, France, Italy, and Germany in June, it was interpreted as an attempt to settle European differences in order that those countries might turn against their common enemies, namely, Russia and the United States.[82] The British, it was said, were encouraging Hitler Germany to act as a spearhead in the coming struggle with the Soviet Union, while Japan was to serve in the same capacity in the east.[83]

Some of the antagonism between England and the Soviet Union in the spring of 1933 could be traced to the Metro-Vickers Affair. Six British subjects working in Russia were arrested and tried on charges of sabotage and economic espionage. Of the five who were found guilty, three were deported and two were sentenced to prison terms. London had strenuously protested throughout the procedure, and, when

[80] The Soviets still hoped for some sort of *modus vivendi* with Germany and at first underestimated the importance and permanence of the Nazi regime, Beloff, *op. cit.*, I, 25-26, 67-68; Edward Hallett Carr, *German-Soviet Relations Between the two World Wars, 1919-1939* (Baltimore, 1951), 110.

[81] For examples, see *International Press Correspondence, Bol'shevik,* and *Kommunisticheskii Internatsional* for spring and summer, 1933.

[82] *International Press Correspondence,* June 16, 1933, 560-561; *Pravda,* August 19, 1933.

[83] R. Palme-Dutt, "Britanskii imperializm, fashizm i antisovetskaia kampaniia," *Kommunisticheskii Internatsional,* July 20, 1933, 46-54.

the verdict was announced, an Embargo Proclamation was issued against Soviet goods. Although the incident was finally settled during the Economic Conference by the commutation of the prisoners' sentences and the simultaneous lifting of the embargo, it served to heighten Soviet suspicions of British designs against the USSR.[84] Soviet-American relations came into the discussion of this event in a rather oblique manner. Soviet commentators suggested that one reason for Britain's desire for a settlement was her fear that the expected Russian rapprochement with the United States would permanently divert Anglo-Soviet trade to America.[85]

In general, the western danger was considered more potential than imminent. It was from the direction of Japan that an attack was most likely.[86] In the face of that increasingly probable eventuality, cooperation with the United States became even more attractive to Russia in 1933. Moscow was pleased with the reports that Roosevelt was undertaking a naval construction program. Karl Radek commented that the Japanese had been mistaken in their expectation that a new American Administration meant less opposition from the United States. On the contrary, Roosevelt was displaying a less wordy but more effective approach to the problems of the Far East.[87] It was felt that America would need some time to arm sufficiently for an outright conflict with Japan, and, in the meantime, would use diplomatic channels as effectively as possible to discourage the Japanese.[88]

International communism also became more outspoken in its desire for closer relations between Russia and the United

[84] For a detailed, albeit one-sided, account of the Metro-Vickers Affair, see W. P. and Zelda K. Coates, *A History of Anglo-Soviet Relations* (London, 1942), 470-505.

[85] Mad'iar, *op. cit.* (See note 73 *supra*), 35; see also *New York Times*, October 24, 1933.

[86] Editorial in *Kommunisticheskii Internatsional*, May 20, 1933, 3-11.

[87] *Izvestia*, July 2, 1933.

[88] G. Safarov, "Bor'ba za novyi razdel Kitaia," *Bol'shevik*, August 31, 1933, 72-83.

States in the interests of strengthening the defensive position of the Bolshevik homeland. America's future policy was characterized as a question of "critical importance."[89] A realization of the common immediate aims of the two nations most concerned about Nipponese aggression was reflected in the theoretical discussion among Communists as to the most probable direction of Japan's initial blow: toward Russia or toward America.[90] All Soviet comment pointed to the inevitable conclusion that whatever the reasons for the growing antagonism between Washington and Tokyo, it was a fact that could be used advantageously by Russia to strengthen her position in the Far East.

[89] *International Press Correspondence*, March 2, 1933, 242; *ibid.*, March 17, 1933, 307.

[90] Sen Katayama, "Iaponskii imperializm i voina," *Kommunisticheskii Internatsional*, July 20, 1933, 23.

CHAPTER 5

ROOSEVELT TAKES THE INITIATIVE

FROM the beginning of his Administration, Franklin D. Roosevelt was determined to alter the anomalous situation which had existed between the Soviet Union and the United States for nearly sixteen years. He was convinced that there was no longer any excuse for the two great nations to be without normal relations.[1] He believed that, as a diplomatic device, nonrecognition had become outmoded as applied to a well-established, independent government influential in international affairs. The United States could not afford to prolong an unrealistic policy that possibly contributed to world unrest.[2]

But in the first months after March 4, 1933, Roosevelt was faced with far more urgent problems than that of Russia. Foreign affairs were only incidental to the consideration of emergency measures to restore economic confidence and morale at home. Millions of Americans stood on the brink of disaster; many had already fallen into the abyss. Thus, the Administration was immediately occupied with ways and means of checking the progress of the depression. Yet the President did find time in those frantic days to set the wheels in motion toward recognition.

It is difficult to reconstruct accurately the exact form of those first steps. Apparently, Roosevelt had several people working on the problem and, apparently also, they were at times unaware of each other's activities. Even before his elec-

[1] Interview with Mr. William Phillips, Boston, Massachusetts, June 7, 1949. Hereafter cited as Phillips Interview.

[2] Henry Morgenthau, Jr., "The Morgenthau Diaries," Part III, *Colliers,* October 11, 1947, 20.

tion, he had given the subject consideration. In the early summer of 1932, William C. Bullitt visited several countries of Europe, including the Soviet Union, primarily at the request of Roosevelt, who had sent word through Colonel Edward M. House that he would like to have information on the latest developments abroad.[3] During his brief stay in Moscow, Bullitt talked with Karl Radek, who later published his account of their conversation. According to Radek, Bullitt expressed the view that the Soviet Union alone marched "manfully forward" in the midst of world economic and political disorganization. Roosevelt, the American visitor asserted, would be the next President of the United States and could be expected to "carry out the will of America; to establish not only normal but friendly relations with [Russia]."[4]

Upon his return to the United States later in the summer, Bullitt reported orally to Roosevelt in Albany, briefing the future President on the current situation in Europe.[5] What he had to say about Russia is unknown, but it is more than probable that he relayed his favorable impression and, in the confident expectation that Roosevelt would be elected, urged a serious investigation of Russian-American relations after March 4.

Soon after his inauguration, the new President called in Henry Morgenthau, Jr., whom he had appointed Farm Credit Administrator, and, after informing him of his desire to alter the existing relations between the United States and Soviet Russia, asked Morgenthau to investigate quietly the possibilities of a reconciliation. This was an early example of Roosevelt's partiality for personal emissaries in preference to the

[3] Letter to the author from Mr. William C. Bullitt, February 2, 1950. Hereafter cited as Bullitt Letter.

[4] *Pravda*, November 9, 1933. Radek no doubt embellished Bullitt's words, but Bullitt's friendliness toward Russia was well-known at the time. See Cordell Hull, *The Memoirs of Cordell Hull* (New York, 1948), I, 296.

[5] Bullitt Letter.

usual channels of government. Morgenthau was a friend and associate of some years and the President was sure from past experience that the matter would be handled with delicacy. According to Morgenthau, Roosevelt sensed opposition to his plans in the State Department and thus moved in such a way as to avoid any obstructionism from that direction.[6] It is possible that the President did have this impression, but available evidence indicates that, although the policy-making members of the Department believed the whole problem should be approached with caution, they were not opposed to recognition.[7]

Morgenthau, following the instructions from his chief, made contact with Amtorg in New York through two intermediaries and began exploratory conversations. But the hesitancy of the Russians approached to assume responsibility for positive action hindered the achievement of any real results. The fruitless talks continued through the summer, while the President became more and more impatient with the dilatoriness of the proceedings.[8] One suspects that the Soviet commercial representatives were never given a straightforward offer of recognition, and on the other hand that, though they realized what Morgenthau and his representatives were hinting at, they were holding out for a bid through official channels. There is also some reason to believe that the Russians were being offered *de facto* recognition through Morgenthau with the added promise of credits. But Moscow's goal was *de jure* recognition with full diplomatic relations, for Russia's eager-

---

[6] "The Morgenthau Diaries," 21.

[7] Hull, *Memoirs*, 292-296. Phillips Interview. On the other hand, Professor Samuel N. Harper of the University of Chicago, who was well acquainted with several members of the Eastern European Division of the State Department as well as with Under-Secretary Phillips, felt at the time that the State Department was "not very enthusiastic about extending recognition." Samuel N. Harper, *The Russia I Believe In* (Chicago, 1945), 200. Harper's strong sympathy for the Soviet experiment may, however, have led him to mistake caution for opposition.

[8] "The Morgenthau Diaries," 21. Jesse Jones alludes to these negotiations in a letter to the President on June 24, 1933, concerning the R.F.C. cotton credits to Russia. Roosevelt Papers.

ness to strengthen her international position was then greater than her desire for commercial benefits.[9]

In any case, by midsummer, Roosevelt was considering the method of personal negotiation which he eventually used. "If I could only, myself, talk to one man representing the Russians," he said to Morgenthau, "I could straighten out the whole question." Late in September, he asked Morgenthau what he thought "of bringing this whole Russian question into our front parlor instead of back in the kitchen?" When Morgenthau replied that of course it must be the President's decision, Roosevelt disclosed that he had "a plan in mind."[10]

On the day following this conversation, Morgenthau discussed the problem with Bullitt, who had been appointed a special assistant to the Secretary of State in April. From that time on, according to Morgenthau, Bullitt took a more and more active interest in the subject and soon, with the President's consent, assumed the responsibility for further developments.[11] Morgenthau's account gives the impression that it was only after this conversation that the State Department had any knowledge of the President's plans for recognition. The facts do not support his allegation, though it is possible that the Department was unaware of the conversations Morgenthau was conducting. It is necessary, therefore, to return to the less exotic development of the Russian problem in the normal channels of foreign policy.

Morgenthau emphasized the opposition of the Department of State to any consideration of recognition,[12] and other

---

[9] This information was found in a letter from Russia printed in *Sotsialisticheskii Vestnik* (Paris), No. 19 (304), October 10, 1933, 14. At that time the *Vestnik* still had remarkably well informed correspondents within the Soviet Union. On August 8, 1933, the Department of Agriculture called a conference of industrialists and agriculturists interested in Russian trade to discuss the formation of a government sponsored corporation to extend credit for Soviet purchases in the United States. It is possible that the meeting was connected with the negotiations of Mr. Morgenthau. Roosevelt Papers.

[10] "The Morgenthau Diaries," 21.

[11] *ibid.*   [12] *ibid.*

sources have made the same assertion.[13] Yet Secretary Hull has implied quite the opposite. In his *Memoirs*, Hull indicated that he favored a rapprochement with Russia from the beginning. He saw many reasons for a change in the American policy. Russia had shown a commendable desire to cooperate with other nations in the cause of peace and had participated in the various conferences which had been called in an effort to reduce the dangers of world conflict. The Secretary felt that the strained relations of both countries with Japan might be eased by a rapprochement, and he was hopeful that the European situation might also be stabilized through the combined efforts of England, France, and a reconciled America and Russia.[14]

In fact, Hull believed that in many respects the United States had more to gain from recognition than did the Soviet Union. Under the existing conditions, Moscow was at least able to keep informed on American affairs through Amtorg, the Soviet Information Bureau in Washington, and the American Communist Party. The United States Government, on the other hand, had no comparable channels of information. The Department relied chiefly on the voluntary reports of American engineers who had spent time in Russia and on the opinions of private visitors to the Soviet Union.[15]

The Secretary and his immediate associates in the Department were convinced, however, that the Russian question should be handled with great circumspection. Like every other departure in foreign policy, recognition had to be approached with an eye to American public opinion. Care had to be taken not to frighten the people with any measures which might lead to a belief that the United States was involving itself in international affairs beyond the conventional limits. American opinion was still overwhelmingly isolationist.[16] Also, despite the more favorable attitude toward Russia which had

[13] Harper, *loc. cit.*
[15] *ibid.*, 296.

[14] Hull, *Memoirs*, I, 292-293, 304.
[16] *ibid.*, 176-177.

been developing during the past few years, communism was still a very ticklish matter with which to deal and opposition to recognition was strong in many quarters. It was imperative that a rapprochement, when it came, must be so conducted as to minimize American fears of Communist contamination. All these factors were of vital importance, and the Department was well aware of the delicacy of the situation.[17]

In the first weeks of the Roosevelt Administration, the White House referred a number of requests for appointments to discuss the Russian question, and forwarded materials received dealing with the problem, to Assistant Secretary of State Raymond Moley for study.[18] On April 4, 1933, at the request of both the President and Hull, Colonel Hugh Cooper filed his views on recognition with the Secretary.[19] Later in the same month, the appointment of William Bullitt as a Special Assistant to the Secretary indicated that further developments on the recognition front might be expected.[20] Meanwhile, Hull was discussing the question with ambassadors and ministers in Washington whose countries had diplomatic relations with Russia. He was interested in ascertaining how their governments had handled the negotiations and what special difficulties might be encountered.[21]

His interrogations were continued at the London Economic Conference. The Secretary discussed the subject "elaborately" with a "number" of the foreign ministers attending the meeting. In particular, Hull tried to sound out Sir John Simon, the British Foreign Secretary, concerning his views, but Hull

[17] Phillips Interview; interview with Mr. Robert F. Kelley, Washington, D.C., June 15, 1949. Hereafter cited as Kelley Interview.

[18] Memorandum to Miss Margaret Le Hand, secretary to the President, from "G.E.F.," March 17, 1933, Miss Le Hand to Mr. Percy Shepard, March 27, 1933, Louis McH. Howe to Professor Jerome Davis, March 23, 1933, Roosevelt Papers.

[19] *New York Times*, July 1, 1933.

[20] *ibid.*, April 21, 1933. Mr. Phillips also suggested that Bullitt was appointed primarily to work on the recognition problem. Phillips Interview.

[21] Hull, *Memoirs*, I, 293-294.

wrote that "for some reason" Sir John was most reticent.[22] Perhaps the explanation lay in the current unpleasantness between Russia and Great Britain over the Metro-Vickers Affair, which was only at that moment being settled. While at the Conference, Hull also had several conversations with Maxim Litvinov, chiefly on economic matters. Apparently, however, some reference was made to the possibility of recognition, for Hull recalled that during those talks the "groundwork was laid for our later personal discussions at the time of recognition."[23] At the London meeting, both Bullitt and Raymond Moley also had conferences with the Soviet Commissar.[24] Although both men favored recognition,[25] it does not appear to have been a subject of discussion between them and Litvinov.[26]

On his return to Washington, Secretary Hull reported to the President on his conversations in regard to recognition, and they reviewed the subject in a "general way."[27] Soon thereafter, Robert F. Kelley, the Chief of the State Department's Division of Eastern European Affairs, drafted a memorandum on recognition for the White House, presumably at the request of the President. Kelley, an astute student of Russian history who knew the language well,[28] had no misconceptions about the difficulties involved in a rapprochement.

Kelley advised the President that the experiences of other

[22] ibid.   [23] ibid., 294.

[24] New York Times, July 3, 1933.

[25] Louis Fischer, Men and Politics, An Autobiography (New York, 1941), 214. Mr. Moley declared his advocacy of recognition to Mr. Fischer early in 1933.

[26] Moley denied that recognition had been discussed when questioned by newsmen after his conference with Litvinov. New York Times, July 3, 1933. Mr. Bullitt has no recollection of discussing recognition with Litvinov during his several meetings with the Soviet representative at the London Conference. Bullitt Letter.

[27] Hull, Memoirs, I, 294.

[28] Professor Samuel Harper, who was a leading Russian scholar in the United States, had a very high opinion of Kelley's knowledge and abilities. His only criticism was that Kelley was inclined to be too legalistic and unemotional in his approach to Russia, traits which more objective evaluators would be inclined to list as assets. Harper, The Russia I Believe In, 201.

nations had clearly shown the necessity for a settlement of all outstanding issues between the two governments. "Until a substantial basis of mutual understanding and common principles and purposes has been established," he wrote, "official intercourse, with its increased contacts is bound to lead to friction and rancor." Kelley then enumerated the problems which had to be resolved before diplomatic relations were resumed. First and foremost was the question of Communist activity. In his opinion, it was essential for friendly relations that Moscow cut all ties with communism in the United States. A satisfactory settlement of the Russian debt should also precede recognition, Kelley recommended, for once relations were established there would be little chance of the Soviet Government's making an adequate arrangement to pay the monies owed. To support his statement, he cited the history of the fruitless French and English attempts at settlement after recognition had been accorded. Finally, Kelley urged that a prior understanding be reached on the legal rights of Americans in Russia in order to protect them from the hazards inherent in the great divergence of the two legal systems.[29] The memorandum was a sound appraisal of the situation and wisely counseled firmness as the requisite of a successful negotiation.

At the end of September 1933, Roosevelt asked Secretary Hull to put his views on recognition into writing. In general, the requested letter from Hull reiterated the points emphasized by Robert Kelley. The Secretary, however, directed the President's attention to Russia's great desire for credits and recognition. That fact, said Hull, offered the United States "two powerful weapons" with which to force Soviet adherence to a settlement of the basic problems before recognition. Of the two, credits, according to Hull, were possibly the most eagerly sought after by Russia, and therefore no loans should be extended except as part of a general agreement on all

[29] *Foreign Relations, 1933,* II, 782-788.

points. The Secretary was also aware that Moscow believed recognition would help deter Japan from attacking the Maritime Provinces, and would generally strengthen the international and domestic position of the Moscow government.[30]

On the basis of the facts now available, it is doubtful if Hull correctly assessed the relative importance of Soviet aims. A careful analysis of Russian statements and actions through 1932 and 1933, as well as the course of postrecognition negotiations, support the theory that by 1933 Moscow was interested first in diplomatic relations and only secondarily in credits. But both Hull and Kelley were justified by the experience of other governments in their recommendations on procedure.

By this time, Hull had definitely made up his mind in favor of opening recognition negotiations. But when, several days after the receipt of the above memorandum, the President asked Hull to look over the correspondence that had come to the White House for and against the projected action, the Secretary delayed stating his opinion until he had read the material. Hull then returned to the White House and told Roosevelt that he favored recognition, despite the continued opposition from many quarters.[31] Russia, he told the President, had shown herself to be "peacefully inclined." With the world "moving into a dangerous period both in Europe and in Asia .... [she] could be a great help in stabilizing ... [the] situation as time goes on and peace becomes more and more threatened." The President replied: "I agree entirely."[32] Having received the concurrence of his chief lieutenant, Roosevelt was ready to act.

[30] *ibid.*, 789-790.

[31] Hull, *Memoirs*, I, 297. In the light of subsequent events, it is interesting to note that Henry A. Wallace, then Secretary of Agriculture, expressed to the President his opposition to recognition on religious grounds. Roosevelt was puzzled by Wallace's remarks and told Morgenthau that the Secretary of Agriculture was "a kind of mystic." The Morgenthau Diaries," 21.

[32] Hull, *Memoirs*, I, 297.

Before turning to the subsequent steps toward recognition, it is necessary to examine more carefully the motives that had led the President and his advisers to favor setting aside the sixteen-year policy of the United States toward the Soviet Union. What were the influences that had brought them to the view that nonrecognition was no longer practicable?

At the time of recognition, the great majority of the American people justified the action of their government on the grounds that Russo-American trade would stimulate economic recovery. And since Washington said nothing to discount that view, it was generally accepted as the primary reason for recognition. But a study of the statements made then and later by the participants shows a surprising paucity of evidence to support that theory. The publication of documents and memoirs dealing with the event, and the correcting perspective of time, reveal that other factors played the paramount role. No doubt the President hoped that the reestablishment of relations would bring some trade, and no doubt he considered that fact an important reason for taking the initiative with regard to recognition. But increased commerce was not his primary objective. As one of the negotiators later expressed it, trade was a necessary "cloak" for recognition, which made it easier for the Administration to secure a favorable public opinion.

Secretary Hull in his account clearly emphasizes the effect of the international situation upon his favorable decision, mentioning the unsettled conditions both in Europe and in Asia. Normal relations with Russia, he wrote, opened the way to possible collaboration between the United States, England, France, and the Soviet Union for the preservation of peace. The implication that the President shared Hull's view was corroborated by Henry Morgenthau, who wrote that Roosevelt "felt . . . that the continued isolation of Russia might destroy his hopes of preventing war through the collective moral sense of the nations of the world."[33]

[33] "The Morgenthau Diaries," 20-21. Morgenthau also observed in his

Logically the next query is: to what extent were particular areas of unrest and instability considered in the motivations toward recognition? Was the primary concern betterment of conditions in the Far East or did the President have Europe uppermost in his mind? These are difficult questions to answer, but it would seem that Roosevelt had no specific design which he hoped to put into operation as the result of normal relations with Russia, but rather believed that all world problems might be eased by the abolition of one more obstacle to international cooperation. It is of course natural to assume that Japanese aggression in China, which was already an actuality and a present danger to peace, loomed as the most immediate problem upon which recognition might have an alleviating effect. Washington was well aware of Russia's hopes in that direction and undoubtedly cognizant of the fact that a reestablishment of relations would be interpreted by many observers as an attempt to check Japan in the Far East.

Pressure from abroad to recognize, when predicated on international factors, continued to be argued almost exclusively on the basis of Far Eastern considerations. The Chinese continued to impress upon the United States Government the healthy influence a resumption of Russo-American diplomatic relations would have on the troubled course of Far Eastern affairs.[34] In July 1933, the Soviet Ambassador to China told the American Minister that he considered the absence of relations a source of great weakness to both the Russian and American positions in the Far East. As long as Washington refused to recognize the Moscow regime, he asserted, Japan would feel less hesitation in striking at Russia, since the war promoters

---

Diary that few people realized how early Roosevelt became aware of the potential threat to United States security from German and Japanese aggression. *Ibid.*, 72.

[34] Editorial in the *Chinese Republican* (Shanghai), as quoted in the *Literary Digest*, May 6, 1933, 11. The Chinese Ambassador to Russia urged recognition to Hull at the London Economic Conference. Hull informed him that the matter was under advisement. *Foreign Relations, 1933,* III, 495.

could emphasize the anti-Communist angle with more confidence of American support.[35]

Secretary Hull voiced his concern over the Far Eastern problem in his first months in office when he wrote: "When I entered the State Department I had two points on the Far East firmly in mind. One was the definite interest the United States had in maintaining the independence of China and in preventing Japan from gaining overlordship of the entire Far East. The other was an equally definite conviction that Japan had no intention whatever of abiding by treaties but would regulate her conduct by the opportunities of the moment."[36]

Although the Roosevelt Administration aimed no notes of protest at Japan and, in contrast to the Hoover regime, appeared to take a friendlier attitude toward Tokyo,[37] it also made clear from the beginning that it did support the program of its predecessor. The fleet was not withdrawn from the Pacific; a naval building program was inaugurated;[38] and all of Tokyo's efforts to promote public acts reflecting friendship between the two countries were diplomatically rejected by Washington. The offer to exchange good-will missions was quietly turned down and the suggestion for an arbitration treaty made by Viscount Ishii to Roosevelt was left to die aborning.[39] Finally, the United States Government was well

[35] *ibid.*, 377-378.

[36] Hull, *Memoirs*, I, 270. According to James A. Farley, Roosevelt discussed the possibility of war with Japan during the second cabinet meeting of the new Administration. James A. Farley, *Jim Farley's Story: The Roosevelt Years* (New York, 1948), 39.

[37] Ambassador Grew reported, in June 1933, that there was a definite feeling in Japan that the Roosevelt Administration was more friendly to her than its predecessor. Joseph C. Grew, *Ten Years in Japan* (New York, 1944), 92.

[38] Hull, *Memoirs*, I, 287.

[39] The Japanese plan for an exchange of "good-will" missions was advanced in mid-October. *Foreign Relations, 1933*, III, 430-431, 433-434. Viscount Ishii suggested an arbitration treaty to the President, and later to Hull at the London Conference, but Washington discouraged his advances. *Ibid.*, 745-748.

aware of Japanese apprehensions over the ramifications of a Russian-American rapprochement.[40]

Yet there is impressive evidence to show that the Far East did not enter directly into Washington's recognition considerations. Three of the participants in the event, William Phillips, William Bullitt, and Robert Kelley, have stated that Japanese relations did not figure prominently in the decision to recognize, though all admit that they were on the periphery of the deliberations.[41] In fact, two of the negotiators declared that the primary area of concern was Hitler Germany. Henry Morgenthau expressed the thesis with caution, suggesting that Roosevelt "must have perceived that Russia would be a natural ally in any conflict against . . . Germany."[42]

But William Bullitt, who next to Roosevelt was the most prominent and influential figure in the subsequent recognition negotiations, stated emphatically in 1950 that: "By that time [early fall of 1933] both the President and I were convinced that Hitler would eventually make war unless England, France, and the Soviet Union should stand together against Nazi aggression. It seemed in our national interest to prevent the outbreak of a Hitler war and, therefore, to resume relations, somewhat skeptically, with the Soviet union. . . . The primary objective was to prevent the launching of another world war by Hitler."[43]

If such was the case, the President displayed great foresight. The fact that Bullitt enunciated his opinion with such conviction leads to a belief that the German question was a factor in the President's decision. Nevertheless, it is possible that the course of history since 1933 has in some measure influenced Mr. Bullitt's recollection of the motives behind recognition. Although the voluminous section in *Foreign Relations* for 1933 testified to Washington's concern over the threat-

---

[40] *ibid.*, III, 709.
[41] Phillips Interview; Bullitt Letter; Kelley Interview.
[42] "The Morgenthau Diaries," 21.   [43] Bullitt Letter.

ening resurgence of Germany, the subject matter indicated no anxiety over the imminence of aggressive moves on her part. Germany's intentions were becoming more and more obvious as 1933 wore on, but they were potential dangers.[44] Japan was already on the march. It is difficult to see why Roosevelt recognized Russia solely on the basis of a future contingency, when the present was fraught with a danger which recognition might avert or postpone. It would seem safer, therefore, in the absence of more concrete evidence, to conclude that both considerations were present in the President's decision and part of his awakening interest in ways and means of assisting the machinery of peace.

Apparently, no American official questioned the advisability of settling the major issues before or at least contemporaneously with the granting of recognition. The unsatisfactory experiences of other nations which had left negotiations until after relations were established, together with the realization

[44] See the section on "Germany" in *Foreign Relations, 1933*, II, 183-543. When Ambassador William Dodd left the United States in June 1933, to take up his duties in Berlin, President Roosevelt discussed with him the issues in German-American relations which were of present concern. Dodd's account of the interview does not indicate that the President feared German aggression at that time. William E. Dodd, Jr. and Martha Dodd (eds.), *Ambassador Dodd's Diary, 1933-1938* (New York, 1941), 4-6. Dodd, an outspoken anti-Nazi, discounted the predictions of the French Ambassador in the summer of 1933 that Germany might march at any moment. He noted that Germany had first to re-arm before she could contemplate any aggressive moves. *Ibid.*, 35. Joseph E. Davies describes a conversation with Roosevelt in August 1936, which, if correctly recorded, would indicate that even at that late hour the President was not sure whether Germany had a "Will for peace" or a "Will for conquest." Joseph E. Davies, *Mission to Moscow* (New York, 1941), XIII-XIV. Mr. Bullitt himself wrote, in April 1936: "The only actual threat to the Soviet Union is the Japanese. All Litvinov's propaganda trumpetings to the contrary, the Soviet Government knows very well that Germany cannot be in a position to make war on the Soviet Union for many years." *Foreign Relations, The Soviet Union, 1933-1939*, 293. Yet Secretary Hull recalls that in "my first year in the State Department I had no doubts as to Hitlerite Germany's intentions and capacities." Hull, *Memoirs*, I, 235-242.

that the American public demanded all proper precautions be taken before extending the hand of friendship to Russia, were the basic considerations affecting that decision.

At the request of Hull, Assistant Secretary of State R. Walton Moore and William Bullitt each wrote a memorandum for the information of the President, covering certain aspects of the forthcoming negotiations. Moore gave his attention primarily to the problem of securing Russian guarantees at the time of recognition. Although he advised the signing of a treaty simultaneously with recognition, he acknowledged that such a procedure might not be workable. As an alternative, he suggested some kind of limited representation in each country to continue until the governments were mutually assured of each other's good faith in regard to the informal commitments. Unconditional recognition he discarded as offering little prospect for a satisfactory future relationship between the two countries.[45]

Bullitt agreed with his colleague, writing that "before recognition and before loans we shall find the Soviet Government amenable. After recognition or loans, we . . . [shall] find the Soviet Government adamant." The issues which he felt should be covered were by and large the same as those presented in the Kelley memorandum. In connection with the debt settlement, he suggested that the United States try to obtain a waiver on the inevitable counterclaims which would be presented by the Soviets for damage suffered from the Siberian, Archangel, and Murmansk expeditions. Bullitt also recommended that guarantees be obtained to secure the religious rights of American citizens resident in Russia.[46]

This point had not appeared in the Kelley memorandum nor in the letter of the Secretary of State to the President. It was, in fact, the President's own addition to the list of prerequisites to recognition. Although the issue had been mentioned in the

[45] *Foreign Relations, 1933*, II, 791-793.
[46] *ibid.*, 793-794.

public discussions,[47] the Department had not considered it worthy of particular emphasis until the President insisted upon its inclusion in the negotiations.[48] According to Mrs. Eleanor Roosevelt, her husband took particular pride in the fact that he had been instrumental in bringing the point to the attention of his advisers. He was most anxious to assure the right of American nationals to perform the rites of their churches in freedom while resident in Russia.[49]

Recent events had brought one other special problem to the attention of the government. The Metro-Vickers Affair, which had strained Anglo-Soviet relations, demonstrated the need to include in the section of the agreement relating to legal rights a clarification of the question of "economic espionage." In view of the British experience, proper precautions were deemed advisable to prevent a similar misunderstanding between Russia and the United States.[50]

Meanwhile, attention was being given to the ways and means of approaching the Soviet Government. Secretary Hull recommended to the President that contact should at first be made secretly with the Russians and the points at issue settled. Only then would it be wise to invite Moscow publicly and officially to send a representative to the United States to conclude the formal recognition.[51] In fact, some members of the Department, including the Under-Secretary and perhaps Hull as well, felt that it should be so arranged that Moscow would take

[47] The subject had been brought to the attention of the State Department also by a letter from the American Committee on Religious Rights and Minorities, as well as by a public statement from Bishop Michel d'Herbigny, President of the Pontifical Commission for Russia at the Vatican. *New York Times*, April 10, September 24, 1933.

[48] Kelley Interview.

[49] Eleanor Roosevelt, *This I Remember* (New York, 1949), 134.

[50] Bullitt made this point in his memorandum. *Foreign Relations, 1933*, II, 791-793. At the London Economic Conference, Hull told the Chinese Ambassador to Russia that the Metro-Vickers Affair had not been encouraging to the United States in its study of recognition. *Ibid.*, III, 495.

[51] Hull, *Memoirs*, I, 297.

the initiative and open the negotiations.[52] In either case, the Department preferred that the procedure be handled through normal channels and not by some personal emissary of the President.[53]

Roosevelt, however, had a predilection for direct communications between heads of states. He was determined to address the Russian government openly and personally. And he saw no reason for preliminary conversations. Some exchange of opinion was necessary, nevertheless, to guarantee that the method adopted would be satisfactory to Russia. For this task, Roosevelt turned to Bullitt, who during the late summer had become Roosevelt's closest adviser on the Russian question. Morgenthau's assertions to the contrary, Bullitt had been taking an active part in the recognition preparations since August at least.[54] Although Bullitt was a member of the State Department, his work in this matter was directly under the President, and during the exploratory stages before the invitation was dispatched, the Department was not cognizant of many of his activities.[55]

The first approach to the Soviets was made by Bullitt through Boris E. Skvirsky, the Director of the Soviet Information Bureau in Washington,[56] the unofficial embassy of the Russian government in the United States. Skvirsky had come to America in 1921 as a delegate to the Washington Conference from the Far Eastern Republic. After the Conference, when the Far Eastern Republic was incorporated in the Soviet Union, he remained in Washington as Director of the Information Bureau. The primary function of his organization was to establish contacts with American officials and to disseminate information on the Soviet Union. To further its aims,

[52] Phillips Interview; Robert Walton Moore, *Recognition of the Union of Soviet Socialist Republics*, Radio Address, November 22, 1933 (Washington, United States Government Printing Office, 1934), 2.
[53] Hull, *Memoirs*, I, 297-298.
[54] *Foreign Relations, 1933*, II, 788.
[55] Kelley Interview; Phillips Interview.   [56] Bullitt Letter.

the agency published a monthly magazine, the *Soviet Union Review*, which carried news on Russian life under the new regime and endeavored to foster closer relations between the two countries. Although Skvirsky's contacts with the State Department were naturally somewhat limited, he had close relations with several members of the press and with officials from other branches of the government.[57]

Working through Skvirsky, Bullitt made known to the Russians the desire of the President to open negotiations, and attempted to ascertain if Moscow was willing to discuss the issues outstanding between the two countries.[58] From the subsequent course of the conversations in Washington, it is safe to assume that the assurances from Moscow were of a very general character. Although recognition was greatly desired, the Kremlin was apprehensive of the exact nature of the demands America would make in return, and was also apparently concerned about the psychological effect of sweeping concessions on the Communist rank and file in Russia.[59] It was a negotiation which necessitated particular finesse, and, very likely, the Russian agreement on terms was couched in noncommittal phrases of acceptance.

The President and Bullitt were presumably satisfied, however, for Bullitt turned next to the drafting of a note of invitation for Roosevelt to send to Moscow. Among other factors determining the form of the message was the conviction of Bullitt that the success of the recognition negotiations depended upon the Kremlin's choice of a Soviet statesman of first-rate importance for the American mission, preferably Litvinov himself. The text was worded and reworded with the object of insuring the appointment of Litvinov.[60]

When the note was completed and approved by the Presi-

[57] Hull, *Memoirs*, I, 296.
[58] *ibid.*, 296-297; Bullitt Letter.
[59] Letter from Russia signed "A," *Sotsialisticheskii Vestnik* (Paris), No. 22 (307), November 10, 1933, 16.
[60] Kelley Interview.

dent, Bullitt went to Skvirsky and asked him to transmit it to Moscow unsigned in his most secret code to ascertain if it was acceptable to the Soviet Government. If so, it would be signed and retransmitted officially; it not, then Skvirsky must pledge himself not to make any public revelation of the exchange.[61] Moscow did approve of the form of the invitation, and it was resent, addressed to Mikhail Kalinin, President of the Central Committee of the USSR, signed by Roosevelt, and dated October 10, 1933.

In the communication, the President disclosed that since his inauguration he had been desirous of altering the "abnormal" situation existing between the two countries. He referred to the long tradition of Russian-American friendship before the Revolution, and expressed the belief that the problems standing in the way of friendly relations were "serious but not, in my opinion, insoluble." They could be resolved, he thought, by "frank, friendly conversations." If President Kalinin agreed with this view, Roosevelt wrote, he would be pleased to receive a Soviet representative "to explore with me personally the questions outstanding between our countries." Roosevelt carefully added that the acceptance of the invitation would in no way commit either country to any future course of action[62]—a necessary protection against false hopes on either side.[63]

The apparent concern of the Soviet Government over the possible demands of the United States in the forthcoming negotiations affected the choice of the Russian representative. There is evidence that considerable interest was shown in high government circles in Moscow over the appointment.

[61] "The Morgenthau Diaries," 21; Kelley Interview. A notation on the State Department copy of Kalinin's answer to Roosevelt reads: "Correct. Boris Skvirsky." *Foreign Relations, 1933*, II, 795n.

[62] *ibid.*, 794-795. For the complete text see Appendix B.

[63] Hull states that the President was careful not to commit the United States to recognition in the message. Hull, *Memoirs*, I, 298. Roosevelt told the press that the exchange of letters meant "just what they say and no more." *New York Times*, November 14, 1933.

Many Communists felt that a member of the Old Bolsheviks should be sent to insure a firm hand in the conversations, rather than an expert from the Narkomindel. Yet when the task was handed to Litvinov, who met both qualifications, certain of his enemies saw reason to rejoice, for, they said, the seeds of his undoing lay in the mission whether he was successful or unsuccessful. If he bungled such an important negotiation either by failing to achieve recognition or by giving too much in return for it, he would be ruined. If, on the other hand, he achieved a spectacular success and the plaudits of the people, his popularity would be most distasteful to Stalin.[64] Whatever truth there was in the analysis, it did reflect two interesting facts on the Soviet approach to the Washington parley. It mirrored concern for the proper publicity attendant on an agreement which would probably entail concessions beyond those the Soviets had previously been willing to make for recognition. And at the same time, it emphasized the importance that the Kremlin attached to the establishment of diplomatic relations with the United States.

The reply of Kalinin was dated October 17, 1933, and both his and the President's communications were released to the press on the twentieth. Expressing his complete agreement with Roosevelt on the abnormality of relations between the two governments, Kalinin slyly noted that he had held that opinion for sixteen years. He was sure that all the problems then existing or which might arise in the future could be solved once normal relations were restored, a phraseology that suggested Russia still hoped to gain recognition before the issues involved were settled. The Soviet President then touched briefly on the aspect of recognition which most concerned his government. He ventured to suggest, he said, that the absence of relations had had "an unfavorable effect not only on the interests of the two states involved, but also on the general

[64] *Sotsialisticheskii Vestnik* (Paris), No. 22 (307), November 10, 1933, 16.

international situation, increasing the element of disquiet, complicating the process of consolidating world peace, and encouraging forces tending to disturb that peace"—an unmistakable reference to the Far East. In conclusion, Kalinin informed the American government that Russia would be represented in the forthcoming conversations at Washington by Maxim Litvinov.[65]

Among all the other facts which Roosevelt had taken into account before he sent his historic invitation to Kalinin, none perhaps was more instrumental in deciding him to act when he did than his realization that American public opinion in the main supported a resumption of relations with Russia.[66] The President was remarkably sensitive to public opinion and throughout his tenure as Chief Executive seldom moved politically or diplomatically until he was sure that the majority of his countrymen would follow either from previous conviction or, on occasion, because they were fascinated by the boldness of his action.

The months of speculation and unofficial prophecy that preceded the invitation had prepared the American people for some step in the direction of recognition. The release of the exchange between Roosevelt and Kalinin came, therefore, as no surprise. Although dissenting voices were raised, the response in general was either favorable or restrained, pending the outcome of the negotiation.[67] The *Christian Science Moni-*

[65] *Foreign Relations, 1933*, ii, 795. For the complete text see Appendix B.

[66] Phillips Interview. Besides the American Foundation newspaper poll, Roosevelt had for his information a survey of press opinion taken by the Department of State in September and October. The latter showed that the New England and North Atlantic states were not enthusiastic over recognition, the majority of Southern and Midwestern states were in favor of recognition, and the Pacific states "somewhat indifferent." Under Secretary of State William Phillips to Franklin D. Roosevelt, with enclosures, October 19, 1933, Roosevelt Papers.

[67] Of eleven newspaper editorials on the Roosevelt-Kalinin exchange from all sections of the country quoted in the *New York Times*, October 22, 1933, only one was adverse, that in the *Los Angeles Times*.

tor commented that it had become more and more evident during the past year that Washington's Russian policy was "ineffective and artificial." It warned against "expecting too much" from the conversations or even from recognition. Trade and cooperation in the Far East would depend upon the removal of many troublesome hurdles.[68] The *New York Times*, while approving, also cautioned against unduly optimistic trade hopes, reminding its readers that recognition was not necessarily "a guarantee of large sales to Russia." But propaganda and debts, the editor declared, could no longer be considered real barriers to an understanding,[69] a view which was shared by William Phillip Sims, foreign editor of the Scripps-Howard press.[70] In the opinion of the *San Francisco Chronicle*, the Far Eastern situation was the most urgent reason for the President's move, although it agreed that Roosevelt was wise in not mentioning it since, "unlike Kalinin," he had "a Senate to deal with."[71]

Business groups interested in the potentialities of the Soviet market were pleased that the President had acted to facilitate commerce.[72] According to *Business Week*, "conservative opinion in the United States looked forward confidently to a first year's sale of fifty to seventy-five million dollars to Russia, provided the Reconstruction Finance Company was willing to grant three and four year term credits."[73] American steamship owners, likewise hoping to profit by the expected flow of trade, urged the stipulation that at least fifty per cent of the goods sent to the Soviet Union must be carried in American bottoms.[74]

Naturally, the liberal journals hailed the exchange as a tri-

[68] *Christian Science Monitor*, October 25, 1933.
[69] *New York Times*, October 22, 1933.
[70] *Literary Digest*, November 4, 1933, 15.
[71] *San Francisco Chronicle*, October 21, 1933.
[72] *New York Times*, October 21, 1933.
[73] *Business Week*, October 23, 1933, 8.
[74] *New York Times*, October 22, 1933.

umph of their policy. The *New Republic* pointed out that it had been recommending recognition for sixteen years. In the opinion of the editors, the Far East was as compelling a motive to the Administration as was the desire for new markets.[75] Louis Fischer, writing in the *Nation*, expressed his pleasure at the turn of events, but regretted that the President had considered it necessary to conduct negotiations before recognition. The insistence on preliminary discussion and agreements, he felt, was rather insulting to the USSR.[76]

The opposition vacillated between resignation and violent protest. Bowing to a *fait accompli*, the *Boston Evening Transcript* nevertheless hoped "that we will make it clear to the Russian conferees that the first sign of subversive operations by Communist agents on American soil will result in the immediate severance of friendly relations."[77] The *Commonweal* was convinced that the prestige given the "forces of atheism" would far outweigh the gains of the United States in trade and international affairs.[78] Emphasizing the same objection, the *National Republic* saw recognition as a "welcome to the 'Society of the Godless'," with the anticipated result that " 'In God We Trust' will soon be scraped from our coinage and likewise from our minds."[79] The *Chicago Tribune* considered Roosevelt's initiative "humiliating in its implications."[80]

Despite these indictments and the continued opposition of such groups as the American Legion and the American Federation of Labor,[81] the volume of protest was evidently considerably less than the Administration had anticipated.[82] Even

[75] *New Republic*, November 1, 1933, 325.
[76] *Nation*, November 15, 1933, 559.
[77] *Boston Evening Transcript*, October 21, 1933.
[78] *Commonweal*, November 3, 1933, 6.
[79] *National Republic*, November, 1933, 21. The article was entitled "Recognition or God."
[80] *Chicago Tribune*, October 26, 1933, as quoted in *National Republic*, November 1933, 29.
[81] *New York Times*, November 3, 16, 1933.
[82] *ibid.*, October 24, 1933.

Father Walsh counselled against embarrassing the President with too much public debate of the issue. In a surprisingly mild statement, Walsh advised the people to wait and see what could be achieved in the forthcoming negotiations. If the "obstacles" which stood in the way of a satisfactory relationship could be overcome, he suggested that he might support recognition.[83]

In Moscow, needless to say, the reaction to the letter of the President was wholeheartedly favorable. For four days after the public announcement, the front pages of the two leading newspapers were devoted to comments and reports on the significance of the exchange. This perhaps more than the actual contents of the editorials attested to the importance of the event to the Soviet Union. Welcoming Roosevelt's initiative, *Pravda* considered that it reflected a long-delayed change in the attitude of the American bourgeoisie. They had finally become "convinced" that it was impossible to ignore the growing importance of the Soviet Union in world affairs. But Russia was most gratified that the revaluation had finally taken place. The significance that the Soviet Government attached to the conversations in Washington, the editors pointed out, was clearly evidenced by the choice of Litvinov as the official envoy. "Who can doubt," the editorial concluded, "that normal relations between the usa and the ussr could create such a correlation of forces that it would be impossible for the adventurist groups to consider attempts to break the peace?"[84]

Noting that all recent efforts to preserve peace by international conference had proved unsuccessful and that the nations of the world were hurrying down the road to war, *Izvestia* found the President's invitation a source of great

[83] Several days before the release of this statement, Father Walsh had an appointment with the President, who apparently asked his advice on the conduct of the negotiations. The meeting appears to have caused Walsh to become temporarily more conciliatory. Father Edmund Walsh to Marvin H. McIntyre, October 21, 1933, Roosevelt Papers.

[84] *Pravda*, October 21, 1933.

hope for all peoples who desired a tranquil world. The American public, the newspaper continued, was at last aware that Soviet foreign policy was based on noninterference in the affairs of other countries and the fostering of friendly political and economic relations with all peace-seeking nations. "We would like to believe," wrote the editors, "that the establishment of official contacts will be only the first step toward a rapprochement between the two great countries, which will undoubtedly be welcomed by all true friends of peace."[85]

International communism also greeted the event with little equivocation, seeing as "the most important result of recognition . . . the discouragement of the enemies of the Soviet Union." But the national parties were warned that a Russian-American reconciliation should not be used as an excuse to relax the fight against imperialist war. Rather the struggle should be intensified to add to the new force which had been thrown in the balance on the side of Russia.[86]

Foreign reactions to the exchange were carefully reported in the Russian press. Both the French and the English newspapers were quoted as considering the development one of great consequence, with particular emphasis being placed upon its effect on the situation in the Far East.[87] A significantly large number of dispatches dealt with the Japanese reaction to Roosevelt's action. Although the Foreign Office in Tokyo expressed its pleasure that two of its most important neighbors were in the process of a reconciliation, Moscow accepted the assurance with tongue in cheek. The same officials, according to the Russians, were privately expressing concern. Tokyo saw a disturbing relation between the President's invitation, the recent Soviet publication of Japanese documents on the Chi-

---

[85] *Izvestia*, October 21, 1933.

[86] *International Press Correspondence*, October 27, 1933, 1033-1034.

[87] See *Pravda* and *Izvestia* for October 21, 22, 23, 24, 25, 1933. In every case where economic considerations were mentioned by the foreign press, as quoted in the Soviet newspapers, they were relegated to second place.

nese and Eastern Railway plot, and the continued refusal of the United States Government to exchange a good-will mission with Japan.[88]

Washington was not unaware of Japan's apprehension.[89] Ambassador Grew informed the State Department of Japanese Foreign Minister Koki Hirota's comment on the news. Hirota doubted if the conversations would lead to actual recognition, but he made it clear that: "If there is a man who observes that the possible American-Soviet agreement means pressure on Japan's position in the Far East, he knows nothing of the Far Eastern situation." Saburo Kurusu, the Chief of the Commercial Bureau of the Foreign Office, had confidently, and with a touch of the same indifference, told the Counsellor of the American Embassy that it would be very unfortunate if Russia or China got the idea that the United States would support them in their relations with Japan. He assured the Counsellor that the Foreign Office itself was quite unconcerned, but if such an idea were to gain currency in Japan, public opinion and the military elements might make it difficult for the government to continue its efforts to limit the war budgets.[90]

Speaking with less discretion, the new Japanese Ambassador to Sweden, Toshio Shiratori, who was crossing Canada en route to his new post, frankly admitted that recognition would be a very serious blow to Japan. Any American loans to Russia,

[88] *ibid.*, October 22, 1933; see also *Pravda*, November 4, 5, 1933.

[89] Hull was cognizant of Japan's opposition to the reestablishment of relations between Russia and the United States. Hull, *Memoirs*, I, 276.

[90] Grew sent a long dispatch covering the various reactions in Japan to the Roosevelt-Kalinin exchange. *Foreign Relations, 1933*, II, 796-798. Shortly after the release of the correspondence, it was announced that the Japanese Ambassador to the United States Katsuji Debuchi, had been recalled and would return to Japan in mid-November. *New York Times*, October 24, 1933. That the summons may have been prompted by the desire of the Japanese Foreign Office to consult with Debuchi on the anticipated Russo-American rapprochement is suggested by the fact that in the previous month, in announcing the anticipated recall of key ambassadors for consultation, Tokyo specifically excluded Debuchi. *Japan Times and Mail*, September 26, 1933.

he feared, would be used to further the Communist cause in China.[91] The Tokyo newspaper, *Asahi*, also spoke more openly, cautioning Russia and the United States that: "Our policy is fixed and efforts to change it will only cause discord."[92]

Whatever hopes the Administration might have had regarding the beneficial effect of recognition on the Far East, they were in no way prepared to have it worsen relations between the United States and Japan.[93] In view of the dispatches of Grew and the definite anti-Japanese interpretation the Russians were giving the Roosevelt-Kalinin exchange, Stanley Hornbeck, Chief of the Far Eastern Division of the State Department, recommended to the Secretary that assurances be given Tokyo that the forthcoming negotiations were in no way motivated by Far Eastern problems.[94] Efforts were, in fact, made to calm Japanese fears, the most obvious being the announcement in early November that a considerable part of the American Fleet would soon be transferred to the Atlantic for maneuvers. News of the order was apparently received with satisfaction by all groups in Japan, with the exception of the Navy, which refused to attach any importance to it.[95]

[91] *New York Times*, October 26, 1933.

[92] As quoted in *ibid.*, October 25, 1933.

[93] This was especially true since the appointment of Koki Hirota to the Japanese Foreign Ministry. Hirota, who had just returned from the post of Ambassador to the Soviet Union, declared his policy to be one of closer and more friendly relations with both Russia and the United States. *Japan Times and Mail*, October 2, 1933. Ambassador Grew thought he observed a trend in Tokyo toward friendlier relations with America, but he suggested as one reason Japanese fear of a Soviet-American rapprochement. *Foreign Relations, 1933*, III, 706-709.

[94] *ibid.*, II, 801-802. Grew informed the State Department during the negotiations that Russia had taken a much firmer stand toward Japan since the first of November, causing relations between Moscow and Tokyo to become more strained than they had been for some period of time. He observed that some Japanese believed that Russia's increased confidence was traceable to the Washington conversations. *Ibid.*, III, 458-462.

[95] *ibid.*, III, 449. For favorable Japanese editorial comment in *Nagaya Shinachi, Jiji* and *Asahi*, see *Trans-Pacific* (Tokyo), November 16, 1933,

Official attention, however, was centered upon the approaching conference in Washington. On October 26, Litvinov had left Moscow for the United States, hopeful that the next weeks would see the end of the sixteen-year silence between his country and the United States. As evidence of the long-standing desire of the Soviet Union for recognition, he carried with him his commission as diplomatic representative to the United States, dated June 21, 1918, and signed by Lenin and Chicherin.[96]

---

8. A week later, however, *Nichi Nichi* called the order a meaningless gesture of friendship. *Foreign Relations, 1933*, III, 463. It is interesting to note that Louis Fischer had written in March 1933: "If the United States is afraid to ruffle Japan by establishing relations with Moscow, it should transfer half the Navy back to the eastern seaboard." *Nation*, March 29, 1933, 342.

[96] *New York Times*, November 5, 1933. This interesting document may be found in Louis Fischer, *The Soviets in World Affairs* (London, 1930), I, facing p. 300. The text is in French and Lenin signed his name using the French spelling—V. Oulianoff (Lenine).

CHAPTER 6

RECOGNITION

THE departure of Commissar Litvinov was shrouded in secrecy to avoid publicity and the necessity of meeting correspondents. The second objective was successfully accomplished, but the universal interest in his mission defeated the attempt at concealment.[1] Accompanied by Constantine Umanskii, Press Director of the Foreign Office, and Ivan Divilkovskii, Secretary General of the Foreign Office Collegium, Litvinov traveled by way of Warsaw, Berlin, and Paris to take the transatlantic steamer for the United States.

At Berlin, he finally agreed to grant an interview to American correspondents. Evidencing confidence in the outcome of the conversations with Roosevelt, he told the newsmen that as far as the Soviet Delegation was concerned an agreement could be reached in "a half an hour"[2]—a gambit much publicized in the United States, where it made a most unfavorable impression. It is possible that Litvinov's blunder was purposeful. Anticipating a long session in Washington, he may have foreseen his casual answer would give the prolonged discussions the semblance of concession on his part and thus ease the way to public acceptance of the agreement in America.[3] He certainly did not wish to give the same impression in Russia, and it is perhaps significant that this remark was not reported in the Soviet press, which otherwise followed his progress and statements carefully. In the course of the interview, Litvinov

[1] William Henry Chamberlin in the *Christian Science Monitor*, November 18, 1933.
[2] *New York Times*, October 29, 1933.
[3] See Arthur Upham Pope, *Maxim Litvinoff* (New York, 1943), 294.

was also asked to comment on the effect of recognition upon the Far East. His reply was guarded, but nevertheless revealing. "It might be reasonably assumed," he said, "that friendly relations between the Moscow and Washington governments would react on such a special situation as that involving Russo-Japanese relations."[4]

Meanwhile, in Washington, last minute arrangements were under way to receive the Soviet envoy. Secretary Hull postponed his sailing to the Montevideo Conference in order that he might be on hand to welcome Litvinov and participate in the first three or four days of the negotiations.[5] The experts in the Department were engaged in work on the agreements which were to be presented to the Russians for approval before recognition. All relevant treaties between the Soviet Union and other nations were carefully examined for possible borrowings and to ascertain the limits to which Moscow had gone in the past in the direction of concessions. In some cases, as many as twenty drafts of proposed texts were drawn up in an effort to achieve wording that would be binding and at the same time acceptable to Litvinov.[6] On the evening of November 6, an eleventh hour briefing was held at the White House. Present besides the President were Hull, Phillips, Bullitt, Morgenthau, and Moore. All agreed, according to Secretary Hull, that the "two most important precautions were against Soviet propaganda and illegal activities in the United States and freedom of worship for Americans in Russia."[7]

The *Berengaria*, with Maxim Litvinov and his party aboard, steamed into New York harbor on November 7, 1933, the sixteenth anniversary of the Bolshevik Revolution. At quarantine, the liner was met by the official welcoming party and representatives of the press.[8] Litvinov read a prepared statement

---

[4] *New York Times*, October 29, 1933.

[5] Cordell Hull, *The Memoirs of Cordell Hull* (New York, 1948), I, 300.

[6] *ibid.*, 298-299.   [7] *ibid.*, 300.

[8] *New York Times*, November 8, 1933.

which dealt for the most part with his hopes for a mutually profitable relationship between the two countries and emphasized the many similarities in the history and development of the United States and of his country since 1917.

The most interesting section of his text referred to the possibility of collaboration in the cause of peace. "The efforts of both countries . . . ," he observed, "have so far proceeded along parallel lines, but the absence of normal means of continuous intercourse has prevented that linking up of these efforts which would have made them one of the most solid guarantees of peace. The opinions expressed all over the world on the message . . . between our Presidents have shown the hopes raised among all the friends of peace, at the very thought of the establishment of solid friendly relations between the peoples of the two greatest republics in the world."[9]

Prompted by this reference to international conditions, the reporters asked the Commissar to comment on the connection between recognition and the Far East. But, displaying more discretion in America than he had in Berlin, Litvinov refused to answer. Significantly, he did repeat his assertion that a half hour would be sufficient to resolve the difficulties between the two governments. "Perhaps less," he added.[10]

Boarding a Coast Guard cutter, the official party proceeded to Jersey City and there entrained for Washington. At Union Station in Washington, Litvinov was met by Secretary Hull and his entourage who, after an exchange of greetings, escorted the Russians to the Skvirsky residence. There the Commissar changed into formal attire and, at 5:30 P.M., was called for by Mr. Hull, who accompanied him to the White House for his reception by the President. During the entire trip from the *Berengaria* the route had been heavily guarded. Correspondents noted that there were more police at the Union Station in Washington than there were onlookers when Litvinov

[9] *Soviet Union Review*, XI (1933), 255.
[10] *New York Times*, November 8, 1933.

arrived.[11] American officials were taking no chances on an untoward incident.

President Roosevelt received Litvinov in the Blue Room, although he is said to have jokingly suggested the Red Room as more appropriate. After the diplomatic conventions had been met, the two men chatted briefly. Outside, Litvinov affably saluted the press and made an extemporaneous statement of his pleasure in meeting the President. From the White House he returned to the Skvirsky residence.[12] The amenities of arrival were over. It was time to turn to the business at hand.

The words of R. Walton Moore offer an appropriate introduction to a discussion of the negotiations which took place in Washington between November 7 and November 16, 1933. Moore said: "There were no stenographers present and no reports made, and thus, so far as the conferences are concerned, there will be a bare outline and not a full picture exposed to the eye of the future historian."[13] Although the factual skeleton can now be given form by the use of published memoirs, recently opened private papers,[14] and the official documents released by the Department of State,[15] much that transpired will probably always remain unknown, for the most vital decisions were made in private conferences between the President and Mr. Litvinov. In accordance with his usual custom, Roosevelt made no memoranda of these sessions, and, if Mr. Litvinov did so, it is not likely that historians will ever have the advantage of using them.

The first conversations took place at the State Department on the morning of November 8. Together with Phillips, Moore,

[11] ibid.   [12] ibid.

[13] Robert Walton Moore, *Recognition of the Union of Soviet Socialist Republics*, Radio Address, November 22, 1933 (Washington, United States Government Printing Office, 1934), 4-5.

[14] Notably the Roosevelt Papers.

[15] *Foreign Relations, 1933*, II, 778-840. The author has also been fortunate in receiving the cooperation of several of the participants, who gave him the benefit of their personal recollections of the event.

Bullitt, Kelley, and Morgenthau, Secretary Hull discussed with Litvinov the guarantees which the United States Government expected on propaganda, religious rights, and legal prerogatives. The conference opened in a very friendly manner, but it soon became evident that the Soviet envoy was in no way prepared to approve the commitments the American negotiators desired. The meeting adjourned for lunch, with no progress having been made.[16] Later in the afternoon, a second meeting was held at the Department which lasted until six o'clock.

At the close of this session, results were still most unsatisfactory. At one point during the discussions on religious rights, Litvinov, who spoke and understood English, misinterpreted the proposals of Hull as a demand that religious freedom be granted to all Russians in the Soviet Union. Considerable acrimonious debate resulted before the matter was clarified to the satisfaction of the Commissar.[17] Very probably it was also at this first meeting that Litvinov was presented with the draft agreement on propaganda and Communist activity which had been drawn up by Kelley. Kelley had prepared the text with great care, as it was considered the most important single prerequisite to recognition. Intentionally, the Third International had not been mentioned nor the word "communism" used. Kelley and his associates reasoned that if the organization were specifically referred to it would be an easy matter to simply change the name and thus violate the spirit but not the letter of the agreement. It was an iron-clad document, and upon reading it, Litvinov insisted that his government could never agree to such a pledge. But when it was pointed out to him that Moscow already had agreed in several instances, since the wording was taken from other treaties signed by the

[16] Phillips Interview. The following account of the first three days of the negotiations is based largely upon the diary of Mr. William Phillips, which Mr. Phillips read to the author during the interview.

[17] *ibid.*; see also Hull, *Memoirs*, I, 301.

Soviet Union, the Commissar expressed surprise and asked for time to study the matter.[18]

Apparently, at least one hurdle was eliminated during the meeting on the eighth; thereafter there was no question of recognition before negotiation. Litvinov had arrived still hopeful that that procedure would be followed, and he seemed to have found justification for his assumption in the wording of the President's letter. In the first discussions, however, he was quickly and decisively disabused of the idea. Only when it was clear that the American formula of settlement first and recognition second would be the basis of negotiation, could the conversations proceed to the issues in question.[19]

The joint communiqué issued on the first day gave no hint of the difficulties encountered, referring to "friendly private discussions" and noting that the talks would be continued the following day.[20] The negotiators assembled again in the morning on November 9, and remained in session for two hours. No communiqué was issued. In the afternoon, Litvinov was scheduled to see the President, but the appointment was canceled and, instead of receiving the Commissar, Roosevelt met with the State Department negotiators.

The Department had, in fact, asked the President for the meeting in order to acquaint him with the fruitless negotiations so far. Litvinov, they reported, was highly uncooperative, stubborn in his refusals to meet the American proposals, and suspicious of the motives behind them. Secretary Hull and Mr. Phillips suspected that one reason for the intransigence of the Commissar was his desire, for purposes of prestige, to deal directly with the President rather than through the State Department. In any case, the conferences had reached an impasse on the major issues, namely, religion and propaganda. The only answer seemed to be for Roosevelt to take over the

[18] Kelley Interview; Hull, *Memoirs*, I, 299-301.
[19] Moore, *op. cit.*, 3; Phillips Interview; Hull, *Memoirs*, I, 300; Kelley Interview.
[20] *Foreign Relations, 1933*, II, 802.

negotiations and try to break the stalemate. This the President agreed to do, and Secretary Hull arranged to bring Litvinov to the White House on the following day.[21]

Accordingly, around noon, Hull and Phillips, and possibly Bullitt, accompanied Litvinov to his meeting with the President. The conference, which lasted about an hour, began with Roosevelt reviewing the problems under consideration and the course of the negotiations to date. In his most affable and winning manner, the President drew the threads of the negotiation together, expressed the sincere interest of the United States in a just settlement and, to break the ice, injected a measure of humor into his remarks. By the end of the discussion Litvinov had noticeably thawed. Roosevelt suggested that he and the Commissar meet again in the evening alone and continue their conversation in private, where they could, if need be, insult each other with impunity. Litvinov laughed heartily. The Roosevelt touch had succeeded, and the prospects for continued and profitable negotiations were greatly enhanced.[22]

That evening the Commissar was closeted with the President for three hours, during which time the difficult questions of religious freedom and propaganda were apparently resolved satisfactorily.[23] The evidence that only minor textual changes

[21] Mr. Phillips told the author that no minutes were taken of the first two days' conversations at the State Department largely because of the completely unsatisfactory progress that was being made. Phillips Interview. William Bullitt later declared that Litvinov's persistent refusal to agree to the guarantees prompted the negotiators to hand him a schedule of steamship sailings with the choice of sign or go home. William C. Bullitt, "How We Won the War and Lost the Peace," Part I, *Life*, August 30, 1948. If Mr. Bullitt's memory was correct, the State Department was most certainly resorting to drastic action.

[22] Phillips Interview. It is tempting to speculate on the extent to which this early demonstration of the efficacy of the Roosevelt charm on stubborn Russians influenced the President's later confidence in his ability to wheedle Marshal Stalin, given the opportunity of a personal meeting.

[23] Memorandum and enclosed drafts from Green H. Hackworth, Legal Adviser, the Department of State, to Franklin D. Roosevelt, November 11, 1933, Roosevelt Papers. See also Hull, *Memoirs*, I, 301; and *Foreign Relations, 1933*, II, 802.

were made to satisfy the Commissar supports the explanation for Litvinov's earlier obduracy suggested by Hull and Phillips.

The next day the Secretary of State left for the Montevideo Conference. In Mr. Hull's absence, his duties devolved upon Under-Secretary Phillips. But as far as the Russian-American negotiations were concerned, Bullitt then became the principal representative of the State Department and the President, aided by Kelley and Moore. Mr. Bullitt was Roosevelt's chief adviser and emissary and most of the materials which passed between the White House and the State Department in the succeeding negotiations were handled directly by Bullitt with the President.[24]

On November 11, Litvinov met with Phillips, Moore, Bullitt, and Kelley for an hour at the Department.[25] At this conference, some of the details of wording in the agreements concluded between the President and the Commissar on the night before were doubtless discussed. The following evening, Litvinov spent two hours with Roosevelt at the White House.[26] Neither of these meetings was clarified or even announced by official press releases, although Mr. Bullitt assured reporters that progress was being made. Bullitt facetiously compared Roosevelt and Litvinov to two bookworms working from either end of a shelf. In time they would come together, he said.[27]

For the next two days, the Commissar rested at the Skvirsky residence and took sight-seeing trips in the surrounding countryside. No conferences were held with the President or with members of the State Department. Whether Litvinov was awaiting final approval from Moscow for the settlements he had made is not known, but very likely such was the case. In the meantime, State Department officials were redrafting the commitments in accordance with the alterations made during the preceding discussions.[28] Agreement had been reached on

[24] Kelley Interview.
[25] New York Times, November 12, 1933.
[26] ibid., November 13, 1933.
[27] ibid.   [28] ibid., November 15, 1933.

all but one of the points of dispute, and final action waited on the formulation of the texts.

The remaining unresolved issue was the question of the debts. At this point, it is necessary to give some attention to the intricacies of that problem. The total figure included a number of different categories, the most important, of course, being the monies owed the United States Government by the former Provisional Government of Russia. The first credit established for the Provisional Government by Washington amounted to $100,000,000 and was available as of May 16, 1917. From this sum, $35,000,000 was forwarded as the first advance on July 6, 1917. Other credits were subsequently established and by November 1, 1917, the total amount was $450,000,000. As of the latter date, however, only $186,400,000 had actually been drawn in cash by the Provisional Government. One week after the Bolshevik Revolution the first interest payment was due and, in order to facilitate payment, the Treasury Department advanced $1,329,750 against an obligation signed by Ambassador Bakhmetev, which the Ambassador immediately paid back into the Treasury as interest on the cash advances from the credit account. After that date, no further cash payments were made to the Provisional Government and the remaining credit funds were withdrawn. The total debt was, therefore, $187,729,750.[29]

At the time of the November Revolution, the Russian Embassy in Washington had a number of contracts for materials with American manufacturers. In the following months, the Treasury and the Embassy set about liquidating as many of these agreements as possible, making monetary adjustments on the basis of work completed, and canceling as many contracts as possible. An attempt was made to facilitate at least partial completion of nonmilitary supply contracts, but strictly

[29] "Leffingwell Memorandum," June 28, 1919, *Loans to Foreign Governments,* Senate Document No. 86, 67th Congress, 2nd Sess. (Washington, United States Government Printing Office, 1921), 92-94. Hereafter cited as *Loans to Foreign Governments.*

war material contracts were canceled whenever practicable. As a result of these operations, most of the private obligations of the Provisional Government were successfully settled. In the latter part of 1918, shipments of nonmilitary goods, produced under the above mentioned contracts, were resumed to Russia by the Embassy in Washington. By January 1, 1920, most of these supplies had been disposed of in that manner. The destination of these shipments was Siberia, and the northern and southern regions of Russia, all of which were areas under the control of non-Bolshevik Russian governments. Owing to the lack of separate accounts for the monies originally belonging to the Provisional Government in the United States and those derived from the advances of the American government, the Embassy was unable to state definitely that only Russian funds had been used in payment for these supplies.[30] But inasmuch as the Russian funds before American advances amounted to only $21,000,000, and the value of goods shipped after November 7 equaled between $25,999,000 and $50,000,000,[31] it is logical to assume that some materials were paid for from the American loan.

These facts to a certain extent gave credence to the Soviet claims that they were not obligated to honor the debt of their predecessor because it had been used to aid the forces fighting the Bolsheviks. It must be noted, however, that a very small part of the total loan was apparently so used, and secondly, that the supplies were not military materials but food, medical stores, and rails. Furthermore, Washington did try to take the Soviet argument into account when it calculated the sum owed by the Soviet Government. Obligations to the amount of $4,871,547.37 were disallowed, since they represented surplus war materials sold to the Kolchak government. Washington was also willing to recognize the territorial losses of the So-

[30] Letter of Ambassador Boris Bakhmetev to Acting Secretary of State Frank L. Polk, March 4, 1920, *ibid.*, 96-97.
[31] "Leffingwell Memorandum," *ibid.*, 93-94.

viet Government, and accordingly, to adjust the debt down-ward.[32]

Besides the government loans, there were two other debt categories to be considered. One included the claims of American holders of pre-Revolutionary bond issues, which were repudiated by the Communists, and the other consisted of the claims of American citizens whose properties and other interests in Russia had been confiscated by the Soviet Government at the time of the Revolution. The rough totals under these two headings were $106,884,157 and $336,691,771 respectively, without interest.[33]

In a memorandum on the debt problem, written shortly before the arrival of Commissar Litvinov, Robert Kelley pointed out that all of the government debt and a large part of the private debts were contracted by the Provisional Government, in contradistinction to the Russian debts owed to the other Allies, which were, in the main, accounts of the Tsarist government. For that reason, Kelley suggested that the Soviets could settle with the United States without establishing a precedent for the settlement of their other debts.[34] Kelley had reference to the frequently reiterated contention of the Soviets that any payment to the United States would reopen the debt issue with their other creditors. Kelley's proposal was the more interesting for being completely opposed to the basic doctrine upon which the American government based its claim for the Soviet payment of the Provisional Government's debt, i.e. that succeeding governments were responsible for the payment of international obligations contracted by their predecessors. Still, it was an argument that could be used to persuade Moscow to settle the American debt. For that matter, only one creditor government was legally in a position to demand Russian payment should the Soviets settle with the United States. According to the Treaty of Rapallo, Russia and

[32] *Foreign Relations, 1933*, ii, 800-801.
[33] *ibid.*, 787-788.   [34] *ibid.*, 801.

Germany canceled their debts to each other, but if at any time the Soviet Government settled its other international debts, it was obligated to pay those owed to Germany.[35] The other creditor nations could only exert moral and diplomatic pressure on the basis of an American settlement.

The Department of State strongly recommended to the President that a definite settlement be made on the debt before recognition. Otherwise, it warned, the United States would undoubtedly find itself in the same position as England and France, both of which had waited until after establishing relations with Russia and neither of which had ever been able to negotiate a settlement.[36] And, apparently, the original intention was to follow the recommended course, for the Treasury Department cooperated with the State Department in drawing up tentative agreements on the debt.[37] But as the other negotiations continued longer than had been anticipated, and Litvinov was unwilling to make a specific commitment on the issue at that time,[38] it was decided to draw up a declaration of intent in principle which would serve as the basis for further negotiations after recognition.

It was in order to draft such a memorandum that the President saw Litvinov again on the morning of the fifteenth. But no decision was reached. After leaving Roosevelt, Litvinov and Bullitt continued the discussion.[39] The difficulty lay in trying to arrive at a minimum figure acceptable to the Soviet Government. Even after the abandonment of recognition as a lever for settlement, the United States had a weapon of persuasion left—the almost certain passage of the Johnson Act by Congress in the near future. The pending legislation would

[35] Leonard Shapiro (ed.), *Soviet Treaty Series* (Washington, D. C., 1950), I, 169.

[36] *Foreign Relations, 1933*, I, 785, 789, 793.

[37] Hull, *Memoirs*, I, 300.

[38] Henry Morgenthau, Jr., "The Morgenthau Diaries," Part III, *Colliers*, October 11, 1947, 21, 72.

[39] *Foreign Relations, 1933*, II, 802.

make it impossible for the United States Government to lend money to any nation which had defaulted on previous debts owed America.

Making use of the Johnson Act argument, Bullitt advised Litvinov not to make any "absurd offer" of settlement, for it would most certainly be rejected by Congress, which had to pass on the terms. If that occurred and the Johnson Act were in force, the Soviet Union would be "unable to obtain one penny of credit from either the Government or any private corporation or individual in the United States, or their agencies abroad." The sum of $50,000,000 which Litvinov suggested was rejected by Bullitt, who suspected that the Soviet Government would insist that it be accepted as the maximum, once it was down on paper as the minimum. Litvinov maintained that most of the loan had been spent to arm Kolchak, and accused the private creditors of having padded their claims, both of which assertions Bullitt hotly denied. The discussion terminated with Litvinov somewhat more amenable to altering the figure upwards. But Bullitt, reporting to the President on the conference in preparation for a second Roosevelt-Litvinov meeting in the afternoon, urged the President to "endeavor forcibly" to persuade Litvinov to fix $100,000,000 as the lower figure. "I think we were a bit too gentle with him this morning," Bullitt advised.[40]

That afternoon a "gentleman's agreement" between Roosevelt and Litvinov was finally initialed. Litvinov stated that his government would pay a sum "not less than $75,000,000 in the form of a percentage above the ordinary rate of interest on a loan to be granted to it by the Government of the United States or its nationals, all other [mutual] claims . . . to be regarded as eliminated." Roosevelt was confident he could persuade Congress to accept a settlement for $150,000,000, but he was doubtful of approval of any lesser amount. In the opinion of the Commissar, that figure was excessive, but he was willing

[40] *ibid.*, 802-803.

to personally advise his government to pay $100,000,000. He expressed his conviction that the President would see the justice of the Soviet figures upon investigation of the facts of the case. In an effort to arrive at a mutually acceptable sum between the limits of $75,000,000 and $150,000,000, Litvinov agreed to remain after the resumption of relations and continue negotiations with Bullitt and Morgenthau.[41]

Such was the unfortunate debt memorandum which was to be the source of much future ill-feeling between the two governments. Assuming that Washington was sincere in its desire to settle the debt, and there is no reason to doubt that it was, the method adopted was most certainly a mistake. The well-known experiences of other nations should have been sufficient warning that the United States was tempting fate. It was a particularly unfortunate move in the light of the circumstances surrounding recognition. Russia was unusually anxious for diplomatic relations, and it is not at all improbable that if enough pressure had been exerted she would have made a definite settlement then and there. The Soviet Government and Maxim Litvinov would have suffered an immeasurable loss of prestige both at home and abroad if the negotiations had failed. If Litvinov had been given the alternatives of signing an agreement in detail or relinquishing the prospect of recognition, he would very likely have complied with the demand of the United States.

If, however, for undisclosed reasons, a firm stand was not feasible, every effort should have been made to draft a tentative agreement that left no room for misinterpretation. The badly worded memorandum gave the Soviet Government an opportunity later to draw quite a different meaning from it than had been intended. The phraseology would indicate that Roosevelt simply wrote the memorandum down at the moment or perhaps called in a secretary and dictated it. So vital a document should have been carefully worded by experts in the

---

[41] *ibid.*, 804. See Appendix C for the complete text of the memorandum.

State or Treasury Departments. It is only fair to point out that even the most iron-clad guarantee would no doubt have been violated without hesitation by the Soviet Government had it been in its interest to do so. But as it was, the United States Government, by its less than precise action, handed the Soviets a ready-made weapon to brandish in the dispute that followed. If Washington could not have prevented the disagreement, it could at least have avoided the embarrassment of basing its position upon a deceptively worded agreement "in principle."

So far as is known, no further meetings were held until the next evening, November 16, 1933. Following the annual Cabinet Dinner and Musicale, the President asked Mr. Phillips and Secretary of the Treasury Woodin to join him in his study. Waiting there also were Morgenthau, Bullitt, and Commissar Litvinov. At eleven o'clock, Roosevelt came in and read through the agreements that had been drafted by the State Department. Several minor changes, suggested by Litvinov, were dealt with on the spot, a procedure which took some time. When both parties were at last satisfied with the wording, the President and Mr. Litvinov signed the series of documents which were dated November 16. Due to the delay occasioned by the changes, the signatures were actually affixed at 1:14 the morning of the seventeenth. At the conclusion of the ceremony, Roosevelt was visibly pleased with the night's work and all those present toasted the new relationship between Russia and the United States with a glass of newly legal 3.2 beer.[42]

Recognition and the mutual commitments which accompanied it were embodied in an exchange of eleven letters, and one memorandum.[43] The correspondence opened with Roose-

[42] Phillips Interview. The President later told reporters that the documents were signed "at the magic hour of 10 minutes before midnight." *United States News*, November 20, 1933. The exactness of Mr. Phillips' entry in his diary, however, makes his version more credible.

[43] See Appendix D for the complete texts of the Roosevelt-Litvinov exchange.

velt informing Litvinov of the decision of the United States Government to establish diplomatic relations with the Soviet Union and Litvinov's reply expressing Russia's pleasure and willingness to accept the tendered recognition. In the remaining documents, the Soviet envoy agreed to certain undertakings on behalf of his government, most of which were reciprocated by the Chief Executive for the United States Government. The one memorandum had been written by Litvinov, at Roosevelt's request, to clarify the Russian interpretation of "economic espionage."

The second letter included a series of exceptionally detailed pledges by the Soviet Government to refrain from participation in or encouragement of any propaganda or subversive activity which would affect the United States. Article One recognized the unqualified jurisdiction of the United States within its own territory, and guaranteed the noninterference of the Soviet Union in the internal affairs of America. Article Two pledged the Soviet Union to prohibit any subversive activity by the agents of its government, or by individuals or organizations directly or indirectly under its control or receiving any financial aid from it, which aimed at disturbing the tranquillity of the United States. Both of these commitments were taken almost verbatim from the General Treaty signed by Great Britain and Russia on August 8, 1924, regulating British *de jure* recognition of the Soviet Union.[44]

Article Three consisted of a guarantee by the Soviet Government not to permit the residence on its territory of any organization claiming to be the government of the United States or of any military group planning an armed invasion of the United States. The wording of this article was almost identical with that of Part IV, Sections 1 and 2, of the Soviet-Latvian Treaty of August 4, 1920.[45]

[44] *Anglo-sovetskie otnosheniia so dnia podpisaniia torgovogo soglasheniia do razryva (1921-1937 gg.)* (Moscow, Narkomindel, 1927), 76.
[45] Shapiro, *op. cit.*, I, 55.

Undoubtedly, Article 4 contained the most significant pledge. "Not to permit the formation or residence on its [USSR] territory of any organization or group—and to prevent the activity on its territory of any organization or group, or of representatives or officials of any organization or group—which has as an aim the overthrow or the preparation for the overthrow of, or the bringing about by force of a change in, the political or social order of the whole or any part of the United States, its territories or possessions."

There was no question that Article Four applied directly and unequivocally to the Third International, whose headquarters were located in Moscow, and to its operations in the United States through the American Communist party. Although the phraseology was copied from sections of several other treaties made by Russia, including the Latvian Treaty and that with Afghanistan, signed August 31, 1926,[46] in its entirety, it was a more sweeping obligation than any the Soviet Union had previously signed. It was notable that the wording made the Soviet Government responsible for subversive acts by private as well as public and semi-public organizations and individuals.

It is tempting to speculate on the degree of American faith in the strict observance of these articles. Pledges similar in spirit if not as all-embracing and detailed in wording had been extended to other governments by the Soviet Union and their violation had led to strained and even ruptured relations. As a matter of fact, it appears there was considerable skepticism among many of the negotiators as to the exact fulfillment of the pledges.[47] It is probable that the President and Mr. Bullitt were more hopeful than their associates that the commitments would be carried out. In any case, all the American officials were convinced of the necessity for their inclusion in the correspondence in order to obtain a favorable public re-

[46] *ibid.*, 55, 322-323.
[47] Phillips Interview; Kelley Interview.

action to recognition. It was a *sine qua non* for American acceptance of a reconciliation with Russia.[48]

The third exchange in the correspondence dealt with the guarantee of religious rights for American nationals in Russia. In his letter to Litvinov, Roosevelt expressed his especial concern that citizens of the United States be allowed the same privileges of worship and other religious observances that they enjoyed in their own country. When the subject was first presented to the Commissar in the course of the negotiations, he had declared that existing Russian laws adequately protected the points enumerated. Hull insisted, however, that the Commissar give his comments in writing. Accordingly, Litvinov immediately annotated the list, writing "yes" when he agreed with the text and in some cases asking that the wording be changed.[49] The final draft in answer to the President's letter was more detailed. After each of the religious rights, Litvinov quoted at some length the Soviet law which applied, noting its specific stipulations. It is interesting to observe that this was the only pledge which Litvinov did not ask the United States to reciprocate. Although Russia had conceded nothing not already granted to other countries or technically guaranteed by Russian law, the President was apparently satisfied. Whether by intent or not, the document served the Soviet Government as a propaganda weapon in refutation of the charges of religious persecution which had been levelled against it.

[48] This point was emphasized by both Mr. Phillips and Mr. Kelley when they were interviewed by the author. The Administration's awareness of the importance of convincing the American people that all possible measures of protection had been taken was also reflected in Assistant Secretary R. Walton Moore's remarks on the radio soon after recognition. He assured "all of our people who have felt concerned as to what might happen" as the result of renewed relations with Russia that it had been the "President's resolute purpose to safeguard the integrity of our Government and the rights of our nationals." "That," he said, "was the primary purpose to which any strictly material question such as the settlement of debts was altogether ancillary." Moore, *op. cit.*, 4.

[49] Hull, *Memoirs*, I, 301.

The next two letters concerned the legal rights of American citizens resident in the Soviet Union. The Commissar informed the President that his government was prepared to negotiate a consular convention.[50] In the meantime, the Soviet Union would grant the United States all rights accorded to the nation most favored in that respect. The Treaty applicable had been concluded with Germany in 1925,[51] and Litvinov enclosed articles from it to indicate the guarantees which would be enjoyed equally by nationals of the United States. Under the provisions of the Treaty, the authorities were obligated to notify the consul, within a given period of time, of the arrest of an American citizen, and the consul or diplomatic representative was guaranteed permission to visit his incarcerated countryman. The President in his reply assured Litvinov that American officials would be "zealous" in guarding the rights accorded, and would also expect citizens of the United States held by the USSR to be given speedy and fair trials and the privilege of counsel of their own choice.

Both the pledge on legal rights and the document which followed it, a memorandum stating the Soviet Government's interpretation of "economic espionage," were given added importance by their obvious connection with the recent Metro-Vickers case. In that instance, the arrested Englishmen had been held on vague charges of "economic espionage," and their ambassador had been unable for some time to receive permission to visit them in prison.

The final communications concerned claims and counterclaims. Although no final settlement had been reached on those points, Litvinov had made two concessions. First, he had agreed, pending a settlement, to relinquish all the rights of his government to sums awarded it by court decisions in the United States. The reference here was to assets and holdings

[50] No consular convention was ever concluded between the two governments.

[51] For the terms of the Soviet-German Treaty of 1925, see Shapiro, *op. cit.*, I, 302-308.

in the United States of Russian companies and individuals whose property had been confiscated by the Soviets. According to Moscow, assets held outside of Russia were included in the confiscation. What the Soviet Union was doing, therefore, was to turn these cases over to the United States Government, and whatever was realized on them would be subtracted from the final intergovernmental settlement. To prevent recognition from affecting dispositions of Russian property already made by American courts, the Soviet Government, at the behest of the United States, agreed not to contest any prior actions.

The second concession on counterclaims prompted considerable speculation. Litvinov wrote to the President that "following my examination of certain documents of the years 1918 to 1921 relating to the attitude of the American Government toward the expedition into Siberia, the operations there of foreign military forces and the inviolability of the territory of the Union of Soviet Socialist Republics, the Government of the Union of Soviet Socialist Republics agrees that it will waive any and all claims of whatsoever character arising out of activities of military forces of the United States in Siberia . . . and that such claims shall be regarded as finally settled and disposed of by this agreement."

Many readers and commentators then and later thought they saw a clear inference in the Commissar's words. During the intervention, American troops attempted to restrain the anti-Soviet activities of the Japanese. In 1933, Japan was again on the move, menacing both Russia and the interests of the United States. The understanding on Siberian claims was interpreted as an oblique but obvious reference to the mutual alarm and perhaps future cooperation of the two governments in connection with the Far East.

At least two scholars have found significance in the fact that the American officials permitted Litvinov to use the term Union of Soviet Socialist Republics, when there was in fact no USSR at the time of the intervention, and that he was also al-

146

lowed to write "inviolability," whereas the United States had in 1918-1920 insisted only on preserving the integrity of the Russian state. They suggested that, in return for the waiver, Litvinov was allowed to use these studied anachronisms in order to suggest to Japan the continuing interest of the United States in the preservation of Russian sovereignty over all her Far Eastern territories.[52]

These assumptions do not seem to have been justified, at least not as far as the United States was concerned. When Litvinov, as expected, presented the Russian counterclaims at the negotiations, Robert Kelley collected all the documents available in order to convince the envoy that the American forces in Siberia had made a calculated effort to protect both Russian territory and Russian property during the occupation. By virtue of that evidence, the United States was able to persuade Litvinov to agree to the waiver of those claims. He would not do the same for the Archangel and Murmansk claims. There is no evidence to suggest that Washington had the Far Eastern situation in mind in urging the Soviet Government to withdraw its demands for restitution for American actions in Siberia in 1918-1920.[53] It is entirely possible, however, that Litvinov submitted to the American pressure more readily because of its contemporary connotations and the impression his letter would convey.

The final document was a joint communiqué by Roosevelt and Litvinov, stating that there had been an "exchange of views" on debts and claims and that Litvinov would remain

[52] Malbone W. Graham, "Russian-American Relations, 1917-1933; An Interpretation," *American Political Science Review*, xxviii (1934), 408-409; Pauline Tompkins, *American-Russian Relations in the Far East* (New York, 1949), 261-262.

[53] Kelley Interview. The United States Government made a particular effort to relieve Japanese anxiety over recognition. Ambassador Debuchi was handed a copy of the Roosevelt-Litvinov correspondence by the State Department directly after the letters were signed, with the assurance that the reestablishment of relations had "nothing whatever to do with the Far East." *Foreign Relations, 1933*, iii, 463.

in Washington for several days to continue the discussions. The "gentleman's agreement" was not released then nor, in fact, until sixteen years after the event, despite the disagreement that was later to develop over its interpretation.

With the exception of a debt settlement, Roosevelt had managed to achieve almost everything that he had considered necessary to a satisfactory recognition agreement. The propaganda and subversive activity pledges were far more extensive than any before conceded by the Soviet Union, and the religious and legal guarantees were as extensive as could be expected in lieu of a consular convention. The American public had no grounds for objection to the text of the notes which were to protect America against possible Communist contamination, although many citizens might question the good faith in which they were signed by the Soviet envoy. The method adopted, that of recognition simultaneous with settlement of the questions outstanding between the two governments, served to save face on both sides.

The fact that Litvinov agreed to sign such sweeping pledges emphasized the importance Moscow attached to recognition by the United States. And there is considerable evidence to indicate that the Soviet Government regarded these commitments as unusually broad concessions. It is possible also that they expected violations to occur and did not wish the Russian public to be aware of the exact wording of the texts. In any case, so far as is known, none of the letters containing the mutual undertakings by the Soviet and United States Governments was ever published within Russia. The extensive coverage of the recognition in Soviet newspapers did not include the commitments. Vague references were made to the letters, but, as described, they took on a thoroughly unofficial character. They did not appear in the official treaty collection nor in *Sovetsko-amerikanskie otnosheniia*, which was printed soon after the recognition and presumably included all documents of any importance in the relations between the two countries since 1917.[54]

As far as the Soviet reader knew, the exchange had consisted only of the first two letters, those in which the President had granted recognition, and Litvinov had accepted and reciprocated it. Russians undoubtedly gained the impression that the usual assurances on noninterference had been given in an informal manner, but they were given no hint as to the extensive coverage of the pledges. These facts, and the pre-recognition report that the Kremlin was concerned about public reaction to the expected American demands, suggest that the Soviet Government wanted a rapprochement with the United States badly enough to make commitments which it preferred not to publicize in its own territory.

The one reference in the Soviet press to the mutual obligations signed by Roosevelt and Litvinov was in a reprint of sections of the Commissar's address to the National Press Club in Washington on the night of November 17. The phrasing of Litvinov's remarks on that occasion indicated that he was thinking as much of his Russian audience as of his American listeners.

After noting that in response to the President's interest in the legal position and religious rights of Americans in Russia, he had written him a letter "supplying this information," the Commissar continued: "In addition—there was the inevitable question of propaganda. In another letter I assured the President that the relations of the Soviet Government with the governments of other countries were based on the principle of mutual non-interference in internal affairs. I stated the mutual obligations undertaken by the Soviet Government and other governments with which normal relations were established. These obligations were extended to the United States."[55]

[54] *Sbornik deistvuiushchikh dogovorov, soglashenii i konventsii, zakliuchennykh s inostrannymi gosudarstvami* (Moscow, Narkomindel, 1935), viii; and *Sovetsko-amerikanskie otnosheniia* (Moscow, Narkomindel, 1934), give only the first two letters in the exchange.

[55] *Izvestia*, November 20, 1933.

This extremely innocent description in no way conveyed a correct conception of the binding nature of the undertakings. Litvinov's clever wording may not have been noticed by his immediate audience, for they had seen the documents and knew to what he was referring, but the Soviet reader received a most deceiving impression.

Before leaving the United States, Litvinov made two remarks which served notice of Moscow's interpretation of the propaganda pledge. After his address at the Press Club, he was asked what effect the much discussed Article Four would have upon the American Communist party. His answer was illuminating: "The Communist Party of America is not concerned with the Communist Party of Russia and the Communist Party of Russia is not concerned with the Communist Party of America."[56] Three days later he expressed the same idea more bluntly when he admonished newsmen that: "The Third International is not mentioned in the document. You must not read into it more than was mentioned."[57] But these portents were largely overlooked in the general atmosphere of satisfaction over a well-negotiated treaty.

At the Presidential press conference on the afternoon of November 17, when the recognition correspondence was released, Roosevelt also made known the appointment of William C. Bullitt as the first ambassador from the United States to the Soviet Union. The appointment seemed a logical choice,

[56] *New York Times*, November 18, 1933.

[57] *Daily Worker*, November 21, 1933. The ex-American Communist Benjamin Gitlow relates that the American Communist party was genuinely concerned about the effect of the subversive activities pledges upon the future of their organization. According to Gitlow, the OGPU apparatus in the United States arranged a meeting between Litvinov and the Party Secretariat in New York, at which the Commissar assured the American members that the commitments in no way affected the activities of their party or its relations with the International. "After all, comrades," Litvinov was quoted as saying, "you should by this time know how to handle the fiction of the tie-up between the Comintern and the Soviet Government. . . . the letter is a scrap of paper." Benjamin Gitlow, *The Whole of Their Lives* (New York, 1948), 264-265. It seems very surprising that Litvinov would risk such a meeting.

for no other American had done more to facilitate the final agreement. The obvious enthusiasm of Bullitt for a rapprochement was well-known to the Russians. But future events were to suggest that perhaps a man less emotionally involved with the success of the new relationship would have fared better at the Moscow post.

On November 19, Litvinov informed Washington that his government had nominated Alexander A. Troyanovsky to be the Soviet envoy to the United States. Pending Mr. Troyanovsky's arrival, Boris Skvirsky would serve as Chargé d'affaires, and subsequently as Counsellor of Embassy. The previous activities of the Soviet Ambassador singularly qualified him for his new duties in the United States. From 1923 to 1927, he had been President of the State Trading Corporation, and from 1927 to January 1933, he had served as Russian Ambassador to Japan, returning to Moscow to take the post of Vice President of the State Planning Commission. Troyanovsky's recent tour in Tokyo was considered significant by many commentators, including those who were watching events from Japan.[58]

Litvinov remained in Washington until the morning of November 23, continuing his conversations with the State and Treasury officials on the settlement of the debt problem. But at the time of his departure no conclusions had yet been reached. The press release from the State Department blamed the failure on the "intricacy of the questions to be explored," but expressed confidence in an early agreement. Negotiations would be "actively continued" by both governments through their representatives in the two capitals.[59] Already the shades of the French and British experiences were faintly observable in the background of Russian-American relations.

Before his sailing, Litvinov spoke at some length on the results which might be expected from the reestablishment of

[58] Joseph C. Grew, *Ten Years in Japan* (New York, 1944), 107.
[59] *Establishment of Diplomatic Relations with the Union of Soviet Socialist Republics* (Washington, United States Government Printing Office, 1933), 19.

relations between the United States and the Soviet Union. In an address to the American-Russian Chamber of Commerce and the American-Russian Institute in New York on the evening of November 24, the Commissar emphasized first and foremost the stabilizing effect of recognition upon world unrest. Without naming either Germany or Japan, he left no doubt as to their leadership in preparations for war and aggression.

Although Litvinov mentioned other areas of cooperation which had been opened by the resumption of relations, it was significant that even before an organization whose interest lay primarily in the commercial and industrial field he gave first place to the potentialities of Russian-American cooperation in the diplomatic arena. After commenting on the newly cleared roads to economic and cultural collaboration, he added: "What is still more important, can any question arise as to whether both the United States and the Soviet Union will benefit from the joining of their efforts in the cause so important to both of them—the great work of preserving peace? Who can doubt that the combined voices of these two giants will make themselves heard and that their joint efforts will weigh the scales in favor of peace?"[60]

When Litvinov left New York on the following day aboard the *Conte di Savoia*, he had every reason to feel that he had completed a successful mission. True, there had been concessions, at least on paper, but they had no doubt been worth the gaining of what he later termed "not merely one more recognition . . . by a great Power, but the fall of the last position, the last fortress in that attack on [the USSR] . . . by the capitalist world, which after the October Revolution took the form of nonrecognition and boycott."[61]

[60] *Soviet Union Review*, XI (1933), 260-262.
[61] From the text of Litvinov's report on foreign affairs to the Central Executive Committee of the USSR. Maxim Litvinov, *Vneshniaia politika SSSR* (Moscow, 1935), 61-62.

CHAPTER 7

FIRST REACTIONS

THE new era in Soviet-American relations was ushered in with high hopes on both sides for future benefits. The problems which had kept the two nations separated for sixteen years appeared to have been settled to the mutual satisfaction of both parties. For Russia recognition was a triumph of patience, a goal long sought and finally realized. It came at a moment when the rewards seemed more attractive than at any time in the long period of waiting, except for the first months of the regime. For the United States, recognition brought an end to an outdated and hampering policy. It represented an American contribution toward the stabilization of a restless world, and it opened the road to economic advantages which might aid the struggle against depression. Although the United States Government realized the danger of pitfalls in the new relationship, the prevailing mood in Washington was one of optimism and of willingness to make the tie mutually profitable. But Russian reactions, though unanimously favorable, had an undertone of bumptiousness which was foreboding.[1]

Moscow hailed recognition as an unequivocal acknowledgment by the United States that Russia could no longer be

[1] According to Louis Fischer, Stalin believed that as a matter of prestige the Soviet Union should not display too openly its pleasure over recognition, and he consequently instructed the press and public spokesmen to show restraint in their treatment of the event. Louis Fischer, *Men and Politics, An Autobiography* (New York, 1941), 299. If Mr. Fischer's information was correct, and the public reactions were modified, the enthusiasm shown becomes even more striking. Milly Bennett, reporting from Moscow in the *Nation*, wrote that speakers were sent to factories and schools to explain recognition to the people. *Nation*, January 17, 1934, 72.

ignored in the affairs of the world community. The press explained that the Soviet Union was not only a great European power, but a great Asiatic power as well. The United States had a vital interest in the Pacific. Both nations were occupied with the task of preserving peace in that area. Consequently, Washington had come to realize that the absence of relations prevented the possibility of cooperation toward the mutual objective—a conclusion heartily supported by the government and people of Russia. A rapprochement with the United States would be one of the most effective methods of guaranteeing peace and, therefore, must be welcomed as a great victory for Soviet foreign policy.[2]

Referring with greater directness to the diplomatic effect of recognition, the Red Army organ *Krasnaia Zvezda* editorialized: "At a time when the danger of military aggression has become an actuality and when the sharpest antagonisms in the imperialist camp have taken on the most menacing dimensions, the establishment of normal relations between the USA and the USSR will bring about a fundamental change in the correlation of forces in the international arena, a change which the adventurist groups who are attempting to break the peace cannot disregard."[3]

Sotsialisticheskoe Zemledelie likewise directed attention to the fact that Roosevelt had acted when the world was moving into a period of crisis and uncertainty. In the Far East, Soviet-Japanese relations had become increasingly strained, while Japan and America continued their slow-motion struggle for the Pacific with mounting intensity. In Europe, Germany had announced its withdrawal from the League, and the Disarmament Conference had reached a stalemate.[4] The reader was left to draw his own conclusions, but the implications were clear.

The labor newspaper *Trud* flatly stated that Japanese aggres-

[2] *Izvestia*, November 20, 1933.
[3] *Krasnaia Zvezda*, November 20, 1933.
[4] *Sotsialisticheskoe Zemledelie*, November 20, 1933.

sion in the Far East had produced the steadily growing demand for recognition in the United States during the past two years. The final acquiescence of Washington had resulted from the pressure of American public opinion and the cognizance in official circles of the need for normal relations with the Soviet Union.[5] In similar terms, *Pravda* emphasized the diplomatic connotations of recognition. The menace to peace of "certain imperialist powers" and the "ominous portents in the East and West" gave the resumption of Soviet-American relations "a special significance." "The 16th of November," the newspaper phophesied, "will become an important date in the history of the international relations of our epoch."

But the party press was particularly anxious to underline the new prestige which the event had given to Russian foreign policy. The United States, like all the other great powers, had been "forced" to renew relations with Moscow. The growth of Soviet importance in world affairs could be traced by studying the history of Soviet relations with the capitalist nations from the first temporary trade agreements to eventual full recognition and the leadership of Russia in the fight for peace. Compelled by the indisputable economic, political, and military strength of the Soviet Union, the nations of the world had one by one come to terms. "The very fact that the present American Administration has renounced the traditional policy of 'non-recognition,'" *Pravda* proclaimed, "is in itself most significant evidence of the strength and importance of the Soviet Union."[6]

Tying together the matter of prestige and the situation in the Far East, M. Tanin, writing in *Za Industrializatsiiu*, observed that November 16 was a far cry from the Washington Conference of 1921. Then, Russia had been denied the right to attend a pivotal meeting on Far Eastern affairs, whereas sixteen years later the United States had turned to the Soviet Union for aid in maintaining the peaceful *status quo* in the same area. The change in attitude, wrote Tanin, clearly dem-

[5] *Trud*, November 20, 1933.   [6] *Pravda*, November 19, 1933.

onstrated the effect of the new position of Moscow in the international arena on the "ruling classes" of America.[7]

Of perhaps greater interest was an article written by Karl Radek for an American journal early in 1934. Before its publication in the United States, it appeared in the Soviet press. Radek declared that the Soviet Union "does not close the door to the possibility of a deal, or agreement, with imperialistic Powers which are waging a struggle against other imperialistic Powers, if the latter attack the Soviet Union." Written for publication in the United States with the recent recognition fresh in the minds of both author and readers, the article strongly suggested the course of Kremlin thought. It was to the credit of Radek that he continued his discussion with a frank disclosure of Soviet intentions in the event of collaboration with a capitalist nation. "[I]n entering into such agreements," he cautioned, "the Soviet Union would not accept any responsibility for the specific purposes pursued by the imperialistic powers. . . . But against attacking imperialism an agreement is permissible with any opponent in order to defeat an enemy invading Soviet territory."[8] Seldom in that period did Moscow indulge in such candid expositions of its policy. And it was unfortunate, in the light of subsequent events, that foreign statesmen allowed those rare revelations to be obscured by the smoke screen of intervening deception which constantly emanated from the same source.

The chorus of Soviet praise for the new relationship with the United States was unhesitatingly joined by the leaders of the party and government. In fact, on November 7, just as the Washington conversations were beginning, V. M. Molotov told the Moscow Soviet that the significance of the negotiations far exceeded the limits of normal relations between two states. And it may have been noteworthy that he turned next to an

[7] *Za Industrializatsiiu*, November 20, 1933.
[8] Karl Radek, "The Basis of Soviet Foreign Policy," *Foreign Affairs*, XII (1934), 204-205; see also *Izvestia*, December 16, 1933.

unusually bellicose discussion of Soviet-Japanese relations.[9] Later, speaking before the Central Executive Committee of the USSR in December, Molotov characterized recognition as "the greatest achievement of Soviet foreign policy" in the past year. The restoration of diplomatic ties, he noted, had created a favorable basis for the growth of economic intercourse, but, most important, it constituted a "great positive factor in the stabilization of international relations and the furtherance of universal peace." Molotov assured his listeners that the accompanying agreements, which he did not enumerate, were completely in line with the fundamental precepts of Soviet policy. Further along in his address, Molotov alluded with some humor to the frantic reactions of Tokyo to the new balance of power in the Far East. Although he intimated that Japanese fears of an entente between Russia, China, and the United States were groundless, his denial was couched in terms that suggested there was some truth in the assertion.[10]

It is worth noting that here again the absence of Russian concessions had been emphasized. Over a year later, Molotov was still directing attention to the conventionality of the Soviet commitments. In a review of Soviet foreign policy before the Seventh Congress of Soviets in February 1935, he reiterated that Russia "did not find it necessary in establishing these relations [with the United States] to modify . . . [its] position or to make any kind of sacrifice and this also cannot be regarded otherwise than as a very favorable fact."[11] If the government considered the agreements so innocuous, why then were they withheld from the Russian public?

Litvinov did not neglect to give similar assurances when he reported to the Central Executive Committee of the USSR on December 29, 1933. But the outstanding feature of his address was the note of triumph in his comments on recognition. Placing that event first in importance among the successes of the

---

[9] *ibid.*, November 10, 1933.   [10] *ibid.*, December 29, 1933.
[11] V. M. Molotov, *Stat'i i rechi, 1935-1936* (Moscow, 1937), 16-17.

157

year in Soviet diplomacy, Litvinov then briefly traced the history of Soviet-American relations since 1917. The final collapse of Washington's resistance to contact with Russia, he stressed, marked the abandonment of an ideological, not a political stand; thus it was a victory of the first magnitude for the Soviet state. And the exceptional satisfaction and pleasure which the decision had given the Russian government, he opined, was not unrelated to the very long period during which the "defenders" of the American "fortress" had held out against Soviet assaults. Nevertheless, Litvinov declared, once the United States had decided to abandon its position, and had entered into conversations with Moscow, it became obvious that "at the national or governmental level contradictions between her and our Union are absent, and troublesome questions were easily resolved."[12] That phrase was of particular interest because, without describing the contents of the letters exchanged between himself and Roosevelt, Litvinov consciously or unconsciously served notice that Russia would limit the application of the agreement to the governmental structure. Whatever the wording might be, and the subversive activities pledge specifically covered private individuals and organizations, the Soviet Union intended to preserve the fiction of nonconnection between the Moscow government and the Communist International as it had always done in the past.

Stalin also officially pronounced the reestablishment of relations with Washington a major success of Soviet diplomacy. "There can be no doubt," he told the Seventeenth Party Congress, "that this act has very serious significance for the whole system of international relations." Furthermore, he asserted, it would stand as a "landmark between the old, when the United States was regarded in various countries as the bulwark for all sorts of anti-Soviet tendencies, and the new, when this bulwark was voluntarily removed, to the mutual advantage of

[12] Maxim Litvinov, *Vneshniaia politika SSSR* (Moscow, 1935), 61-62.

both countries."[13] A month earlier, on Christmas Day, 1933, Stalin had granted an interview to Walter Duranty to whom he also had expressed his pleasure at the reestablishment of relations. The advantages to both sides were manifold, he told the correspondent: "politically . . . it increases the chances of preserving peace: economically . . . it removes complicating factors . . . finally it opens the road to mutual cooperation." In the course of his remarks, he paid tribute to Roosevelt as a "resolute and courageous politician," a "realist" who saw things as they were.

Duranty questioned Stalin on the possibilities for increased Soviet-American trade as the result of recognition. In reply, the Russian leader referred to the Litvinov speech at the London Conference. Moscow was prepared to order and to pay for a great quantity of goods. But, he added, in order to do so, the Soviet Union had to have favorable credit conditions and, "more important," a market for its exports. "We cannot import without exports," he said, "because we do not want to place orders unless we are confident we can pay on time." If necessary, he observed, Russia could herself produce the equipment needed.[14] In other words, Stalin was clearly implying that recognition alone was not sufficient to stimulate Russian-American trade. And, although he looked to the growth of commercial intercourse between the two countries as a desirable goal, he did not appear particularly concerned about that aspect of the new relationship.

In fact, even economic circles in Russia gave first attention to the international and diplomatic advantages accruing to Russia and the United States from recognition. *Ekonomicheskaia Zhizn* mentioned the new opportunities for economic collaboration at the end of a long discussion emphasizing the blow struck against aggressive forces in the world.[15] Substantially the same treatment was accorded the event by *Za*

[13] *Izvestia*, January 28, 1934.   [14] *ibid.*, January 4, 1934.
[15] *Ekonomicheskaia Zhizn*, November 20, 1933.

Industrializatsiiu, which, while acknowledging the commercial possibilities, nevertheless cautioned that recognition did not automatically create trade.[16] Both newspapers did, however, devote considerable space elsewhere in their pages to the economic potentialities in the resumption of relations. Yet their coverage of the event made it clear that despite their own and their readers' specialized interest in the economic side of recognition, the most important over-all result was in the area of foreign policy.

An interesting feature of what might be called the recognition edition of *Za Industrializatsiiu* was a series of statements by directors of Soviet industrial enterprises. All of them expressed their hopes for profitable intercourse with American manufacturers, but the desired imports were not goods and materials but techniques and expert assistance. Little mention was made of the need for trade, and much was made of the advantages Soviet enterprises could derive from access to advanced American methods and skills. In the two instances where increased purchasing in the United States was prophesied, the writers were careful to specify that its volume would depend on the reciprocity of American import from Russia.[17] Similarly, N. Borev, reviewing the past and discussing the future of Soviet-American trade in *Ekonomicheskaia Zhizn*, advised that mutual exchange and favorable credit facilities must be present before trade could reach any substantial volume.[18] Yet every editorial comment in the Russian press carefully noted the importance of the commercial motivation in altering attitudes toward Russia in the United States. The triumphal manner in which they interpreted recognition as a tribute to Soviet economic strength was offset by the relatively mild interest they displayed in the trade boom that the American public expected.

Personalities also received their due from the Russian com-

---

[16] *Za Industrializatsiiu*, November 20, 1933.   [17] *ibid.*
[18] *Ekonomicheskaia Zhizn*, November 29, 1933.

mentators. Karl Radek sang the praises of "Our Commissar of Foreign Affairs," who had once again scored a victory for Soviet diplomacy. Litvinov, Radek wrote, was schooled in the principles of Lenin, but well acquainted with the capitalist world: a man of firmness who had captured the admiration of foreign statesmen, and the living proof "that in the realm of diplomacy we have already fulfilled the instructions of Comrade Stalin 'to overtake and surpass'" the western nations[19]— a rather ominous remark when applied to the Commissar's recent activities in Washington.

Nor were the American toilers in the vineyard of Russian-American reconciliation overlooked. Elsewhere, Radek paid his tribute to Bullitt and Colonel Raymond Robins for their long struggle in the cause of recognition and gave credit to Borah, Louis Fischer, and Duranty for their support of the Russian fight for a resumption of relations with the United States.[20] *Za Industrializatsiiu* devoted half a page to photographs and biographical sketches of Moscow's advocates in America, including besides the individuals already mentioned: Alfred Smith; the La Follettes, father and sons; Speaker of the House Henry Rainey; Colonel Hugh Cooper; Theodore Dreiser; John Dos Passos; and Sherwood Anderson.[21]

The news organ of world communism also saw manifold advantages accruing to the Bolshevik homeland from the extension of recognition by the United States. Hailing the event as a "victory of the World Revolution," the editors of *International Press Correspondence* gave primary importance to the effect within Soviet Russia, where it would "increase the courage and confidence of the workers and peasants and deliver the deathblow to the inner counterrevolution [an interesting admission]." Abroad, the results would be most evident in the Far East, where the rebellious Asiatic masses would take new hope from the enhanced prestige and strength of Moscow, and

[19] *Izvestia*, November 20, 1933.   [20] *Pravda*, November 19, 1933.
[21] *Za Industrializatsiiu*, November 20, 1933.

where Japan would hesitate in her threatening advance. There was always the chance, the magazine warned, that Japan and other plotters of intervention might move swiftly before Russia was able to profit from her recent success. Even if that occurred, the psychological encouragement given to all friends of Russia would be a powerful weapon against her attackers. In any case, the editors concluded, in an unrestrained manifestation of loyalty, the real significance of "the victory of the Soviet Union in securing American recognition [is that the] victor is the heart and brain of the world revolution."[22]

Writing in the same news organ a month later, R. Palme-Dutt saw the Russo-American reconciliation as the chief deterrent to an alleged plan of Great Britain to cooperate with Germany, Japan, and possibly France in a diplomatic and eventually military campaign against the Soviet Union and the United States.[23] Another contributor refuted socialist accusations that recognition and cooperation between Moscow and Washington would be the basis of an alliance, that is an alliance in the capitalist sense of the word. Russia might temporarily collaborate with an imperialist nation for reasons of defense, but she could never share the goals required for a true alliance with any non-Communist nation.[24]

In mid-December, the Soviets had a second opportunity to play up the reestablishment of relations with the United States, when William Bullitt arrived in Moscow to present his credentials and make a survey of the accommodations available for the new Embassy. The arrival of the Ambassador was heralded by a long biographical sketch of his service in the cause of a Russian-American rapprochement.[25] On December 13, Bullitt presented his credentials to Kalinin, emphasizing in his

[22] *International Press Correspondence*, November 24, 1933, 1137-1138.
[23] *ibid.*, December 8, 1933, 1213-1214.
[24] *ibid.*, December 1, 1933, 1116. For some reason neither *Bol'shevik* nor *Kommunisticheskii Internatsional* had any specific comment on recognition.
[25] *Izvestia*, December 12, 1933, reprinted from the *New York Times*, November 26, 1933.

accompanying remarks that the "close collaboration of our governments in the task of preserving peace will draw our peoples together." The United States and its Ambassador, he averred, wished to establish not only normal "but genuinely friendly relations" between the two countries. The reply of Kalinin echoed Bullitt's hopes for a mutually profitable association, and referred particularly to Bullitt's personal efforts toward the goal of recognition.[26]

Although the exchange of amenities involved in offering and accepting the diplomatic credentials followed the stereotyped phrases common on such occasions, there was a special atmosphere of cordiality in the proceedings. And the newspapers attached importance to the words of the American Ambassador. It was pointed out that, as Bullitt had stated, the significance of the new relationship lay in the fact that both countries desired a much closer tie than mere normal diplomatic intercourse offered. The basis for the cooperation of Russia and the United States, a mutual interest in the avoidance of a new war, was applauded as the highest aim upon which to found a profitable friendship.[27]

Meanwhile, Bullitt was receiving exceptional manifestations of friendship from the Russian leaders. President Kalinin, in an informal conversation following the credentials reception, bestowed liberal praise upon the Ambassador and upon Franklin Roosevelt. Lenin, he said, had spoken many times of Bullitt's sincere interest in the Soviet Union, and for that reason he felt that he was greeting an old friend. As to President Roosevelt, Kalinin assured the Ambassador that Russia saw a vast difference between the American executive and other

---

[26] *Izvestia*, December 14 1933; *Foreign Relations, 1933*, ii, 827-828. Ambassador Troyanovsky presented his credentials to President Roosevelt on January 8, 1934. On this occasion also, the opportunities for cooperation in the cause of peace were emphasized in the remarks of both the President and Troyanovsky. Department of State, *Press Releases*, x (January-June, 1934), 9-11; and a draft, with corrections, of the President's statement, Roosevelt Papers.

[27] *Izvestia*, December 14, 1933.

capitalist statesmen. The people of Russia knew that Roosevelt was truly interested in the well-being of "laboring men and the farmers and that he was not engaged in protecting the vested interests of property."[28] Unfortunately, Kalinin did not disclose the channels through which the Soviet public had been apprised of that information. Certainly they did not receive it via the press or other Russian periodicals, which had consistently castigated the methods of Roosevelt as semi-fascist and pictured in lurid terms the ruthless disregard of the American governing classes for workers and agriculturists in the United States.

Joseph Stalin also outdid himself in according Bullitt a warm personal welcome. He made the unprecedented gesture of receiving the Ambassador formally, and further evidenced his good will with even more unusual actions. At a dinner given by Voroshilov for Bullitt, attended, as Litvinov expressed it, by all the "inside directorate," Stalin was among the guests and offered a toast: "To President Roosevelt, who in spite of the mute growls of the Fishes, dared to recognize the Soviet Union." Again Bullitt was informed, this time by Stalin, that Roosevelt was "one of the most popular men in the Soviet Union." And, as if to give the occasion a final grand touch, the Russian leader, before his departure from the banquet, drew the American envoy aside and said: "Is there anything at all in the Soviet Union that you want?" When Bullitt replied that he was interested in the bluff property overlooking the Moscow River as a location for the United States Embassy, Stalin unhesitatingly responded: "It is yours."[29]

To judge by the enthusiastic reports of his short visit to the USSR in December, Bullitt was highly flattered by the attentions he received. In fact, he was somewhat concerned over the reaction of other diplomats in Moscow to his exceptional reception. After the Voroshilov banquet, he suggested to Litvinov that the press be told only that Stalin "dropped in," a

[28] *Foreign Relations, 1933*, II, 834.   [29] *ibid.*, 837-838.

circumlocution which he felt would avoid drawing the jealousy of his foreign colleagues. "It is valuable to have the inside track," he wrote to the Secretary of State, "but it seems to me not desirable to emphasize the fact to the world."[30] Bullitt would have been wiser to have waited until the Russian authorities were asked to give something more tangible than words to the cause of Soviet-American friendship before he accepted their protestations of assistance so uncritically. Although he was later to revaluate drastically his opinion of the Soviet Union, there seems little question that he went to his new post full of high hopes for the future of Russo-American relations and with a strongly developed sympathy for the men and the objectives of the new Russia.[31]

Russia was not alone in emphasizing the international political aspect of recognition. Foreign observers for the most part interpreted the rapprochement as a counterweight to German militarism in Europe and especially to Japanese aggression in the Far East. When economic motivations were acknowledged, they were relegated to a distinctly secondary position. The *Times* of London declared that the situation in the Far East "would alone have justified him [Roosevelt] in restoring diplomatic connexion between Moscow and Washington." But the same newspaper on the strength of bitter British experiences warned the United States to beware of the

[30] *ibid.*

[31] Louis Fischer quotes a remark by Bullitt soon after his arrival in Moscow which throws some light on the Ambassador's outlook at that time. "After all," said Bullitt, "the President, Jack Reed [prominent American Communist in the early postwar period; author of *Ten Days that Shook the World*] and I are of the same American strain." Fischer, *Men and Politics*, 299. Litvinov was apparently skeptical from the beginning of the fitness of Bullitt for the Moscow post. The Soviet Government would have preferred a businessman who had less personal interest in the regime and would have approached problems on a strictly practical basis. Interview with Mr. Louis Fischer, New York, June 14, 1949. It should be stressed, however, that the attitude of Mr. Bullitt toward Soviet Russia was shared by many American liberals in the early 1930's before the worst features of the Bolshevik government became manifest.

Russian promises on propaganda and subversive activities.[32] The *Manchester Guardian Weekly* granted that America might gain some measure of support in the Far East from closer ties with the Soviets and anticipated she would also benefit commercially, but in both areas, the editors predicted, present expectations would not be realized. No doubt, Russia would profit more directly from the new balance of power in the Far East than would the United States.[33]

In France, recognition was attributed almost entirely to considerations of foreign policy. Had it not been for the increasing complications in the Far East, the danger of a Russo-Japanese war, and the continuing problem of Manchuria, suggested *Le Temps*, Washington would have hesitated a great deal longer before offering the hand of friendship to the Soviet Union.[34] Another newspaper theorized that "the most important and most secret feature of the conversations dealt with the international situation and particularly with the Far East."[35] A journal published in Paris by and for Russian émigrés speculated that the rapprochement foreshadowed a military alliance in the Far East.[36] Even two years later, when there had been time to observe the results of the reestablishment of relations, Paul Miliukov, writing from his French exile, interpreted the event as a clever and to some extent successful effort on the part of both Russia and the United States to halt Japanese aggression and forestall collaboration between Tokyo and Berlin.[37]

The German press readily admitted the connection between recognition and the Far East, but chose to ignore the possible implications for the Reich. In the opinion of the *Vossische Zeitung*, there could be no question but that the move was

[32] London *Times*, November 19, 1933.
[33] *Manchester Guardian Weekly*, November 24, 1933.
[34] *Le Temps*, November 19, 1933.
[35] *Petit Journal*, as quoted in the *New York Times*, November 18, 1933.
[36] *Sotsialisticheskii Vestnik*, No. 22 (307), November 10, 1933, 1-2.
[37] P. Milioukov, *La politique extérieure des soviets* (Paris, 1936), 453-454.

"strongly anti-Japanese" in character.[38] And the Berlin *Tageblatt* declared that the world was well aware, despite misleading publicity, that problems of the Pacific area had been thoroughly discussed in the Washington meeting.[39] Similarly, the editor of the Nazi organ, *Angriff*, predicted that the resumption of relations between Soviet Russia and the United States insured the prolongation of peace in the Far East. Japan was faced with new conditions, and henceforth every forceful act would draw Moscow and Washington closer together.[40]

As the focal point of international speculation on the ramifications of the Russian-American reconciliation, Japan reacted uneasily. Although the Foreign Office officially gave no credence to predictions that American policy toward Japan would undergo a change, it did acknowledge that Russia might take a firmer stand in the Far East following her diplomatic accomplishment.[41] The press assurances that the recognition was of no importance to Japanese-American relations were so unequivocal as to make their sincerity doubtful. *Nichi Nichi* declared that: "If there is any political effect, it will be on the European situation." But the same newspaper displayed veiled apprehension when it noted that the Washington agreement indicated Soviet willingness to make almost any concessions to gain the diplomatic friendship of the United States.[42] Likewise, *Asahi* expressed first its lack of concern over the event, finding "little foundation" for Japanese fears of increased tension in the Far East.[43] Then, some weeks later, the editors pointed to the recognition as evidence of the incompetence of the government in properly explaining Japan's role in the Pacific. They warned that the diplomats would have only themselves to

[38] As quoted in the *Living Age*, CCCXLV (1933), 369.
[39] As quoted in the *New York Times*, November 18, 1933.
[40] As quoted in Milioukov, *op. cit.*, 453-454.
[41] *Foreign Relations, 1933*, III, 475-476. Ambassador Grew described Japan's state of mind by quoting from the Japan *Advertiser*. The nation was "calm but apprehensive," the editors had observed. *Ibid.*
[42] As quoted in *Trans-Pacific*, November 30, 1933.
[43] As quoted in *ibid.*

blame if continued world misunderstanding of the activities of Japan led to a further aggravation of the Far Eastern situation.[44]

Other Japanese commentators were more openly pessimistic about the new development. They pointed out that the recent Russian bellicosity, evidenced in the publication of the Chinese Eastern Railway documents and in the Molotov speech of November 7, as well as in the general stiffening of the attitude of Moscow vis-a-vis Manchuria, tended to support the view that recognition would have a noticeable effect upon the Far East.[45] Apparently, some sections of the military took an even darker view of recognition. In a highly bombastic article, Vice-Admiral Nobumasa Suetsugu, Commander-in-Chief of the Japanese Combined Fleet, gave the event a sinister connotation, linking it with certain other suspicious actions of the United States. Flights by American aviators across the Pacific, he hinted, were in reality spying expeditions. Topographical and geodetic surveys of the Aleutians and the reenforcement of American forces in China suggested that the recent rapprochement with Russia was part of a plan to surround Japan with hostile military activity. But Suetsugu assured the Japanese that the Imperial forces were ready for any contingency. Whether the article actually reflected the concern of the military or not, it occasioned considerable comment in the Japanese press.[46]

Whereas the European and Japanese press reflected a combination of government-inspired and privately-held opinion, the Russian reactions had of course all been carefully dictated from the Kremlin. Thus Soviet comment on recognition was

---

[44] As quoted in the *Japan Times and Mail*, November 28, 1933.

[45] See, for example, an article by Dr. S. Washio in *Trans-Pacific*, November 30, 1933.

[46] *Gendai*, as reprinted in *ibid.*, January 25, 1934. Both the editors of *Trans-Pacific* and Ambassador Grew in his diary, noted the wide publicity the article had received. *Ibid.*; and Joseph C. Grew, *Ten Years in Japan* (New York, 1944), 111-112.

not an indication of public opinion, but rather a key to the views of the Russian government or at least to the pattern in which the Soviet leaders wished to mold public opinion. On the other hand, American reactions found in the newspaper and periodical press and in the statements of individuals did, to an appreciable degree, represent the attitude of the people toward the action of their government. Unlike Moscow, Washington is highly sensitive to the free expression of its citizens' views and must conduct its foreign policy within the bounds which are sanctioned by those it governs. In the United States, the mirror of public opinion reflects the nation and is consulted by the government.

The majority of the American public appeared either to favor the recognition of Russia or to accept it without apprehension. When faced with an accomplished fact, even those organizations and individuals who had opposed a reconciliation lapsed into temporary silence or were content to caution against future hazards. The American Legion had received the news as "good soldiers," said National Commander Hays, but it would continue the fight against atheism and communism.[47] Father Walsh counseled his followers to withhold judgment until there was evidence to show whether Moscow intended to live up to the agreements. If Russia repudiated the Third International, a step which she was obliged to take under the terms of her pledge, then, he declared, her good faith would be manifested.[48] Matthew Woll, Vice-President of the American Federation of Labor, admitting that he was not optimistic as to the future of the new friendship, announced that as far as he could see the reasons against recognition were still as valid

---

[47] *New York Times*, November 18, 1933.

[48] Radio address by Father Walsh, December 9, 1933, as quoted in the *Congressional Record*, 73rd Congress, 2nd Sess., 309. Of course Russia was not obligated to repudiate the Third International under the provisions of the agreement, but only the activities of its American section both in the Soviet Union and in the United States.

as they had been for the past sixteen years.[49] And Hamilton Fish refused to adjust himself to the new situation. The United States, he stated, had been "betrayed and sold for thirty pieces of silver and commercial propaganda."[50]

Several newspapers and journals were outspokenly opposed to the President's decision to acknowledge Soviet existence. The *Boston Evening Transcript*, concluding that it was too late to avert the unfortunate misstep, could only hope that the results would not be too disastrous.[51] Likewise, the *Los Angeles Times* entertained grave misgivings as to any profit accruing to the United States from closer relations with Russia.[52] Nor did the *National Republic* disappoint its readers. In two articles entitled "Reds Win as U. S. Holds Bag" and "Profits Stained with Blood," the editorial staff denounced the Washington agreement in scathing sentences.[53] In the two Roman Catholic organs consulted a more reasoned atmosphere prevailed. While neither magazine displayed much confidence in the Russian promises, they did not indulge in diatribe or accusation.[54]

But the voices of foreboding were exceptions. Although some members of Congress deplored the action of the White House, more of their number approved. Naturally, Senator Borah was greatly pleased that his long fight had come to a victorious conclusion, and many of his colleagues joined him in public statements endorsing the restoration of relations with Russia.[55] Prominent businessmen expressed their high hopes

[49] Radio address by Matthew Woll, December 2, 1933, as quoted in *ibid.*, 183-184.

[50] *New York Times*, November 19, 1933.

[51] *Boston Evening Transcript*, November 18, 1933.

[52] As quoted in the *New York Times*, November 18, 1933.

[53] *National Republic*, December, 1933, 12, 13, 14.

[54] *Commonweal*, cxxxviii (1933), 114-115; *Catholic World*, December 3, 1933, 357. It is interesting to note that Cardinal Hayes expressed to the President his satisfaction with the conduct of the negotiations, especially with the achievement of the religious guarantees. Monsignor Keegen to Franklin D. Roosevelt, November 18, 1933, Roosevelt Papers.

[55] *New York Times*, November 18, 1933; telegram from Senator Borah to Franklin D. Roosevelt, November 17, 1933, Roosevelt Papers.

for the future of trade with the Soviet Union. In an address lauding the constructive move taken by the President, Thomas J. Watson, President of International Business Machines, asked "everyone in the United States," in the cause of amicable relations with Moscow, to "refrain from making any criticism of the present form of government adopted by Russia." At the same time, he expressed the hope that the Soviets would "not allow any criticism to be spread in this country against the form of government we operate."[56] Apparently, he did not see the distinction between domestic criticism of a foreign regime and foreign agitation within the United States.

Commercial and industrial prognosticators, even in their most cautious predictions, anticipated large sales to Russia, ranging from $120,000,000 to $520,000,000 in the first year.[57] *Business Week* anxiously awaited the settlement of credit details so that the orders might begin to affect the American market.[58] Three of the influential financial organs indicated their confidence that the expected trade agreements would be of great advantage to both nations, though they acknowledged that there would be many difficulties to overcome. It would not all be "smooth sailing."[59] But two of their competitor journals were highly skeptical of the material results of recognition, pointing out that Soviet promises were suspect and that in any case Russia could offer little that the United States needed in the way of goods.[60] A continuing profitable commercial relationship had to depend on something more than

[56] *Economic Review of the Soviet Union,* ix (1934), 59.

[57] The higher figure was advanced by ex-Senator Smith W. Brookhart of Iowa, Special Adviser to the Agricultural Adjustment Administration. *New York Times,* November 18, 1933. Francis T. Cole, Executive Vice-President of the American Manufacturers Export Association considered 120 to 150 millions a year more reasonable. *Ibid.,* November 19, 1933.

[58] *Business Week,* November 25, 1933.

[59] *Wall Street Journal,* November 20, 1933; *Journal of Commerce,* November 18, 1933; *Commercial and Financial Chronicle,* November 25, 1933.

[60] *Forbes,* December 1, 1933, 7.

credits, an article in the *Magazine of Wall Street* soundly advised.[61]

In general, the influential press organs favored the rapprochement with the Soviet Union. The *Christian Science Monitor* accepted the agreement as "a common sense" arrangement, which was preferable to nonrecognition even if future relations did not prove to be as rewarding as some advocates hoped.[62] The *Louisville Courier-Journal*, previously an opponent of a change in American policy, admitted that it could see "no valid reason for withholding recognition," while the *Baltimore Sun* heartily endorsed the move.[63] In the deep South, the *Charleston News and Courier* scoffed at the fears of Communist penetration into the United States, suggesting that America had better look to her health if she saw danger in "Communist germs." The *New Orleans Times-Picayune* agreed, and termed the guarantees secured by the government "safe and reasonable."[64]

Several journals, although in favor of recognition, tried to prepare their readers for possible disappointments in the benefits promised. The *Philadelphia Public-Ledger* felt that the resumption of relations would facilitate trade, but could not be expected to cause a commercial boom, and the *New York Herald Tribune* contended that intercourse with Russia would be advantageous as long as the United States did not become involved in such "financial tangles" as long-term loans and trade subsidies.[65] Just how the editors of the *Herald Tribune* expected to increase Soviet purchasing in America without credits when Russia had so little to offer the United States in desired products, the editors did not disclose. The *New York Times* discussed the recognition in extremely measured terms,

---

[61] John C. Cresswell, "What Will Russia Use for Money?," *Magazine of Wall Street*, December 9, 1933, 183.
[62] *Christian Science Monitor*, November 18, 1933.
[63] As quoted in the *New York Times*, November 18, 1933.
[64] As quoted in the *Literary Digest*, December 2, 1933, 13.
[65] As quoted in *ibid*.

avowing doubts as to the effect on trade and conceding its suspicions of the vague statements issued on the debt settlement. The editors were hopeful, however, that contact with America might in some way aid the people of Russia.[66] In the far west, the *San Francisco Chronicle* was satisfied with the Soviet pledges and pleased with the compromise on procedure, but aware that complications might arise over the "two embarrassing questions that await . . . final solution," debts and loans.[67]

As was to be expected, the *New Republic* found recognition "extremely good news." The editors, stressing the international ramifications of the diplomatic reconciliation, opined that the further isolation of Germany and Japan would be a blow struck for peace.[68] Seconding its liberal companion, the *Nation* suggested that a united policy in the Far East might allow Russia and the United States to change the whole course of Japanese imperialism. Recognition, predicted the *Nation*, "will stand out as the major accomplishment of the New Deal."[69] The relatively conservative *Literary Digest* called attention to the "strange comradeship in foreign policy between the two nations." Both Russia and the United States had made a separate peace with Germany after the last war, remained out of the League of Nations and the World Court (comparisons which must have made Wilson stir uneasily in his grave), urged disarmament, and consistently opposed Japanese aggression in China. The action of Roosevelt was, in the opinion of the news magazine, merely an official recognition of established mutual interests.[70]

Perhaps the most interesting reactions were found in the Socialist, and especially the Communist press. Both acclaimed recognition, but disagreed with each other as to the meaning

---

[66] *New York Times*, November 19, 1933.
[67] *San Francisco Chronicle*, November 18, 1933.
[68] *New Republic*, November 29, 1933, 61.
[69] *Nation*, November 29, 1933, 607.
[70] *Literary Digest*, November 18, 1933, 10.

of the Litvinov pledges and the reasons for Roosevelt's decision to recognize. According to the Socialists, the Third International had been outlawed in the United States under the terms of the agreement and the Communist party itself given a death blow.[71] Technically, the Socialists were correct, but it was surprising that they attached so much importance to the letter of the guarantees. As to the motivations that had decided the White House for recognition, Norman Thomas listed the realization of the worthlessness of the old policy, the natural desire to promote trade, and the mutual interest of the two countries in checking the imperialism of Tokyo.[72]

The Communists, however, preferred to interpret Roosevelt's move as an admission of Soviet greatness and American failure in the fields of economics and diplomacy. And the editorial in the *Daily Worker* would have made unwelcome reading to those citizens who put unquestioning faith in the Russian promises. Defiantly, the Party organ proclaimed that "in this country the Communist Party, section of the Communist International, basing itself on the principles of Lenin and Stalin, will more than ever strive to win the American workers for the revolutionary way out of the crisis, for the emulation of the Soviet Union and its revolutionary victories."[73]

In the same vein, a second editorial continued: "The capitalist press knows it, Roosevelt knows it, and the capitalist class knows it. . . . They know that every attempt to claim that article 4 of the Litvinov pact applies to the Communist International will meet with defeat. Just as every attempt of the British government, for example, to do that failed. The Communist International . . . will grow in power and force."[74]

But from Moscow, Ambassador Troyanovsky, evading the full implications of the agreement Litvinov had signed, assured his American hosts that: "Of course, no propaganda of any

[71] *New Leader*, November 25, 1933.   [72] *ibid.*
[73] *Daily Worker*, November 20, 1933.   [74] *ibid.*, November 21, 1933.

sort will emanate from the Soviet Embassy."[75] The State Department, perhaps with inner doubts, assured the public that the President had secured effective guarantees against the Communist evils that many Americans feared would penetrate their country via the reopened diplomatic channels.[76] And President Roosevelt, speaking at Savannah on his way south for a vacation at Warm Springs, explained his recent action in the homely phrases he so often employed to report on matters of state.

Emphasizing diplomatic rather than commercial benefits, Roosevelt told his audience: "I have had a good example of the effect of honest statement and simple explanation of the fundamental American policy during the past weeks in Washington. For sixteen long years a nation, larger even than ours, has been unable to speak officially with the United States or to maintain normal relations. I believe sincerely that the most impelling motive that has lain behind the conversations which were successfully concluded . . . was the desire of both countries for peace. . . ."

Then, after quoting a statement of Thomas Jefferson to the effect that Russia and the United States had a common interest in promoting peace, the President concluded: "And so in the spirit of Thomas Jefferson, Mr. Litvinov and I have believed that through the resumption of normal relations the prospects of peace over all the world are greatly strengthened."[77]

[75] *New York Times*, November 22, 1933.

[76] Robert Walton Moore, *Recognition of The Union of Soviet Socialist Republics*, Radio Address, November 22, 1933 (Washington, United States Government Printing Office, 1934), 4.

[77] Franklin D. Roosevelt, *The Public Papers and Addresses of Franklin D. Roosevelt* (New York, 1938), II, 492.

CHAPTER 8

DEBITS AND CREDITS

To judge by the public and official reception, the establishment of relations between Russia and the United States had inaugurated a period of fruitful cooperation in many fields. The documents signed by President Roosevelt and Commissar Litvinov offered a sound legal basis for diplomatic and political intercourse. But trade awaited further agreements, and the debt issue was still unsolved. Even the reciprocal commitments were of questionable value until time and temptation had tested their worth. It remained to be seen whether words and pledges would be matched by deeds.

Although any real expansion of commerce between the two nations was dependent upon the extension of government loans or credits in return for a debt settlement, in conformity with the memorandum drawn up by Litvinov and Roosevelt, both governments immediately after recognition set about freeing the trade channels of the encumbrances which had been raised in the past sixteen years. For the Soviets this involved few changes. In fact, the only important discriminatory measure directed against American goods was the higher tonnage duty on United States' vessels in Russian ports. On November 21, 1933, Counsellor Skvirsky informed Mr. Phillips that these fees had been reduced to give the United States preferential treatment. In return, the President, by a proclamation of January 21, 1934, removed similar discriminatory levies against Soviet ships in American ports.[1] Acting from the same motives, the Treasury Department announced that the anti-dumping orders

[1] *Foreign Relations, 1933*, II, 817-818.

176

and the convict labor rulings had been annulled.[2] With the evidences of past friction thus removed, it was possible to begin the building of a new economic relationship .

The Russian government believed that progress in this direction could be facilitated by the appointment of a trade commissioner or representative, resident in New York, who would concentrate in his hands the placing of Soviet orders in the United States and the accepting of American orders for Russian goods. As a member of the Embassy staff, the trade representative would be entitled to the privileges and immunities granted to diplomatic personnel. Since the practice was well established in Soviet commercial relations,[3] and since the Russian system of trade monopoly was unique, Moscow was hopeful that Washington would agree to the innovation in the United States. But the State Department received the request with little enthusiasm and, after several weeks of deliberation, refused its approval. The Department, Phillips informed Skvirsky, had no objection to the appointment of a Commercial Attaché to perform the usual duties of that office nor was there any objection to his residing in New York. The United States Government could not, however, permit him or any other official representative to engage in actual business and commercial activities with American citizens.[4] Such transactions would have to continue to be handled by Soviet agencies not accredited to the United States Government. In other words, the practical aspect of commercial relations must remain outside diplomatic channels.

This Russian overture suggested an eagerness to begin buying in America. But the report of Ambassador Bullitt on a conversation with Litvinov in December was less encouraging. The Commissar estimated that at best the United States could not take more than $60,000,000 worth of Russian goods in one year and pointed out to Bullitt that if America wished to sell

[2] *Treasury Decisions*, LXV (1934), 119-120.
[3] *Vnesh. torg.*, 91. [4] *Foreign Relations, 1933*, II, 824-825, 829.

more than that amount to the Soviets, long-term credits would be necessary. In short, the United States could not expect to sell more than it purchased, unless acceptable financing was arranged. Litvinov had continued by saying that the USSR was really not particularly interested in building up a large export-import trade, as it wished to attain as much self-sufficiency as possible. Nevertheless, if America was willing to grant favorable credit facilities, Moscow would be "glad" to place orders to a "considerable" amount in the United States[5]— hardly an enthusiastic exposition, and one that contrasted strangely with the "billion dollar" address in London six months before.

After his return to the United States, Bullitt made an effort to caution American business and financial leaders against overestimating the volume of trade that could be expected without reciprocal buying in the Soviet Union. Speaking to the Philadelphia Chamber of Commerce on January 19, 1934, the Ambassador warned that too much reliance should not be put on the efficacy of credits to stimulate Soviet buying. "Credits in some measure are no doubt justifiable," he advised, "but credits merely postpone the day when goods have to be taken, and therefore credits in excessively large amounts must be avoided."[6] His remarks were prompted no doubt both by his Moscow impressions and by concern in Washington over the undue optimism in many industrial circles.

But hopes were not easily dimmed. Private business groups immediately set about formulating plans for facilitating Soviet credit in the United States. Banks and industrial and commercial organizations discussed projects to form amalgamations for the financing of Russian orders.[7] Before any definite

[5] *ibid.,* 850.

[6] William C. Bullitt, *The Establishment of Normal Relations Between the United States and the Union of Soviet Socialist Republics,* An address before the Chamber of Commerce of Philadelphia, January 19, 1934 (Washington, United States Government Printing Office, 1934), 5.

[7] E. C. Ropes, "American-Soviet Trade Relations," *The Russian Review,* III, No. 1 (1943), 92.

steps could be taken, however, the government itself answered the need by creating through executive order, on February 2, 1934, the First Export-Import Bank. Established as a District of Columbia banking corporation, administered and financed by the government, the organization had the power to advance credits, borrow money and negotiate discount notes, as well as other bona fide evidences of indebtedness. The First Export-Import Bank was founded specifically to assist in the antici-pated trade with Russia.[8] But its facilities were rendered use-less almost from its inception.

The debts had still not been settled. Accordingly, to make clear the position of the American government, the Export-Import Bank passed a resolution stating that credits for Soviet purchases in the United States would be withheld until a satisfactory debt arrangement had been presented to the Presi-dent by Moscow.[9] Soon thereafter the Johnson Act completed its passage through the Congress and became law. Obviously, Russia could expect neither government credits nor loans until it offered an acceptable agreement on the American claims. But one opening did remain. Presumably at the request of the White House, the Johnson Act as passed included an amend-ment excluding from its provisions government controlled or financed public corporations, i.e. the Export-Import Bank.[10] Consequently, if the Soviets submitted a plan which met with executive approval, or showed sufficiently convincing evidence to the President of intent to pay, it was possible for the Export-Import Bank to revoke its resolution and extend credits to Russia.

There was even some question as to whether the Johnson Act provisions applied to the Soviet Union, since the debt had been contracted by the Provisional Government and negotia-

---

[8] Franklin D. Roosevelt, *The Public Papers and Addresses of Franklin D. Roosevelt* (New York, 1938), III, 79.
[9] The resolution is quoted in Benjamin H. Williams, *Foreign Loan Policy of the United States Since 1933* (New York, 1939), 24-25.
[10] *ibid.*, 25.

tions were in progress to reach a settlement. The question was submitted by the Department of State to the Attorney-General for a ruling. The reply was definite; neither fact nullified the provisions of the Act. Russia had to begin payment on her debt before she would cease to be considered in default.[11]

Needless to say, the Russians were most disgruntled by the course of events. It is very probable that they were more disturbed by the diplomatic rebuke inherent in the American actions than by their inability to receive a loan or credits. An indication of their displeasure was the appearance of two interesting and significant editorials in *Za Industrializatsiiu* which revealed the Soviet arguments. The first editorial appeared on April 17, 1934, and directed attention to the tremendous opportunities for Soviet-American trade, which recognition had made possible. According to the editorial, export and import planners had immediately begun revising their schedules in order to increase Russian purchases in the United States. But "through no fault of ours," Soviet readers were informed, unjustifiable obstacles had been thrown in the path of the expected development, namely, the Johnson Act and the Export-Import Bank resolution.

It was incorrect, the newspaper continued, to compare the Soviet Union, which had itself incurred no debt and which had paid all its own obligations promptly, with governments which had made "formal agreements with the United States . . . but later refused to pay." Did the members of Congress and the directors of the Export-Import Bank realize what a disastrous effect their actions would have upon Russo-American trade? Debt negotiations were always long and complicated and, in any case, the amount involved was much less than that asked by other creditors of the USSR.

In conclusion, the editors held out the usual bait. Final plans were being formulated for import during the entire Second Five Year Plan. Until the recent actions of the United States,

[11] *Press Releases*, x (January-June, 1934), 265-266.

those plans had had a "definite 'American slant.'" "However, in view of the circumstances which have now arisen, we are forced to remind our industrialists that this tendency must be corrected. The expansion of our foreign trade contacts abroad has . . . opened up many diverse possibilities to us. And most important, we have achieved great success in our struggle for technical-economic independence."[12]

The second editorial, published some ten days later, went a step farther and contested the validity of the debt itself. By the use of figures, the source of which is unknown, *Za Industrializatsiiu* calculated that the maximum sum which had been loaned by the United States to the Provisional Government was not more than $90,000,000. Of that amount, the newspaper contended, a large part had been used to arm Kolchak, Denikin, and other White Guard generals in their struggle against the very government that was now asked to pay. "Is it possible," the editors asked, "that it will be demanded of the working masses of the USSR that they pay for shells and bullets used to shoot them down?" Finally, *Za Industrializatsiiu* threw the inevitable counterclaims in the balance, and concluded that "as a whole the matter concerns only very insignificant and generally disputable and problematical claims." As an indication of how the pendulum had swung away from the pre-recognition arguments, the newspaper pleaded for the lifting of the bans on loans and credits in order that "a solid material base [be created] under the political rapprochement of the two great countries, which in the present troublous times are bound together by a common interest in the maintenance of peace."[13]

Yet, despite this and other indications that the Soviet Government continued to consider the debts invalid, conversations were under way to reach a settlement on the basis of the Roosevelt-Litvinov memorandum. On February 20, 1934, the

[12] *Za Industrializatsiiu*, April 17, 1934.
[13] *ibid.*, April 28, 1934.

Department of State handed to Ambassador Troyanovsky a draft proposal, which set the debt figure at $150,000,000 and recommended that it be paid off through additional interest on commercial credits granted to the Soviet Union. The debt principal was to bear interest at 5 per cent, beginning on July 1, 1934, and Russia would pay 10 per cent above the normal interest on credits in order to retire the debt.[14] The Ambassador accepted the note for transmittal to Moscow, where negotiations were to be conducted by Bullitt and Litvinov, with the ominous comment that the "gentleman's agreement" made no mention of interest on the principal.[15]

The reply of the Kremlin confirmed the suspicions thus aroused and set the stage for the tortuous and unsuccessful negotiations that were to follow. Litvinov informed Ambassador Bullitt that his government took exception to a number of items in the draft. As it stood, the proposal would lead to the reopening of the debt issue with every other creditor nation. More specifically, he declared that the USSR was unprepared to discuss any sum greater than $100,000,000, that no agreement had been made to pay interest on the debt, and that he had been promised a loan, not credits, by the President. Although he objected to other conditions which figured in subsequent discussions, such as the rate of interest on loans or credits, these points continued to be the major sources of disagreement in the subsequent negotiations.[16]

Of course, it is impossible to ascertain exactly what verbal commitments Roosevelt and Litvinov made in private conferences, but Litvinov was obviously correct in his assertion that the document itself made no reference to interest and that the word loan rather than credit was used. Secretary Hull, in his account of postrecognition negotiations, did not state directly that interest payment was part of the understanding. He did, however, definitely imply that the Amer-

---

[14] *Foreign Relations, The Soviet Union, 1933-1939*, 78.
[15] *ibid.*, 65-66.   [16] *ibid.*, 66-67.

ican officials considered it accepted by both sides as part of the final settlement.[17] No doubt it was, but knowing the reluctance of Moscow to pay any of the sums owed, the American negotiators were inexcusably careless not to include a statement to that effect in the memorandum.

Likewise, on the question of a loan, there is ample evidence that Litvinov while in Washington was fully aware that his government must be satisfied with credits. Bullitt had made it clear that the inevitable passage of the Johnson Act would rule out the possibility of a loan, and the American negotiators were positive that the Commissar had understood this condition.[18]

But, however loosely Roosevelt, and presumably Litvinov, had interpreted the word loan at the time of signing, the fact remained that the Russians could point to the memorandum as proof of the justice of their claim. The American representatives, including the President, manifested surprising naïveté in assuming that they could base their case against the Russian interpretation on impressions or oral understandings. Evidence of their embarrassment and of Litvinov's realization that he held a trump card was shown by the Commissar's desire to publish the memorandum when the discussions broke down and the refusal of the United States Government to make the document public.[19]

Disconcerted but not discouraged by the unexpected barriers Litvinov had thrown in the path of settlement, Bullitt advised Hull that he remained hopeful and was inclined to believe that the Russians would back down after a certain amount of bargaining.[20] And, in fact, the Commissar did present an alternative solution in the beginning of April 1934, which, on the surface, appeared to be a step in the direction

[17] Cordell Hull, *The Memoirs of Cordell Hull* (New York, 1948), I, 303.

[18] Kelley Interview; *Foreign Relations, The Soviet Union, 1933-1939,* 110.

[19] *ibid.*, 184-185.   [20] *ibid.*, 69.

of compromise. The Soviet Union would agree to a twenty-year credit instead of a loan, the credit to be for double the amount of the debt and to bear interest at 4 per cent for the first four years with no extra interest toward retiring the debt. During the following sixteen years the normal interest would be supplemented by a 3 per cent additional charge to cover the claims. Hull's reaction was one of disgust as he pointed out that under such terms the completion of debt payments would find Russia still owing twice as much as at the beginning of the transaction.[21] Informed by Bullitt of the American reception of his proposal, Litvinov angrily stated that he had made his last offer and that, since Russia could get along very nicely without goods from the United States, Washington harmed only itself by such a stand.[22] So ended the first round of proposal and counterproposal. Those that followed were but variations on the same theme.

After a month of silence, Litvinov reopened the subject with Bullitt. His suggestions, though unacceptable, indicated an apparent desire to come closer to the American demands, and Hull accordingly indicated a willingness on the part of the United States to scale the debt figure down to $125,000,000, and to extend credit to twice that amount over a twenty-year period, with each transaction to be paid off in five years.[23] Presented with this compromise on the eve of his departure for Geneva, Litvinov indicated agreement in principle,[24] but when the matter was taken up with his subordinates, the wind had shifted again and Bullitt found no sympathy for the proposal in the Foreign Commissariat.[25] Litvinov's return rather than easing the situation led to an acrimonious exchange, on June 16, between him and the American Ambassador. Accusing the President of an attempt to violate the terms of the "gentleman's agreement," the Commissar bluntly stated that: "No nation today pays its debts. Great Britain has defaulted.

21 *ibid.*, 75-77. 22 *ibid.*, 79-81. 23 *ibid.*, 93-94.
24 *ibid.*, 95-96. 25 *ibid.*, 97-98, 104-105.

Germany is defaulting. And no one will be able to make propaganda against the Soviet Union if we do not pay one dollar on a debt we did not contract."[26]

Still anxious to find some solution to the problem, Secretary Hull suggested that the conversations be transferred to Washington.[27] Hope was fading that the Soviet Union would agree to the figure originally proposed by America, but it was considered vital that some settlement be made to satisfy both the prestige of the United States and public opinion within the country.[28] Therefore, after some preliminary discussions, Ambassador Troyanovsky opened the Washington phase of the diplomatic marathon by presenting, on August 24, 1934, a new proposal from his government. Inasmuch as this proved to be the last formal offer of the USSR, it deserves rather more attention than its predecessors.

Russia agreed to recognize the debt principal at $100,-000,000 and to begin repaying it on condition that the United States extend to her a commercial credit for an equal amount, with the term of each transaction under this credit to vary according to the type of goods purchased, no terms to be less than five years. In addition, the Soviet Union asked for a financial credit of $100,000,000, repayable in twenty years and renewable as repayments were made on the sums drawn. On both credits, Moscow was prepared to pay a total interest of 7 per cent, 3 per cent of which would go to retire the debt and to meet a 1 per cent interest charge on the principal of the debt.[29]

For whatever concessions had been made on interest, Litvinov retained his demand for a loan which was now euphemistically termed a financial credit. The proposal made it disappointingly clear that Russia was not prepared to meet the United States on workable terms. Troyanovsky was advised that the draft was unacceptable, and the American people

[26] *ibid.*, 109.
[28] *ibid.*, 119-120.
[27] *ibid.*, 103.
[29] *ibid.*, 136-137, 141.

were at last informed by means of a Department press release that "it was not possible to be optimistic that any agreement will be reached."[30] Nevertheless, one last effort was made,
this time by Assistant Secretary Moore with the President's
blessings. Would Russia be willing to pay $100,000,000, bear-
ing not less than 2 per cent interest, in return for a commercial credit which could total up to $200,000,000 at any
one time, with the average term of each transaction five years?
Troyanovsky was noncommittal.[31]

The next month saw an interlude during which confusing
cross-currents alternately raised hopes and brought further
discouragement. In Moscow, Radek suggested to Bullitt that
Stalin had been misinformed by Litvinov as to the course of
the negotiations. A flicker of optimism came from the Ambassador, unshared by Secretary Hull, only to be snuffed out
when Radek reported back that Stalin was after all aware of
the facts. The journalist explained to Bullitt that, with Japan
menacing in the East, Russia could not afford to antagonize
France and Great Britain in Europe by favoring the United
States with a debt settlement. Consequently, so ran the argument, the American solution must be unique. Inasmuch as
neither France nor Great Britain could grant Russia a loan
double or even equal to the debt owed them, the Soviet plan
would insure no complications from third power creditors.
Bullitt was inclined to give some credence to this reasoning,
but unable to find an answer which would be acceptable to
both parties.[32] Meantime, Vice Commissar of Foreign Affairs
Krestinskii no doubt voiced more accurately the Kremlin's
desire when he suggested that the best answer was to let the
whole matter drop.[33]

But just as the last hopes for agreement were vanishing, a
new development caused a final burst of optimism. Ambassa-

[30] *Press Releases,* xi (July-December, 1934), 64.
[31] *Foreign Relations, The Soviet Union, 1933-1939,* 138-141.
[32] *ibid.,* 143, 147-148.   [33] *ibid.,* 149-150.

dor Troyanovsky announced that he was returning to Moscow to consult with his government on the entire issue.[34] All the evidence at the disposal of the State Department indicated that he was making the trip at his own request in an effort to convince his superiors of the reasonableness of the last American proposal.[35] On the basis of this information and in order to avoid any interference that might mitigate against the success of the mission, Bullitt was advised to continue with his plans for a vacation during Troyanovsky's visit.[36] The atmosphere of optimism spread to the American press and prompted considerable speculation on the nature of the proposals and counterproposals under consideration.[37] However, Bullitt, on the scene, must have entertained doubts concerning the success of the Troyanovsky journey. Certainly, his last meeting with Litvinov, before leaving Moscow, made it evident that if the Ambassador prevailed it would be over great odds. The Commissar once again bitterly accused Roosevelt of violating his word, "grew purple" in his anger, and flatly declared that whatever proposal Troyanovsky carried back to Washington would be the last from Russia. If Washington did not accept, it could consider the negotiations at an end.[38]

As it proved, Litvinov's stubbornness was a more accurate gauge of things to come than Troyanovsky's hopeful pilgrimage. The belated return of the Ambassador to the United States in January, after frequent postponements, bespoke a hard fight in Moscow.[39] His confident statements en route gave the American public encouragement that he had won the battle.[40] But the true state of affairs was soon made known. Before delivering his message to Secretary Hull, Troyanovsky

[34] *ibid.*, 151, 153.   [35] *ibid.*, 153, 159.

[36] *ibid.*, 153; Assistant Secretary of State R. Walton Moore to Marvin H. McIntyre, September 29, 1934, Roosevelt Papers.

[37] The Russian press, on the other hand, had little to say on the negotiations after the spring of 1934.

[38] *Foreign Relations, The Soviet Union, 1933-1939*, 155.

[39] *ibid.*, 162.

[40] *New York Times*, December 26, 1934.

nervously hinted to Ambassador Bullitt, still in Washington, that his news would be unwelcome. Obviously, he disliked the task before him.[41]

The meeting with the Secretary on the following day, January 31, 1935, was as short as it was disappointing and conclusive. The Ambassador reported that he was unable to improve upon the last offer he had made before his departure. Russia must have a loan; otherwise she could not pay off her debt. Hull pointed out that the attitude of the USSR in this matter appeared to preclude any cooperation on issues of world significance, observed that the negotiations "would seem to have come to an end," and terminated the conversation.[42] A press release of the same day informed the world of the failure to reach a settlement, and briefly reviewed the nature of the American proposals without reference to the Soviet demands or objections.[43] A despatch to the Moscow Embassy notified the Chargé that the Export-Import Bank would be abolished, the Naval and Air attachés to the Soviet Union withdrawn, the Consulate-General in Moscow closed, and that reductions in the Embassy staff could be expected.[44] In this fashion, the American government quickly gave material evidence of its anger and disillusionment.[45]

In Moscow, Litvinov, apparently disconcerted by the tone and content of the Department release,[46] issued to the press his own version of the disagreement. Avowing he had left Washington confident that all but the details of the debt problem had been settled, he accused the United States of subse-

[41] *Foreign Relations, The Soviet Union, 1933-1939*, 169.
[42] *ibid.*, 170-171.
[43] *Press Releases*, XII (January-June, 1934), 62-63.
[44] *Foreign Relations, The Soviet Union, 1933-1939*, 171.
[45] S. R. Bertron, who was frequently consulted by the Russians, wrote Louis McH. Howe on February 4, 1935, that he had warned them that their demand for a loan would never be met by the United States and could lead only to failure. Roosevelt Papers.
[46] *Foreign Relations, The Soviet Union, 1933-1939*, 175.

quently repudiating "one of the fundamental points of the agreement . . . namely that of a loan."

But the statement of Litvinov was much more conciliatory than that of Hull, indicating that Moscow was still desirous of American friendship and anxious to gloss over the unpleasantness as much as possible. Expressing the hope that the failure to reach an agreement would not continue to hamper trade relations, the Commissar declared that "the USSR and the USA along with other peace-loving nations are faced with more serious common aims, for which it is possible to work without damaging the material claims of either state. The difficulty of solving the problem of mutual financial claims between states has now become a common phenomenon of international life, but it does not interfere with international collaboration in the development of trade relations or in the preservation of peace."[47]

Among other indications that Moscow wished to minimize the entire affair was the lack of recrimination in the Soviet press. Usually, Russian newspapers took advantage of such diplomatic unpleasantnesses, which were always interpreted as attacks on the USSR, to launch a bitter campaign against the offending nation. Nothing of the sort occurred on this occasion. Brief news accounts stated the bare facts in a tone of hurt sufferance, and the editorial writers maintained silence.[48] One receives a very definite impression that the Kremlin made every effort to avoid antagonizing the United States any more than the act of repudiation had made necessary, and at the same time to impress the Russian people with the unimportance of the event. This evidence would suggest that the government was in no way prepared to endanger the hard-earned American recognition. Both internationally and domestically, such a development would have been a blow to the prestige of the Kremlin.

[47] *Izvestia*, February 3, 1935.
[48] See *Pravda* and *Izvestia*, February 3, 4, 5, 8, 9, 1935.

As a matter of fact, the Soviets did have some reason for concern. The long-drawn-out negotiations had irritated certain members of the United States Congress to the extent that resolutions were presented in the House and Senate recommending the severance of diplomatic relations with Russia.[49] Although neither measure came to a vote, probably due to the unofficial intervention of the State Department, they did reflect the disillusionment and anger felt by many Americans.[50] The failure of the Soviet Union to honor its obligations was "a disappointing and even humiliating outcome of a Russian policy launched in the midst of so many fine sentiments and rosy hopes." The Russians, said the *New York Times*, "sat back and killed time and gravely went through the forms of negotiations while laughing in their sleeves at American simplicity. Now they add a touch of irony by explaining that they no longer want the . . . goods which they professed to be so anxious to obtain."[51]

Indeed, Russia seemed to be intentionally rubbing salt into the diplomatic wounds by her forthright expression of disinterest in American products. A number of Soviet declarations to that effect were made about the time of the final breakdown of the debt negotiations. *Za Industrializatsiiu*, echoing Litvinov's earlier diplomatic statements, asserted that Russia could afford to wait without concern for America to make up her mind whether or not to encourage economic relations. No harm was being done to the Soviet Union by the intransigence of Washington; only the United States suffered from its own

[49] *Congressional Record*, 74th Congress, 1st Sess., 58, 790.

[50] Congress could, of course, do no more than express its wishes in the matter, as the conduct of foreign relations is the prerogative of the executive branch of the United States Government. Secretary Hull directed Congressional attention to this point in a public letter to Senator Key Pittman, Chairman of the Senate Foreign Relations Committee, at the same time advising Pittman that the President did not intend to break off relations with the Soviet Union. *New York Times*, March 21, 1935.

[51] *ibid.*, February 3, 1935.

190

stubbornness.[52] It was not that Russia wished to cut off for-eign trade, a later editorial explained, but rather that she had reached a level of domestic production which enabled her to curtail her buying abroad when conditions were unfavorable. As to the United States, the newspaper continued, it would do well to note the experience of other nations which had finally been forced to disassociate the debt problem from sub-sequent commercial arrangements. Until that lesson had been learned, there was little chance of the situation improving.[53]

The self-sufficiency of the Soviet Union in 1935 was con-firmed also by A. Rozenholtz, Commissar of Foreign Trade. Russia, he declared, was in a position "to limit herself to very inconsiderable imports," unless highly favorable trading con-ditions were offered.[54] In the United States, Soviet repre-sentatives emphasized that Russia no longer had any "special need for foreign credits to finance . . . current imports," but that she was always prepared to take advantage of long-term arrangements with fair interest rates.[55] Of course Moscow and its spokesmen were only expounding more openly the argu-ments they had advanced ever since the beginning of the Soviet trade decline in 1932. Americans who had been guided by their own desire for trade and misled by Russian pro-nouncements abroad before recognition now became aware of facts which should have been known from the beginning.

It is entirely possible, however, that Russia would have im-ported more than she did from the United States after 1933 had long-term financial credits been available. Although the prerecognition predictions were fantastically exaggerated, there is no reason to question the desire of the Soviet Union

[52] *Za Industrializatsiiu*, December 23, 1934.
[53] *ibid.*, February 4, 1935.
[54] A. Rozenholtz, *Foreign Trade and Economic Independence of the USSR* (Moscow, 1935), 11.
[55] Ivan Boyev, Chairman of the Board of Directors of Amtorg, in an address to the Board of Directors of the American-Russian Chamber of Commerce, January 7, 1935, *Economic Review of the Soviet Union*, x (1935), 3-4.

for loans and credit arrangements to facilitate trade. But the debt problem intervened. It is difficult to say whether or not Moscow ever actually intended to pay the debt, but if so, it undoubtedly conditioned its payment on the reciprocal granting by the United States of a sizable loan, equal to if not greater than the agreed debt payment. Only for such a large reward would it have been worthwhile to invite the reopening of the entire debt problem as it related to other governments. But the Johnson Act made it impossible for the United States to advance a loan first.

Of course, credits were still available through the Export-Import Bank once Russia agreed to a detailed settlement. Why then did Moscow refuse that arrangement? Probably because the terms or the amounts offered were not satisfactory enough or large enough to warrant paying the debt. Or, it is entirely possible that the final refusal indicated that the Soviets had been bluffing—that they never intended to meet their obligation. Secretary Hull seems to have reached that conclusion as early as September 1934, when he wrote Bullitt: "Personally I have little idea that the Soviet officials will come to any reasonable agreement. Litvinoff won his victory when he obtained recognition and regards everything else as of minor importance."[56]

There is also evidence that Moscow counted on the long and fruitless negotiations to build up pressure from business groups in the United States, which would eventually force Washington to raise the loan and credit ban without the debt being paid.[57] The same strategem had been moderately successful with other countries to which the Soviets owed money, and the governments of those countries had been less friendly than the Roosevelt Administration.

Still another factor may have played a role in the Soviet disinclination to make a debt settlement. The Franco-Russian

[56] *Foreign Relations, The Soviet Union, 1933-1939*, 146.
[57] *ibid.*, 111.

rapprochement, which had had its first faint beginnings in 1932, took on new life in the summer of 1933 and by 1934 was well under way. In May 1935, this development culminated in the signing of a Mutual-Assistance Pact between France and the Soviet Union. During this same period, Russia had drawn closer to other western European powers, having in September 1934 entered the League of Nations. Certain it is that Moscow used its recently improved relations with France and England as an excuse for not meeting the American terms. The Russian negotiators argued that a debt payment to the United States would open the road to similar demands by their new friends.[58]

A corollary to this defense was the inference that pressure was being exerted upon Moscow by London and Paris not to endanger their position as defaulters on American debts by betraying the solid front of European repudiation.[59] Other reports to Washington, although perhaps purposely dissimilating, tended to cast doubt on the validity of this plea.[60] In any case, to both of these arguments, Hull answered, not without reason, that had they been mentioned when Litvinov was in Washington, some satisfactory arrangement might have been made.[61]

Finally, the achievement of somewhat better relations with Japan, beginning in the spring of 1934, and the subsequent ebb of Far Eastern fears reduced the importance of the United States in Russian diplomatic calculations and consequently the need to meet the American demand for a debt settlement.[62] Ambassador Bullitt quickly recognized the significance of this factor, writing in July 1934 that: "So long as the Soviet Union feels completely secure I believe that no agreement acceptable to us will be acceptable to the authorities in Moscow."[63] There is some reason to believe, however,

[58] *ibid.*, 115-116, 147-148, 155, 170-171.
[59] *ibid.*, 165.   [60] *ibid.*, 162, 173.   [61] *ibid.*, 170.
[62] *ibid.*, 186-187.   [63] *ibid.*, 100.

that the Soviet military leaders were more uneasy about Japanese intentions than their diplomatic colleagues. On two occasions, Commissar Voroshilov revealed concern over the growing rift in Russian-American relations, indicating by his remarks that he still considered the Japanese threat a real one, necessitating compromises with the United States on minor issues in order to insure its support in any conflict with Nippon. But the Commissariat of Foreign Affairs had, by this time, the further knowledge through experience, that little support, diplomatic or otherwise, could be expected from isolationist America, and that nothing of a practical nature was likely to be gained from courting her favor.[64]

Whatever the motivating factor or factors in Soviet intransigence, the contemplated boom in Soviet-American trade did not materialize. Although America exported approximately twice as much to Russia in 1934 as she had in 1933, the total was only one-seventh of the 1931 figure. There was a further slight rise in 1935, and each succeeding year brought an increase over its predecessor, but the sums were insignificant as far as their effect upon American trade was concerned.[65] But, when examined in the light of Soviet statistics, Russian-American trade takes on a somewhat different aspect. During those years, total Soviet imports reached their lowest level since 1924, dropping from one-third to one-fourth of the figures of the preceding eight years. The limited growth of Russian im-

[64] *ibid.*, 124, 183-184. Litvinov expressed his disillusionment concerning American participation in international affairs to the Chinese Ambassador in Moscow, who relayed the statement to Bullitt. Bullitt to Hull, October 26, 1935, National Archives (RG 59:711.61/574). The author is grateful to Mr. William A. Williams for bringing this dispatch to his attention. During 1937 and 1938, the Soviet Government gave some indication that it was interested in reaching a debt settlement in order to improve diplomatic relations with the United States. American Ambassador Joseph E. Davies discussed the matter with a number of Russian leaders, including Stalin, but evidently no basis could be found for an understanding. Joseph E. Davies, *Mission to Moscow* (New York, 1941), 50-53, 65-66, 220-221, 228, 239-242, 341-343, 344-346. *Foreign Relations, The Soviet Union, 1933-1939*, 567, 594.

[65] See Appendix A, Table III.

ports from the United States was thus of more significance to Soviet foreign trade than to American.[66]

The fact that any noticeable increase at all continued after 1935 was largely attributable to the conclusion of a trade agreement between the two countries in the summer of 1935. The negotiation of this agreement was the only bright spot in the otherwise gloomy postrecognition years. In an effort to obtain some economic profit from the resumption of relations after the collapse of the debt negotiations, Secretary Hull advanced the plan of extending to Russia the tariff reductions granted other nations under his reciprocal trade program.[67] In return for the advantages of lower tariffs, the Soviet Union agreed to purchase in the United States during the next twelve months $30,000,000 worth of goods. On the basis of these terms, the agreement was inaugurated by an exchange of notes between Ambassador Bullitt and Commissar Litvinov in Moscow on July 13, 1935.[68] The success of the arrangement led to its renewal in the years following until 1940, the guaranteed sum rising to $40,000,000 after 1937.

Moscow newspapers had little to say about the trade agreement with the United States. The two leading journals printed only a brief announcement of the event and the texts of the notes.[69] *Za Industrializatsiiu* did devote an editorial to observations on what it termed the first practical step toward improving Russian-American trade relations, but its comments were carefully restrained.[70] Nevertheless, the agreement and its renewals did stimulate Soviet purchasing in the United States to

[66] See Appendix A, Tables I and II.

[67] Hull, *Memoirs*, I, 304-305; *Foreign Relations, The Soviet Union, 1933-1939*, 193ff.

[68] *Press Releases*, XIII (July-December, 1935), 45-48. In a statement to the press, drafted by the Department, Bullitt tried to offset the debt settlement disappointment to American business by emphasizing the promise of increased trade inherent in the agreement. *Foreign Relations, The Soviet Union, 1933-1939*, 210.

[69] See *Izvestia*, July 14, 16, 1935.

[70] *Za Industrializatsiiu*, July 14, 1935.

the extent that in 1937 America captured first place from Germany in the list of exporters to Russia.[71] It was a revealing commentary on prerecognition trade hopes that this distinction was achieved with the sale of only $42,892,000 worth of goods to the Soviet Union.[72]

[71] *Torg. otno.*, 21.
[72] See Appendix A, Table III.

CHAPTER 9

DIPLOMATIC DISILLUSIONMENT

THE diplomatic aftermath of recognition proved to be almost as sterile as the commercial.

In the first months after the reestablishment of relations, the public statements of the representatives of both countries gave promise of a possible rapprochement in the political field, which would have an appreciable influence on the course of world affairs. Ambassador Bullitt returned from his brief initial visit to Moscow to tell the American people that the United States and the Soviet Union could "now work together and shall work together for the preservation of peace," and to predict that the "cooperation of our nations will be a potent force in preserving peace."[1] At the same time, the Soviet envoy, Alexander Troyanovsky emphasized the need for the two countries to concentrate on finding ways and means to "contribute positively to the promotion of the peace of the world."[2]

Speaking in more general terms of the intent of the United States to cooperate actively in international activities which aided the maintenance of world stability, President Roosevelt told the Woodrow Wilson Foundation, in December 1933, that America would give her support to measures which contributed to the "good of the peoples of the world as distinguished from . . . the good of political leaders, of privileged classes and of imperialistic aims." In words that must have raised Russian hopes and sounded startlingly familiar to Rus-

[1] William C. Bullitt, *The Establishment of Normal Relations Between the United States and the Union of Soviet Socialist Republics,* An address before the Chamber of Commerce of Philadelphia, January 19, 1934 (Washington, United States Government Printing Office, 1934), 5-6.

[2] *Economic Review of the Soviet Union,* xi (1934), 3.

sian ears, the President proposed that "from now on war by governments . . . be changed to peace by peoples."[3] The remarks of the Chief Executive did, in fact, prompt Karl Radek to write that "the policy of President Roosevelt . . . which is directed toward avoiding war . . . responds to the interests of mankind . . . is intelligent and farseeing."[4]

The act of recognition in itself appeared to have a noticeably alleviating effect upon the area where the Soviet Union and the United States might expect to achieve most from diplomatic intercourse. Ambassador Grew in Japan expressed his satisfaction with the results of recognition in the Far East, when he wrote in February 1934 that: ". . . American recognition of Soviet Russia has injected an important psychological element into the situation and gives pause to those in authority in Japan, for regardless of the pacific policy of the United States, American action in the event of a Japanese-Soviet conflict would be to the Japanese an unknown and disturbing factor, necessarily to be taken into consideration. . . . American recognition has increased self-confidence in Moscow, but no one believes that the Soviet Union will commence hostilities. I therefore believe that our recognition of the Soviet Union has injected into the situation a restraining influence, probably of greater effect than any other single integral."[5]

Soviet leaders privately revealed similar conclusions in conversation with Mr. Bullitt,[6] while Professor Eugene Varga, the prominent Russian economist, publicly stated in *Bol'shevik* that the reestablishment of relations was "the most important step which the United States has undertaken to weaken the external political position of Japan." Tokyo had displayed its apprehension, Varga noted, by subsequent attempts to ease the

[3] Franklin D. Roosevelt, *The Public Papers and Addresses of Franklin D. Roosevelt* (New York, 1938), II, 547-549.
[4] *Izvestia*, January 1, 1934.
[5] *Foreign Relations*, 1934, III, 34.
[6] *ibid.*, 111.

198

Far Eastern tension and by protestations of peaceful intent.[7]

Thus recognition did have some temporarily beneficial results in the international arena. But in order to have a permanent influence, it required implementation in the form of continued diplomatic collaboration between the Soviet Union and the United States. Moscow was willing and desirous of taking further steps in that direction.[8] Washington no doubt also saw the advantages of more active cooperation through the newly opened diplomatic channels. But Washington was, as always, forced to consider the will of the American people, which was overwhelmingly opposed to closer ties with other nations. Isolationism still reigned supreme. Russia was not unaware of the importance of this factor in the formulation of American foreign policy, but the recent actions of the new Administration had apparently encouraged the Soviet foreign office to believe that the United States might not reject an opportunity to aid in stabilizing the situation in the Far East.

During the negotiations in Washington, Litvinov had suggested to both the President and the State Department that the United States and Russia conclude a bilateral nonaggression pact and inaugurate a series of similar interlocking agreements to include China and Japan. The President firmly rejected the

[7] E. Varga, "O iapono-amerikanskikh protivorechiiakh," *Bol'shevik*, April 30, 1934, 60-63. The Soviets also took cognizance of the belligerent reactions of other groups in Japan, namely, the military. The Chan Chung correspondent of *Asahi* wrote that the United States had been granted oil and gold concessions on Sakhalin, the returns from which would be used to pay off the Russian debt to America. This intimation that Americans would be based so near to Japan was, of course, calculated to arouse Japanese fears. Evidently the rumor was given a certain amount of credence in Japan, for *Pravda* published an official denial along with its account of the story on December 26, 1933, imputing the fabrication to Japanese Army Headquarters and the collaborationist White Russians in Manchuria.

[8] The Soviet Ambassadors in Berlin and Rome, during their initial postrecognition conversations with the American envoys in the two capitals, emphasized almost exclusively the possibilities for active collaboration between Russia and the United States in the Far East. William E. Dodd, Jr. and Martha Dodd (eds.), *Ambassador Dodd's Diary, 1933-1938* (New York, 1941), 80; *Foreign Relations, 1933*, III, 465.

treaty plan because it did not include all of the powers with interests in the Far East,[9] and Acting Secretary of State Phillips pointed out to the Commissar that the Kellogg Pact already served the same purpose. As an international instrument, it had more force than would a number of bilateral agreements. Litvinov did not agree. Individual agreements gave more security than international pacts, he stated, and, in any case, Japan had already violated the Kellogg Pact, negating its further applicability in the Far East. Although Mr. Phillips promised that the government would consider the plan, he carefully refrained from giving Litvinov any encouragement.[10]

Despite this cool reception, Litvinov returned to the subject during the visit of Ambassador Bullitt to Moscow in December 1933. Once again the Commissar was advised of the difficulties which lay in the way of American participation. It was extremely doubtful whether either the government or the people of the United States would consider a step which represented so sharp a deviation from traditional American foreign policy. But Litvinov was not easily dissuaded from his purpose of using Russian-American diplomatic relations as a deterrent to Japan. With considerable frankness, he told Bullitt that "anything that could be done to make the Japanese believe that the United States was ready to cooperate with Russia, even though there might be no basis for the belief, would be valuable." Bullitt listened sympathetically, but could only repeat the reply of Mr. Phillips that the United States would consider the proposal.[11]

Other members of the Russian government underlined the urgency of Litvinov's request by divulging to Bullitt their fears of an outbreak of war with Japan at any moment. Molotov told the Ambassador that an attack by Japan was probable in the spring of 1934, and certainly not later than the beginning of 1935. In a conversation with Bullitt, Commissar of

[9] See *Foreign Relations, 1934*, III, 74, 78.
[10] *ibid., 1933*, III, 464-465. [11] *ibid.*, II, 839.

War Voroshilov, confirming the threat of impending hostilities, asked that the United States send to Moscow military and naval attachés who spoke Russian so that he might talk to them in private. If Washington was agreeable to the idea, the Commissar declared, its military representatives in Russia could "have a relationship of the utmost intimacy with the military authorities of the Soviet Union." Stalin also impressed upon the Ambassador the imminence of Japanese aggression, introducing the Soviet Chief of Staff Egorov "as the man who will lead our army victoriously against the Japanese when they attack us." The Soviet leader made a definite appeal for matériel from the United States, requesting that 250,000 tons of rectified rails be sent from America to double track the Trans-Siberian Railroad. "Without the rails we shall win that war," Stalin observed, "but it will be easier with them."[12]

In the face of this pressure for aid of any kind, Bullitt repeatedly advised the Russians that the United States, while willing to use moral influence in the cause of peace, was in no way prepared to take any action which would involve it in hostilities.[13] But despite the guarded responses of Bullitt and his government, Soviet efforts toward a nonaggression pact continued through the spring of 1934, when the unyielding stand of Washington was finally accepted as definite. Technically, American opposition continued to be predicated upon the necessity for an agreement including all the Pacific powers, and reenforced by an unwillingness to recognize Manchukuo, a prerequisite to Japanese adherence that Moscow was apparently willing to grant.[14] But it was clearly evident that beneath these objections lay the continuing disinclination

---

[12] *ibid.*, 831, 835-837.   [13] *ibid.*, 835.

[14] *ibid.*, *1934*, III, 74-75, 78, 82-83, 292. On July 7, 1934, the *New York Times* revealed the Russian demands for a nonaggression pact and the American refusals, citing the State Department as its source of information. Two days later *Pravda* was authorized by the Commissariat of Foreign Affairs to state that "Comrade Litvinov never made any kind of proposal either in Washington or in Moscow for a bi-lateral Soviet-American nonaggression pact." *Pravda*, July 9, 1934.

of the United States to become involved in international complications. In any case, by the summer of that year, Japanese-Russian tension had eased and the Soviet Government had heard reassuring views expressed by France and England concerning their attitude toward a possible attack on Russia from the east. The Kremlin could afford to be less concerned about American aid.[15]

There remains to be recounted the closing chapter of this attempt at Soviet-American collaboration in the Far East. In the summer of 1935, Ambassador Bullitt, following a year of direct contact with Moscow diplomacy, and very likely also under the influence of the discouragements both personal and official of his post, had some succinct observations on the Russian attitude toward Japan and the United States.

In a message to the Secretary of State, which deserves quotation in full, he wrote: "It is, of course, the heartiest hope of the Soviet Government that the United States will become involved in a war with Japan. If such a war should occur it would be the policy of the Soviet Union to remain outside the conflict and to gain whatever wealth might be acquired by supplying the United States with war materials via the west and supplying Japan with war materials in the east. To think of the Soviet Union as a possible ally of the United States in case of war with Japan is to allow the wish to be father to the thought. The Soviet Union would certainly attempt to avoid becoming an ally until Japan had been thoroughly defeated and would then merely use the opportunity to acquire Manchuria and Sovietize China."[16]

Although there are some predictions in the above passage which stretch the imagination, for example the picture of industrially backward Russia furnishing war materials to the United States, or the inference that such a conflict would take place in a vacuum without the complicating participation of

[15] *Foreign Relations, 1934*, III, 96-97, 230-232.
[16] *ibid., The Soviet Union, 1933-1939*, 227.

other powers, especially in Europe, the tenor of the argument constitutes a rather remarkable prophecy of things to come.

The desire of Moscow to achieve some kind of diplomatic result from the resumption of relations with the United States was demonstrated again later in 1934. In May of that year, Litvinov had made a last effort to salvage something from the disintegrating Disarmament Conference with a proposal to transform the Conference into a permanent organization, which would consider and act on all threats to peace, working parallel to the League, but unhampered by its restrictions and limitations.[17] Pursuing his plan even after the entrance of Russia into the League, Litvinov approached the United States Government in December 1934, through the Soviet Embassy in Washington, with the suggestion that America take a leading role with Russia in setting up the new international body. The Commissar believed that the organization would offer the United States an opportunity to take a more active part in international affairs while still remaining outside the League. But Secretary Hull, who evidently favored the project personally, regretfully informed the Soviet Ambassador that Washington could not accept the offer.[18] Once more Russia had come up against the stone wall of American isolationism.

Although the Soviet Union should have realized that the United States was not yet ready to abandon its tradition of insularity, the failure to supplement recognition with positive acts of cooperation was undoubtedly a disappointment to Moscow. Litvinov was later to comment sadly to an American visitor to Russia: "Yes, we are always expecting more than we should from America, forgetting that for a variety of reasons, some of a constitutional nature, America is really incapable of drawing the proper organizational conclusions [a Bolshevik

[17] League of Nations, *Records of the Conference for the Reduction and Limitation of Armaments*, Series C (Geneva, 1936), II, 212.
[18] Cordell Hull, *The Memoirs of Cordell Hull* (New York, 1948), I, 304; *Foreign Relations, The Soviet Union, 1933-1939*, 152-155, 189-191, 216.

term meaning to carry out a proposal, to take action on the basis of one's words]."[19] On the other hand, Moscow had done little to inspire confidence in Washington after the reestablishment of relations. The failure of the long and aggravating debt negotiations had severely weakened American confidence in Soviet good faith. That disillusionment was to be followed by a second blow which struck even deeper at the roots of the new friendship.

In July 1935, the long-delayed Seventh Congress of the Third International convened in Moscow. The meeting date had originally been set for the autumn of 1934 by a resolution of the Thirteenth Plenum of the Comintern, which met in December 1933.[20] But in September 1934, the Presidium of the Central Executive Committee announced a postponement until the spring of 1935.[21] Apparently the date was again advanced before the Congress actually convened. It was not difficult to guess the reasons for the repeated delays. If the Congress had met when originally planned, relations with the United States would have been put to the test far too soon after the pledges of Washington. By the summer of 1935, however, Moscow could no doubt reason that the postrecognition failures at profitable cooperation with America left Russia with little to lose by one more antagonistic gesture. Moreover, the Soviet Union had made new and more advantageous friends since 1933.

But it would be incorrect to exaggerate the influence of Russian-American relations on the choice of a date for the Congress. Other factors were undoubtedly more decisive. In 1934 Russia faced many uncertainties, both internationally and

[19] The remark was made to Professor Samuel Harper in November 1936. Samuel N. Harper, *The Russia I Believe In* (Chicago, 1945), 249. See also note 64, Chap. 8 *supra*.

[20] XIII *plenum* IKKI, *stenograficheskii otchet* (Moscow, 1934), 597. Hereafter cited as XIII *plenum*.

[21] *Communist International*, XII (January 5, 1935), 37.

domestically. The rapprochement with France was only in the formative stage and the policy of Russia toward the Nazi regime in Germany was undetermined. Stalin was still concerned with consolidating his power within the Soviet Union and in the Comintern. By July 1935, Russia and France had signed their mutual assistance treaty, which was a part of the Soviet decision to take a clear stand against Hitler. And Stalin, secure in his leadership, could call a Congress with absolute assurance that it would docilely follow his orders.

Nevertheless, the effect of the Comintern meeting on Soviet-American relations was profound, for in attendance at the Moscow Congress were the representatives of the American Communist party, who duly reported on the progress of the revolutionary movement under their leadership in the United States.[22] Washington justifiably considered the incident a direct violation of the noninterference pledge made at the time of recognition and, accordingly, dispatched a protest to the Soviet Government worded in the plainest language.[23] Warning Russia that the "most serious consequences" would result if Moscow were "unwilling or unable . . . to prevent further acts in disregard of the solemn pledge given by it to the Government of the United States," the note stated frankly that the continuation of such activities would "preclude the further development of friendly relations" with America.

The Soviet reply, handed to Ambassador Bullitt by Vice-Commissar of Foreign Affairs N. Krestinskii on August 27, 1935, was a sweeping denial of the Washington charges. Asserting that all the commitments made to the United States had been scrupulously observed, Krestinskii declared that the Soviet Government "cannot take upon itself and has not taken

[22] Reports were made by Gil Green and Earl Browder. vii *Congress of the Communist International, Abridged Stenographic Report of the Proceedings* (Moscow, 1939), 83-88, 245-248. Hereafter cited as vii *Congress.*

[23] The President appears to have taken a direct part in deciding on the course of action. *Foreign Relations, The Soviet Union, 1933-1939,* 242-243, 249.

upon itself obligations of any kind with regard to the Communist International."[24]

Later, Secretary Hull wrote that he had been astounded by the Soviet answer which so blatantly disregarded the undoubted meaning of the pledge.[25] Certainly, the response of the United States Government to Moscow's disavowal was extremely forthright. In a statement issued to the American press, Hull reviewed the recognition negotiations and the attendant commitments, declaring that article 4 of the noninterference guarantee "irrefutably" applied to the Third International. The answer of the Soviet Government, therefore, clearly constituted a repudiation of the pledge. If Moscow continued to ignore the clear stipulations of the commitment, Hull warned, "the friendly and official relations between the two countries cannot but be seriously impaired." The future of Russian-American friendship, he concluded "will depend upon the attitude and action of the Soviet Government."[26]

Ambassador Bullitt in Moscow was equally if not more disturbed by the Russian reply. Throwing aside the amenities of diplomacy, Bullitt called in American and other foreign correspondents at the Soviet capital and urged them to give prominence in their dispatches to the unparalleled treachery of the Russian government.[27] It is probable that the disillusionment of the Ambassador had its roots in the increasingly unsatisfactory results of the recognition he had so enthusiastically promoted. But the Comintern affair proved to be the turning point in his attitude toward the Soviets. From that time on his remarks left no doubt as to his hostility to the Moscow regime. The enmity between the two governments arising out of the pledge violation was greatly intensified by the personal activities of the American Ambassador, so much so in fact, that it was

[24] *Press Releases*, xiii (July-December, 1935), 147-152.
[25] Hull, *Memoirs*, i, 305.
[26] *Press Releases*, xiii (July-December, 1935), 151-152.
[27] Louis Fischer, *Men and Politics, An Autobiography* (New York, 1941), 306, 308.

clear that as long as a definite break in relations was not contemplated, the usefulness of Bullitt in Moscow was at an end. Although Bullitt had great provocation for his abrupt about-face, the bitterness of his reaction while still at his post was unfortunate, and may in large part be explained by the interest he had had in developing a close accord with Soviet Russia. It was a personal as well as an official defeat.[28]

As had been the case at the time of the debt negotiation failure, Moscow made an effort to minimize the tension which grew out of the American protest over the Seventh Congress of the Comintern. The Soviet press refrained from any editorial comment on the incident. The newspapers published only a brief communiqué on the exchange of notes between Bullitt and Krestinskii, and an equally brief report on the public statement of Secretary Hull.[29] It would scarcely have been to the best interests of Russia to have allowed the affair to precipitate a withdrawal of American recognition at a time when Moscow was pursuing a policy designed to improve its relations with the capitalist world—a policy based on an apparent renunciation of the revolutionary aspects of the Soviet regime. Consequently there was no attempt to inflame the public against the United States. Rather, an atmosphere of regret that America had taken the unhappy step of protesting permeated the brief coverage. It should be remembered too,

[28] Ambassador William Dodd in Germany was greatly impressed by the drastic change in the attitude of Bullitt toward the Soviet Union after the Comintern affair. Dodd reported that Bullitt had advised the French against a proposed loan to Russia in December 1935, and had given a newspaper interview on December 1, 1935, in Berlin, supporting the case of Japan against Russia in the Far East. Dodd and Dodd, *op. cit.*, 277-278, 290, 309-310, 372. All of Dodd's observations were used in a later-day attack on Bullitt in V. P. Potemkin (ed.), *Istoriia diplomatii* (Moscow, 1945), II, 609-610. Joseph Davies, who was appointed Ambassador to Russia in January 1937, after an interim in which the United States was represented in Moscow by a Chargé d'affaires, was told by Troyanovsky and Voroshilov of the unpleasant impression left by Bullitt during his last months at his post. Joseph C. Davies, *Mission to Moscow* (New York, 1941), 13-14, 64.

[29] See *Izvestia* and *Pravda* August 28, September 3, 1935.

that the Russian people were still quite unaware of the exact nature of the pledges Litvinov had made in Washington.

In an effort to offset the accusations of Washington, Soviet officials asserted that countercharges could have been made with justification by Moscow. Ambassador Troyanovsky, referring to the various anti-Bolshevik Russian groups with headquarters in the United States, suggested that America look to the beam in her own eye.[30] In March 1936, Joseph Stalin made the same comment in reply to a direct question from Mr. Roy Howard, who had asked, during an interview granted by the Russian leader, why Litvinov signed the commitment if it were impossible for the Russian government to observe it.[31] Still another approach, used by the Soviet envoy, was to disagree disarmingly with the Comintern statements and theses in private conversation with American officials in Washington.[32]

But the most interesting defense was the time-tested insistence upon the nonconnection between the Russian government and the Comintern—an argument obviously unsupported by the terms of the Washington agreement. In answer to the pointed questioning of Mr. Howard, Stalin declared that: "Litvinov signed the letter to Roosevelt, not as a private citizen but as a representative of the state, as did Roosevelt in his letter. This is an agreement between two states and its vital consideration concerns the activities of agents of those two states. The agreement, which is an understanding between two governments, can be interpreted only within this framework."[33]

There can be no question that the proceedings of the Seventh Congress were a clear violation of the guarantees made at Washington, and that the United States had every right to submit a strong protest to the Soviet Union. But the publicized

---

[30] *New York Times*, August 27, 1935.

[31] Copyrighted interview of Mr. Roy W. Howard with Joseph Stalin in the *New York World-Telegram* (and other Scripps-Howard newspapers), March 4, 1936.

[32] *Foreign Relations, The Soviet Union, 1933-1939*, 260-262.

[33] Howard Interview with Stalin, *loc. cit.*

anger of American officials was more the measure of exhausted patience than of surprise and shock. The meeting of the Congress was an open challenge that could not be ignored.[34] The activities of the American Communist Party as a section of the International had been neither discontinued nor pursued in secrecy between the time of recognition and August 1935. Delegates from the American Party had attended a meeting of the Plenum of the Comintern in Moscow within a month of the Roosevelt-Litvinov exchange. At that meeting, Earl Browder, the Secretary-General of the American Communist Party, had reported on the activities of his section and American affairs had been discussed.[35] In the following months, articles by Communist leaders in the United States continued to appear in the official Communist publications. Oral protests to both Litvinov and Troyanovsky concerning these breaches of the pledge had brought no more satisfactory reply than a shrug of the shoulders.[36]

When Ambassador Bullitt warned Litvinov, in October 1934, that the announced Comintern Congress would lead to "the most serious consequences" if American issues were discussed, the Commissar affected ignorance of the projected gathering.[37] When Bullitt pressed the point, Litvinov angrily replied that

[34] It is noteworthy that the Seventh Congress officially endorsed the "United Front" policy against Fascism which had been taking form within the Comintern since 1934. This new tactic of communism strove for the union of all parties, Communist and non-Communist, in a common struggle against Fascism. Revolutionary objectives were deemphasized, and the defense of the Soviet Union against its external enemies became the primary task of all sections of the Comintern. vii *Congress*, 151-152. As part of the new program, the International changed its line on the Roosevelt Administration and reappraised it as a progressive liberal regime with which the Communists might temporarily cooperate. *Ibid.*, 361, 406. It is possible that the necessity to repudiate this unwelcome endorsement in the interests of domestic politics influenced the decision of Roosevelt to make a public protest.

[35] Despite the recent Russo-American reconciliation, the Roosevelt Administration was characterized by the Plenum as a war-seeking, semifascist regime. xiii *plenum*, 105-106.

[36] *Foreign Relations, The Soviet Union, 1933-1939*, 111, 131, 156-157.

[37] *ibid.*, 156.

"no nation ever starts talking about the activities of the Comintern unless it wishes to have as bad relations as possible with us."[38] Although Secretary Hull rejected Bullitt's suggestion that Russia be warned of a possible break in diplomatic relations if the Third International should "get out of hand," he authorized the Ambassador to give notice that a definite lessening of the good feeling between the two countries could be expected in the event of such a development.[39]

As the meeting date for the much postponed Congress approached in the early summer of 1935, Bullitt's intimations of American displeasure were repeated and the Commissar's facetiousness changed to anger. In July, Litvinov first replied to the insistent request of the Ambassador for information with the comment: "Is there to be one [a meeting]? You know more about the Third International than I do. The other day when I was talking to Stalin I said that I had heard there was to be a meeting of the Third International on the 10th of this month. Stalin replied, 'Is there?' He knew no more about it than I do."[40] But when Bullitt expressed doubt as to the sincerity of Litvinov's remarks, the Commissar took another tack. "I remember," he retorted, "I said [in Washington] I could not promise anything about the Third International."[41] Forced into a tacit admission of knowledge, Litvinov thus put forward the defense which the Soviet Government had always advanced in the past and which, lacking a better one, it would use in the coming unpleasantness with the United States, however inapplicable it might be.

Needless to say, the American representations proved unavailing. The Congress met with little or no attempt at secrecy and the Party representatives from the United States gave their addresses. When Bullitt sat down to write his report and make his recommendations to the President and the Department, there was no doubt in his mind that both the spirit and the

[38] *ibid.*, 158.   [39] *ibid.*, 157.   [40] *ibid.*, 221-222.
[41] *ibid.*, 223.

letter of the noninterference guarantee had been violated. But his ire at Soviet audacity was tempered by his concern over the international situation. There could be no question, he affirmed, that the United States would be justified "juridically and morally" in severing diplomatic relations with Russia. Yet he could not recommend such a course. No American interest would be served by the action. Whereas the Soviets would continue to have unofficial agencies reporting on American affairs, the absence of a diplomatic mission in Moscow would leave the United States without any avenue of information on Russia, a vital center in the deepening world crises.

Nor did the Ambassador believe that a written protest would be advisable, since it would inspire a nasty reply and no relief. Rather, he suggested oral rebukes to Troyanovsky and the Soviet Foreign Office, to be accompanied by restrictions on Russian travel to the United States and the closing of Soviet consular offices. Then he urged the President to go before the people of America and lay the case before them, detailing the Russian sins, cautioning vigilance against Communist machinations, and explaining the reasons for the decision of the United States not to take the final step of diplomatic rupture.[42]

The advice of Bullitt to take no step which would be embarrassing if not impossible to repair should the United States at some future date find Russian collaboration advantageous was diplomatically realistic. But his other recommendations appear less well thought out. Would not a written protest, even with its inevitable unsatisfactory reply, be better understood by the people of the United States than a Presidential charge of crimes against Russia, followed by an anticlimactic justification of continued relations? The American public was not yet sufficiently concerned with or sophisticated in its thinking about international affairs to understand the decision. The course suggested would, therefore, not only have irritated the Soviet Union with no resulting compensation to America, but

[42] *ibid.*, 244-248.

more important, weakened whatever support the Administration was receiving in the United States for its foreign policy.

Perhaps the President and the Secretary predicated their decision upon this argument. In any case, Roosevelt felt that the more drastic measures should be "held in reserve,"[43] an indication of the extent to which his illusions of fruitful cooperation with the Soviets had faded. The rather moderate press release by Hull took the place of a Presidential indictment. Still, in the diplomatic usage of this period, the actions of the United States constituted a severe reprimand to Moscow.

Indeed, by this time empty promises had taken their toll. If November 1933 had marked the zenith of Russian-American cordiality, August 1935 recorded the nadir. Disappointment and irritation had replaced hope and good will. As Secretary Hull sadly admitted: "We were . . . back almost to where we had started."[44] In March 1935, Ambassador Bullitt had transmitted to Washington his now famous report composed of excerpts from the dispatches of Neil S. Brown, Minister to Russia in the days of Nicholas I. The nineteenth-century American envoy had complained of the secrecy and distrust, and of the "art of worrying a foreign representative without giving him even the consolation of an insult," which the Russian government had developed to "an exquisite degree." Bullitt, discouraged by the failure of the debt negotiations, already aware of the Soviet disinclination to honor the propaganda pledge, harassed by innumerable annoying slights and provoking delays,[45] admitted his plagiarism and commented: *"Plus ça change, plus c'est la meme chose."*[46]

---

[43] *ibid.*, 254.   [44] Hull, *Memoirs*, I, 304.

[45] There were, for example, a series of complications conjured up by the Foreign Office to prevent the building of the American Embassy on the site so graciously offered to Bullitt by Stalin in the first flush of friendship. The project was finally abandoned in disgust by the United States in September 1935. *Foreign Relations, The Soviet Union, 1933-1939*, 72-74, 268ff.

[46] *ibid.*, 289-291. George Kennan, then a Secretary at the Embassy, is usually credited with the actual drafting of this "borrowed" message.

Before quitting his post in the spring of the following year, the Ambassador wrote his own dispatch of counsel, both sad and wise. Reluctantly, he concluded that the best that could be expected of Soviet-American relations was an uneasy correctness. Real friendship was impossible. Inasmuch as the United States needed a "listening post" at the capital of so great and influential a power, "patience" should be the watchword. "We should neither expect too much nor despair of getting anything at all. We should be as steady in our attitude as the Soviet Union is fickle. We should get what we can when the atmosphere is favorable and do our best to hold onto it when the wind blows the other way. We should remain unimpressed in the face of expansive professions of friendliness and unperturbed in the face of slights and underhanded opposition."[47] Excellent advice which came too late for the problems of 1933-1935, but which could have been followed with profit a decade later.

In the years that followed until 1941, when a measure of cooperation was achieved by the exigencies of a world war in which the Soviet Union and the United States faced a common enemy, albeit with conflicting aims, there was no noticeable improvement in the relations between the two countries. The policy-makers of both nations regretted the sterility of the relationship in a world careening toward a conflict which neither desired. But the United States had no confidence in Russian integrity and Moscow was unprepared to remedy the situation by honoring its obligations—especially when American isolationism indicated that the diplomatic rewards would not be great. The quest for mutual understanding proved futile, and the efforts to bridge the ideological gulf through collaboration in other fields of common interest did not succeed.

[47] *ibid.*, 291-296. Bullitt also recommended that the United States make every effort to keep war from coming to the Far East. If either Japan or the USSR won, he predicted, China would be lost. He also recommended that Washington work for a French-German reconciliation, presumably to prevent a war that would give Russia an opportunity to spread Communism in Europe.

C H A P T E R   10

RECOGNITION ASSESSED

FROM the vantage point of historical perspective, it is possible to discern many elements in the Russian-American rapprochement of 1933 which at the time were distorted by proximity. Some of these factors could have been brought into focus and taken into consideration during the events had the statesmen of either country been more astute or better informed. Others probably had to be revealed through time and experience. And in justice it must be remembered that both nations were confronted not only with a confused international situation, but also with a period of transition and stress at home—all of which served to blur outlines which might otherwise have been clear.

Many of the difficulties which arose after 1933 could be traced to prerecognition misconceptions in the Soviet Union and the United States. Although Moscow had desired recognition by Washington ever since the establishment of the Bolshevik regime in 1917, the years after 1929 brought a new note of urgency to its pleas. At first, economic considerations—the need for American goods to aid in the Five Year Plan—exerted the most influence on Russian policy toward America. But by the time the United States had begun to respond to this demand, the Soviet Union had new and more pressing reasons for achieving a rapprochement. Japan, bent on aggrandizement, had broken the peace in the Far East, overrun Manchuria, and given numerous indications that she sought further territorial acquisitions. Moscow feared that the Soviet provinces in the Far East were next on Tokyo's schedule of conquest.

For many reasons, Russia looked to the United States as the most promising diplomatic partner in any attempt to check Japanese ambitions. Moscow had long recognized the fundamental nature of Japanese-American antagonism, and the opposition of Washington to the actions of Japan in Manchuria had been clearly expressed by Secretary of State Stimson as well as by American public opinion. Furthermore, the United States, like Russia, was not a member of the League of Nations, which had done nothing during the Far Eastern crisis to convince Moscow that the member nations sincerely desired to prevent Japan from moving into Soviet territory. But there were two deterrents to the achievement of the desired cooperation with Washington. The Hoover Administration gave no promise of a change in the American policy of nonrecognition, and the United States continued to depend upon unilateral diplomacy based on moral pressure alone to express its displeasure with Japanese aggressiveness.

After the inauguration of Franklin D. Roosevelt as President of the United States, Russia thought that she perceived the beginnings of a new trend in American foreign policy. The pronouncements of the new Chief Executive hinted at increased activity by the United States in those international matters from which it had previously kept aloof. Hope was the mother of exaggeration, and Moscow let the desire for collaboration with Washington override the more cautious appraisal of American plans and capabilities which a closer examination of the facts would have warranted. This misleading evaluation was accentuated by the evident sympathy of Roosevelt for a reconciliation with the Soviet Union. Combining all these facts, Moscow very likely assumed that Roosevelt had some plan in mind for effective opposition to Japan in the Far East.

Unfortunately, decisions reached behind the Kremlin walls are not disclosed to the historian. But the Soviets have often displayed a tendency to read more into events than is there to be read. Russian moves are so carefully planned that Moscow finds it difficult to understand that other nations do not calculate every step with equal precision. And the evidence available suggests that the Soviets did overestimate the significance of the change in American attitudes toward Russia. The leaders of the Soviet Government were further led astray by their chronic inability to assess correctly American public opinion, or more accurately, to appreciate its braking effect on the policies of Washington. Thus, though Moscow was aware of the presence of isolationism in America, it miscalculated the ability and the desire of the government to ignore the prevailing views of the people. As a result, the Kremlin evidently expected more in the way of active diplomatic cooperation between the two countries than there was any chance of achieving.

No doubt the sixteen-year delay, in itself, exerted a subtle influence on the Russian mind, making the recognition when it did come take on a significance out of proportion to its true value, and lending credence to the belief that it foreshadowed a definite change in American foreign policy. In any case, whatever fruitful political returns Moscow anticipated from the reestablishment of relations, there can be no question that it considered the event a tremendous boost for Soviet international standing and prestige. Evidences of that fact can be found not only in the Russian reactions at that time, but also in the careful manner in which subsequent friction was minimized in order not to endanger the continuance of relations.

On the American side, misconception and naïveté paved the way for future disillusionment. Although the United States Government had withheld recognition from Russia for sixteen years on the basis of Soviet disregard for international obligations and Communist interference in the internal affairs of other nations, when it reversed its stand, it proceeded to place an undue amount of faith in Russian promises on both issues. The experiences of other nations plus the observations of its own diplomats abroad should have convinced Washington that Russia was not prepared to abandon her basic principles of conduct in more than token fashion, even to gain recognition from the United States. Moscow could be expected to use circumspection in conducting Communist activities in America, but there was little reason to believe that it would dissolve its connection with the Communist party in the United States.

Nor did the previous debt negotiations of Soviet Russia with the other creditor nations presage an expeditious settlement of the same issue with the United States. Certainly, the inability to grant a sizeable government loan to the Soviet Union and the insistence upon interest payment made the possibility of an agreement even less hopeful. For despite her past record, Russia might have condescended to make a small payment on the debt in a circuitous manner if the economic rewards had been great enough to warrant a breach in her history of repudiation.

The bases for American trust in Soviet good faith are elusive. But, without any attempt to arrange them in order of importance, several elements are discernible. The surface aura of respectability which Russia had studiously cultivated in the past few years assuredly had some effect. Her soft-pedaling of revolutionary activity, combined with her increasingly evidenced desire to be accepted as a member of the world community, led many observers to believe that Russia had discarded the international aspects of Bolshevik theory and was content with "Socialism in one country." In the face of publicized Soviet statements calculated to encourage that opinion, it was easy to overlook the fact that Moscow had not really sacrificed any of its vital national or Communist interests to the supposedly new trend. Although Russia loudly proclaimed her desire to promote the peaceful coexistence of the two systems, socialist and capitalist, she did not actually renounce her past policies or actions. The Communist International continued to function, and Soviet international obligations remained un-

217

acknowledged—to mention two of the points of conflict between the Soviet Union and the United States.

Moscow was, in fact, more willing to work with other countries in the cause of peace and world security than it had been before. But it was expected that in return other countries would overlook outstanding disputes. Why then was Litvinov willing to sign such sweeping pledges at Washington and to make at least a tentative agreement on the debts? Doubtless, the Soviet Government felt that the Washington concessions were worth the heightened prestige and the anticipated diplomatic aid to be gained from American recognition. Russia may also have suspected that the United States did not really expect the agreements to be scrupulously observed. Aware of Roosevelt's willingness to deal with Russia and conscious of the handicap of a strong anti-Communist sentiment in America, Litvinov may well have concluded that although Washington had to receive the assurances of Moscow to satisfy public opinion, it would not be too strict in its interpretation of them. As to the debts, they were of course left for future discussion. In short, the concessions made at the time of recognition were considered justifiable paper promises—not necessarily to be kept in practice.

Another factor which undoubtedly contributed to the unfounded optimism of Washington was the personality of Franklin Roosevelt. The President had great faith in his ability to conduct foreign affairs. Unquestionably, he was singularly gifted in the art of personal negotiation. But his influence was not consistently efficacious, and in Maxim Litvinov and Soviet diplomacy he faced a man and a system motivated exclusively by practical considerations, unhampered by ordinary ethics. The confidence of Roosevelt in his powers of persuasion coupled with his tendency to look on the bright side of events led him to put an unjustifiable amount of faith in the agreements he and Litvinov had concluded. In this he evidenced an aspect of his character which was to become more and more obvious in the later days of his Administration.

There was also the trade delusion. The anticipated expansion of commercial intercourse with Russia with its concomitant stimulation of industry and reduction of unemployment in the United States was, however, a public fallacy regarded with skepticism by officialdom. Although Moscow continued to use trade as a bait long after its real interest lay in a political rapprochement, the United States Government was not misled by the extravagant predictions advanced by either Russian or American prophets. While the conclusion of a commercial arrangement might be expected to increase trade with Russia, the facts of Soviet foreign trade after 1931 indicated that the expansion would be moderate. But Washington made no attempt to disabuse the public of its exaggerated expectations, at least not until recognition had been achieved. The reluctance to endanger the continuance of a favorable public opinion was understandable, but the silence of the government served to accentuate the subsequent national disillusionment.

In concluding the agreements at Washington, the United States Government neglected to face the historical lessons of other negotiations with the Soviet Union. The American negotiators had little if any basis for believing that Russia would abandon the Comintern or discontinue contacts with the American Section of the International. Nor was Washington justified in assuming that the debt would be settled after recognition. Similar commitments and promises had been made by Moscow with other nations with completely negative results. If a detailed noninterference pledge was the price of public approval for the reestablishment of relations, then the United States should have resigned itself to the acceptance of partial observance by Russia, or it should have been prepared to withdraw recognition if the guarantee was violated. As to the debt problem, the alternatives were settlement before recognition or probable failure. In other words, it should have been clear after sixteen years of observation of Soviet foreign relations that the middle road led only to irritation and friction.

The resumption of relations with Russia was a matter of practical politics, and it should have been understood beforehand that certain aspects of the Soviet system had to be taken into account and accepted if the rapprochement was to work. If the payment of Russian obligations to the United States and its nationals was necessary to insure friendly relations, recognition should not have been granted until a promise and a plan to pay had been arranged. If a settlement was not vital, then the issue should not have been allowed to so strain the new friendship. Admittedly, these considerations were not pleasant to face—especially for the United States. But it was a question of admitting the peculiarities of the situation and acting accordingly, or of continuing a completely negative policy of nonrecognition and thereby eliminating any official contacts between two of the greatest and most influential nations in the world at a time when universal peace was daily more seriously menaced.

Despite the mistakes and misconceptions on both sides and their unhappy effect on the subsequent course of Russian-American relations, the present writer is of the opinion that recognition was both advisable and profitable. No vital American interest was endangered by the reestablishment of relations. Communism was not a threat within the United States, as the strength of the American Communist party at the polls in the years of economic crisis amply proved. And it is extremely questionable whether normal intercourse with Russia increased the strength of communism in America. Official barriers, whether up or down, have never had an appreciable influence upon the health of the Communist movement. In any case, domestic legislation has never outlawed the Communist party in America, a measure which would have considerably more effect upon the activities of that group than the absence or presence of relations with Russia.

Nor was the failure to settle the debt a matter of vital import to the United States. Russia was certainly not alone in the 1930's in her refusal to honor her obligations to the United States. With her in the camp of repudiation stood all of the great powers of Europe. Naturally, the failure of the debt negotiations and the continuance of Communist activity were sources of irritation to America and precluded any degree of real cooperation. But the results of recognition were not all on the debit side of the ledger. With the resumption of official relations, the United States had a method of presenting its views to Moscow and of receiving in return the opinions of Moscow on international developments. By virtue of the residence in Russia of American consular and diplomatic officials, Washington had sources of information on the Soviet Union, previously unavailable to it. In this respect, the United States gained more than Russia from recognition, for before 1933, Moscow had three semi-official organizations reporting on America—the Communist party, Amtorg, and the Soviet Information Bureau. Criticism should therefore be directed not at recognition itself, but at the manner in which it was concluded.

Perhaps potentially the most profitable consequence of recognition was the experience in dealing with the government and diplomats of Russia, especially during the disheartening months from November 1933 to the autumn of 1935. In that period, America had the opportunity to study at first hand the conduct of Soviet foreign policy. Clearly revealed was Moscow's propensity for the clouding of central issues by resort to long and tedious arguments on peripheral points of misunderstanding. Evident likewise was the necessity of securing a simultaneous *sine qua non* for every concession to Russia. Promises for the future brought only frustration and tension. The facts of Soviet diplomacy, evidently unlearned by observation previous to recognition, should surely have been obvious to the United States Government after the events of the next years. But if they were understood and appreciated, they were forgotten by 1941. In the light of past experience, the United States should have entered the World War II alliance with Soviet Russia aware of the methods and principles of Soviet diplomacy and prepared to act accordingly.

Unfortunately, the lesson was badly learned. Many of the same mistakes were repeated at a time when the consequences of error were incomparably more disastrous. In all fairness, judgment should be tempered by an appreciation of the seriousness of the threat which drew the two nations together during the war years, and by the inevitable reservation that Soviet Russia might have pursued her postwar policy regardless of any measures taken by America and her other allies. But it is difficult to avoid the conclusion that a more practical, less idealistic approach to Russia during the Second World War was justified by the experiences of recognition and its aftermath.

APPENDICES

APPENDIX A

TABLE I

Trade of the USSR with the United States, Germany and Great Britain, 1921-1938 (in million rubles)*

Year	Export to U.S.	Import from U.S.	Export to Germ.	Import from Germ.	Export to G.B.	Import from G.B.
1921/22	0	193	36.2	367	78.8	233
1922/23	2.4	19.4	187	269	127	163
1923/24	31.5	223	291	198	358	214
1924/25	124	884	383	450	763	485
1925/26	134	535	489	771	850	567
1926/27	103	639	741	708	882	443
1927/28	123	822	815	1088	678	208
1928 (Oct. to Dec.)	38.9	130	231	213	205	29.4
1929	187	776	942	853	887	240
1930	179	1158	901	1099	1226	351
1931	99.4	1007	567	1799	1165	321
1932	75.3	139	440	1435	607	403
1933	61.2	72.6	376	649	381	134
1934	62.5	78.3	431	126	344	214
1935	116	129	289	95.1	378	190
1936	130	209	117	308	362	204
1937	134.4	244.3	107.7	200.5	566.1	192
1938	96.7	405.9	88.3	67.2	375.1	240.3

* Vnesh. torg. 20 let, 220-223, 226-229, 244-247; Alexander Baykov, Soviet Foreign Trade (Princeton, 1946), Appendix, Table VII.

TABLE II

Total Export and Import of the USSR, 1921-1938 (in million rubles) *

Year	Export	Import
1921	88.5	922.9
1922	357.4	1181.7
1923	954.8	627.2
1924	1476.1	1138.8
1925	2664.4	3620.9
1926	3173.7	3016.5
1927	3267.0	3320.5
1928	3518.9	4174.6
1929	4045.8	3857.0
1930	4539.3	4637.5
1931	3553.1	4839.9
1932	2518.2	3083.5
1933	2167.5	1525.1
1934	1832.4	1018.0
1935	1609.3	1057.2
1936	1359.1	1352.5
1937	1728.6	1341.3
1938	1331.9	1422.9

* *Vnesh. torg. 20 let*, 10; Alexander Baykov, *Soviet Foreign Trade* (Princeton, 1946), Appendix, Table I.

TABLE III

Trade of the United States with the USSR, 1921-1938 (Thousands of dollars) *

Year	Export to USSR	Import from USSR
1921	15,584	1,311
1922	29,896	964
1923	7,617	1,619
1924	42,103	8,168
1925	68,906	13,120
1926	49,906	14,122
1927	64,921	12,877
1928	74,091	14,025
1929	84,011	22,551

1930	114,399	24,386
1931	103,717	13,206
1932	12,641	9,736
1933	8,997	12,114
1934	15,011	12,337
1935	24,743	17,809
1936	33,427	20,517
1937	42,892	30,763
1938	69,691	24,034

* *Foreign Commerce and Navigation of the United States, 1922-1939,* *passim.*

APPENDIX B

Exchange of Letters between President Franklin D. Roosevelt of the United States and Mikhail Kalinin, President of the Central Executive Committee of the Union of Soviet Socialist Republics *

Washington, October 10, 1933.

My Dear Mr. President: Since the beginning of my Administration, I have contemplated the desirability of an effort to end the present abnormal relations between the hundred and twenty-five million people of the United States and the hundred and sixty million people of Russia.

It is most regrettable that these great peoples, between whom a happy tradition of friendship existed for more than a century to their mutual advantage, should now be without a practical method of communicating directly with each other.

The difficulties that have created this anomalous situation are serious but not, in my opinion, insoluble; and difficulties between great nations can be removed only by frank, friendly conversations. If you are of similar mind, I should be glad to receive any representatives you may designate to explore with me personally all questions outstanding between our countries.

Participation in such a discussion would, of course, not commit either nation to any future course of action, but would indicate a sincere desire to reach a satisfactory solution of the problems involved. It is my hope that such conversations might result in good to the people of both our countries.

I am [etc.]

Franklin D. Roosevelt

* *Foreign Relations, 1933,* ii, 794-795.

Moscow, October 17, 1933.

My Dear Mr. President: I have received your message of October tenth.

I have always considered most abnormal and regrettable a situation wherein, during the past sixteen years, two great republics—the United States of America and the Union of Soviet Socialist Republics—have lacked the usual methods of communication and have been deprived of the benefits which such communication could give. I am glad to note that you also reached the same conclusion.

There is no doubt that difficulties, present or arising, between two countries, can be solved only when direct relations exist between them; and that, on the other hand, they have no chance for solution in the absence of such relations. I shall take the liberty further to express the opinion that the abnormal situation, to which you correctly refer in your message, has an unfavorable effect not only on the interests of the two states concerned, but also on the general international situation, increasing the element of disquiet, complicating the process of consolidating world peace and encouraging forces tending to disturb that peace.

In accordance with the above, I gladly accept your proposal to send to the United States a representative of the Soviet Government to discuss with you the questions of interest to our countries. The Soviet Government will be represented by Mr. M. M. Litvinov,* People's Commissar for Foreign Affairs, who will come to Washington at a time to be mutually agreed upon.

I am [etc.]

Mikhail Kalinin

APPENDIX C

Memorandum on the debt question by President Franklin D. Roosevelt and Commissar of Foreign Affairs Maxim Litvinov at Washington on November 15, 1933†

Washington, November 15, 1933—2:45 p.m.

Mr. Litvinov, at a meeting with the President, the Acting

---

* The forms "Litvinov" and "Litvinoff" were both in common use in the transliteration of this name into English. The latter was the spelling which the Soviet Foreign Commisar himself used as his signature. The two spellings as used in the documents have been retained by the editors.

† *Foreign Relations, 1933,* ɪɪ, 804.

Secretary of the Treasury, and Mr. Bullitt, made a "gentleman's agreement" with the President that over and above all claims of the Soviet Government and its nationals against the Government of the United States and its nationals, the Soviet Government will pay to the Government of the United States on account of the Kerensky debt or otherwise a sum to be not less than $75,000,000 in the form of a percentage above the ordinary rate of interest on a loan to be granted to it by the Government of the United States or its nationals, all other claims of the Government of the United States or its nationals and of the Government of the Union of Soviet Socialist Republics or its nationals to be regarded as eliminated.

The President said that he believed confidently that he could persuade Congress to accept a sum of $150,000,000, but that he feared that Congress would not accept any smaller sum. Mr. Litvinov then said he could not on his own authority accept any such minimum, as his Government had already stated that it considered this sum excessive.

Mr. Litvinov said that he had entire confidence in the fair-mindedness of the President and felt sure that when the President had looked into the facts he would not feel that a sum greater than $75,000,000 was justified. So far as he personally was concerned, and without making any commitment, he would be inclined to advise his Government to accept $100,000,000 if the President should still consider such a sum fair.

Mr. Litvinov agreed to remain in Washington after resumption of relations and to discuss with Mr. Morgenthau and Mr. Bullitt the exact sum between the limits of $75,000,000 and $150,-000,000 to be paid by the Soviet Government.

M[axim] L[itvinoff]   F[ranklin] D. R[oosevelt]

APPENDIX D

Exchange of letters between President Franklin D. Roosevelt and Commissar of Foreign Affairs Maxim Litvinov coincident with the establishment of diplomatic relations between the United States and the Union of Soviet Socialist Republics at Washington, November 16, 1933*

Washington, November 16, 1933.

My Dear Mr. Litvinov: I am very happy to inform you that as

* *Foreign Relations, 1933*, II, 805-814.

a result of our conversations the Government of the United States has decided to establish normal diplomatic relations with the Government of the Union of Soviet Socialist Republics and to exchange ambassadors.

I trust that the relations now established between our peoples may forever remain normal and friendly, and that our nations henceforth may cooperate for their mutual benefit and for the preservation of the peace of the world.

I am [etc.]

Franklin D. Roosevelt

Washington, November 16, 1933.

My Dear Mr. President: I am very happy to inform you that the Government of the Union of Soviet Socialist Republics is glad to establish normal diplomatic relations with the Government of the United States and to exchange ambassadors.

I, too, share the hope that the relations now established between our peoples may forever remain normal and friendly, and that our nations henceforth may cooperate for their mutual benefit and for the preservation of the peace of the world.

I am [etc.]

Maxim Litvinoff

Washington, November 16, 1933.

My Dear Mr. President: I have the honor to inform you that coincident with the establishment of diplomatic relations between our two Governments it will be the fixed policy of the Government of the Union of Soviet Socialist Republics:

1. To respect scrupulously the indisputable right of the United States to order its own life within its own jurisdiction in its own way and to refrain from interfering in any manner in the internal affairs of the United States, its territories or possessions.

2. To refrain, and to restrain all persons in government service and all organizations of the Government or under its direct or indirect control, including the organizations in receipt of any financial assistance from it, from any act overt or covert liable in any way whatsoever to injure the tranquillity, prosperity, order, or security of the whole or any part of the United States, its territories or possessions, and in particular, from any act tending to incite or encourage armed intervention, or any agitation or propa-

ganda having as an aim, the violation of the territorial integrity of the United States, its territories or possessions, or the bringing about by force of a change in the political or social order of the whole or any part of the United States, its territories or possessions.

3. Not to permit the formation or residence on its territory of any organization or group—and to prevent the activity on its territory of any organization or group, or of representatives or officials of any organization or group—which makes claim to be the Government of, or makes attempt upon the territorial integrity of, the United States, its territories or possessions; not to form, subsidize, support or permit on its territory military organizations or groups having the aim of armed struggle against the United States, its territories or possessions, and to prevent any recruiting on behalf of such organizations and groups.

4. Not to permit the formation or residence on its territory of any organization or group—and to prevent the activity on its territory of any organization or group, or of representatives or officials of any organization or group—which has as an aim the overthrow or the preparation for the overthrow of, or the bringing about by force of a change in, the political or social order of the whole or any part of the United States, its territories or possessions.

I am [etc.]

Maxim Litvinoff

Washington, November 16, 1933.

My Dear Mr. Litvinov: I am glad to have received the assurance expressed in your note to me of this date that it will be the fixed policy of the Government of the Union of Soviet Socialist Republics:

[Here follows repetition of the four numbered paragraphs in Mr. Litvinov's note printed *supra*.]

It will be the fixed policy of the Executive of the United States within the limits of the powers conferred by the Constitution and the laws of the United States to adhere reciprocally to the engagements above expressed.

I am [etc.]

Franklin D. Roosevelt

Washington, November 16, 1933.

My Dear Mr. Litvinov: As I have told you in our recent conversations, it is my expectation that after the establishment of
normal relations between our two countries many Americans will
wish to reside temporarily or permanently within the territory of
the Union of Soviet Socialist Republics, and I am deeply concerned that they should enjoy in all respects the same freedom of
conscience and religious liberty which they enjoy at home.

As you well know, the Government of the United States, since
the foundation of the Republic, has always striven to protect its
nationals, at home and abroad, in the free exercise of liberty of
conscience and religious worship, and from all disability or persecution on account of their religious faith or worship. And I
need scarcely point out that the rights enumerated below are
those enjoyed in the United States by all citizens and foreign
nationals and by American nationals in all the major countries
of the world.

The Government of the United States, therefore, will expect
that nationals of the United States of America within the territory of the Union of Soviet Socialist Republics will be allowed
to conduct without annoyance or molestation of any kind religious
services and rites of a ceremonial nature, including baptismal,
confirmation, communion, marriage and burial rites, in the English language, or in any other language which is customarily used
in the practice of the religious faith to which they belong, in
churches, houses, or other buildings appropriate for such service,
which they will be given the right and opportunity to lease, erect
or maintain in convenient situations.

We will expect that nationals of the United States will have
the right to collect from their co-religionists and to receive from
abroad voluntary offerings for religious purposes; that they will
be entitled without restriction to impart religious instruction to
their children, either singly or in groups, or to have such instruction imparted by persons whom they may employ for such purpose; that they will be given and protected in the right to bury
their dead according to their religious customs in suitable and
convenient places established for that purpose, and given the right
and opportunity to lease, lay out, occupy and maintain such burial
grounds subject to reasonable sanitary laws and regulations.

We will expect that religious groups or congregations composed of nationals of the United States of America in the territory of the Union of Soviet Socialist Republics will be given the right to have their spiritual needs ministered to by clergymen, priests, rabbis or other ecclesiastical functionaries who are nationals of the United States of America, and that such clergymen, priests, rabbis or other ecclesiastical functionaries will be protected from all disability or persecution and will not be denied entry into the territory of the Soviet Union because of their ecclesiastical status.

I am [etc.]

Franklin D. Roosevelt

Washington, November 16, 1933.

My Dear Mr. President: In reply to your letter of November 16, 1933, I have the honor to inform you that the Government of the Union of Soviet Socialist Republics as a fixed policy accords the nationals of the United States within the territory of the Union of Soviet Socialist Republics the following rights referred to by you:

1. The right to "free exercise of liberty of conscience and religious worship" and protection "from all disability or persecution on account of their religious faith or worship."

This right is supported by the following laws and regulations existing in the various republics of the Union:

Every person may profess any religion or none. All restrictions of rights connected with the profession of any belief whatsoever, or with the non-profession of any belief, are annulled. (Decree of Jan. 23, 1918, art. 3.)

Within the confines of the Soviet Union it is prohibited to issue any local laws or regulations restricting or limiting freedom of conscience, or establishing privileges or preferential rights of any kind based upon the religious profession of any person. (Decree of Jan. 23, 1918, art. 2.)

2. The right to "conduct without annoyance or molestation of any kind religious services and rites of a ceremonial nature."

This right is supported by the following laws:

A free performance of religious rites is guaranteed as long as it does not interfere with public order and is not accompanied by interference with the rights of citizens of the Soviet Union. Local authorities possess the right in such cases to adopt all necessary measures to preserve public order and safety. (Decree of Jan. 23, 1918, art. 5.)

Interference with the performance of religious rites, in so far as they do not endanger public order and are not accompanied by infringements on the rights of others is punishable by compulsory labour for a period up to six months. (Criminal Code, art. 127.)

3. "The right and opportunity to lease, erect or maintain in convenient situations" churches, houses or other buildings appropriate for religious purposes.

This right is supported by the following laws and regulations:

Believers belonging to a religious society with the object of making provision for their requirements in the matter of religion may lease under contract, free of charge, from the Sub-District or District Executive Committee or from the Town Soviet, special buildings for the purpose of worship and objects intended exclusively for the purposes of their cult. (Decree of April 8, 1929, art. 10.)

Furthermore, believers who have formed a religious society or a group of believers may use for religious meetings other buildings which have been placed at their disposal on lease by private persons or by local Soviets and Executive Committees. All rules established for houses of worship are applicable to these buildings. Contracts for the use of such buildings shall be concluded by individual believers who will be held responsible for their execution. In addition, these buildings must comply with the sanitary and technical building regulations. (Decree of April 8, 1929, art. 10.)

The place of worship and religious property shall be handed over for the use of believers forming a religious society under a contract concluded in the name of the competent District Executive Committee or Town Soviet by the competent administrative department or branch, or directly by the Sub-District Executive Committee. (Decree of April 8, 1929, art. 15.)

The construction of new places of worship may take place at the desire of religious societies provided that the usual technical building regulations and the special regulations laid down by the People's Commissariat for Internal Affairs are observed. (Decree of April 8, 1929, art. 45.)

4. "The right to collect from their co-religionists . . .* voluntary offerings for religious purposes."

This right is supported by the following law:

Members of groups of believers and religious societies may raise subscriptions among themselves and collect voluntary offerings, both in the place of worship itself and outside it, but only amongst the members of the religious association concerned and only for purposes connected with the upkeep of the place of worship and the religious property, for the engagement of ministers of religion and for the expenses of their executive body. Any form of forced contribution in aid of religious associations is punishable under the Criminal Code. (Decree of April 8, 1929, art. 54.)

5. Right to "impart religious instruction to their children either singly or in groups or to have such instruction imparted by persons whom they may employ for such purpose."

This right is supported by the following law:

The school is separated from the Church. Instruction in religious doctrines is not permitted in any governmental and common schools, nor in private teaching institutions where general subjects are taught. Persons may give or receive religious instruction in a private manner. (Decree of Jan. 23, 1918, art. 9.)

Furthermore, the Soviet Government is prepared to include in a consular convention to be negotiated immediately following the establishment of relations between our two countries provisions in which nationals of the United States shall be granted rights with reference to freedom of conscience and the free exercise of religion which shall not be less favorable than those enjoyed in the Union of Soviet Socialist Republics by nationals of the nation most favored in this respect. In this connection, I have the honor to call to your attention Article 9 of the Treaty between Germany and the Union of Soviet Socialist Republics, signed at Moscow October 12, 1925, which reads as follows:

Nationals of each of the Contracting Parties . . .† shall be entitled to hold religious services in churches, houses or other buildings, rented according to the laws of the country, in their national language or in any other language which is customary in their religion. They shall be entitled to bury their dead in accordance

---

* Omission indicated in the original.

† Omission indicated in the original letter.

with their religious practice in burial-grounds established and maintained by them with the approval of the competent authorities, so long as they comply with the police regulations of the other Party in respect of buildings and public health.

Furthermore, I desire to state that the rights specified in the above paragraphs will be granted to American nationals immediately upon the establishment of relations between our two countries.

Finally, I have the honor to inform you that the Government of the Union of Soviet Socialist Republics, while reserving to itself the right of refusing visas to Americans desiring to enter the Union of Soviet Socialist Republics on personal grounds, does not intend to base such refusals on the fact of such persons having an ecclesiastical status.

I am [etc.]

Maxim Litvinoff

Washington, November 16, 1933.

My Dear Mr. President: Following our conversations I have the honor to inform you that the Soviet Government is prepared to include in a consular convention to be negotiated immediately following the establishment of relations between our two countries provisions in which nationals of the United States shall be granted rights with reference to legal protection which shall not be less favorable than those enjoyed in the Union of Soviet Socialist Republics by nationals of the nation most favored in this respect. Furthermore, I desire to state that such rights will be granted to American nationals immediately upon the establishment of relations between our two countries.

In this connection I have the honor to call to your attention Article 11 and the Protocol to Article 11, of the Agreement Concerning Conditions of Residence and Business and Legal Protection in General concluded between Germany and the Union of Soviet Socialist Republics on October 12, 1925.

Article 11

Each of the Contracting Parties undertakes to adopt the necessary measures to inform the consul of the other Party as soon as possible whenever a national of the country which he represents is arrested in his district.

The same procedure shall apply if a prisoner is transferred from one place of detention to another.

Final Protocol

Ad Article 11.

1. The consul shall be notified either by a communication from the person arrested or by the authorities themselves direct. Such communications shall be made within a period not exceeding seven times twenty-four hours, and in large towns, including capitals of districts, within a period not exceeding three times twenty-four hours.

2. In places of detention of all kinds, requests made by consular representatives to visit nationals of their country under arrest, or to have them visited by their representatives, shall be granted without delay. The consular representative shall not be entitled to require officials of the courts or prisons to withdraw during his interview with the person under arrest.

I am [etc.]

Maxim Litvinoff

Washington, November 16, 1933.

My Dear Mr. Litvinov: I thank you for your letter of November 16, 1933, informing me that the Soviet Government is prepared to grant to nationals of the United States rights with reference to legal protection not less favorable than those enjoyed in the Union of Soviet Socialist Republics by nationals of the nation most favored in this respect. I have noted the provisions of the treaty and protocol concluded between Germany and the Union of Soviet Socialist Republics on October 12, 1925.

I am glad that nationals of the United States will enjoy the protection afforded by these instruments immediately upon the establishment of relations between our countries and I am fully prepared to negotiate a consular convention covering these subjects as soon as practicable. Let me add that American diplomatic and consular officers in the Soviet Union will be zealous in guarding the rights of American nationals, particularly the right to a fair, public and speedy trial and the right to be represented by counsel of their choice. We shall expect that the nearest American diplomatic or consular officer shall be notified immediately of any arrest or detention of an American national, and that he shall promptly be afforded the opportunity to communicate and converse with such national.

I am [etc.]

Franklin D. Roosevelt

[Washington, November 16, 1933.]

In reply to a question of the President in regard to prosecutions for economic espionage, Mr. Litvinov gave the following explanation:

"The widespread opinion that the dissemination of economic information from the Union of Soviet Socialist Republics is allowed only in so far as this information has been published in newspapers or magazines, is erroneous. The right to obtain economic information is limited in the Union of Soviet Socialist Republics, as in other countries, only in the case of business and production secrets and in the case of the employment of forbidden methods (bribery, theft, fraud, etc.) to obtain such information. The category of business and production secrets naturally includes the official economic plans, in so far as they have not been made public, but not individual reports concerning the production conditions and the general conditions of individual enterprises.

"The Union of Soviet Socialist Republics has also no reason to complicate or hinder the critical examination of its economic organization. It naturally follows from this that every one has the right to talk about economic matters or to receive information about such matters in the Union, in so far as the information for which he has asked or which has been imparted to him is not such as may not, on the basis of special regulations issued by responsible officials or by the appropriate state enterprises, be made known to outsiders. (This principle applies primarily to information concerning economic trends and tendencies.)"

Washington, November 16, 1933.

My Dear Mr. President: Following our conversations I have the honor to inform you that the Government of the Union of Soviet Socialist Republics agrees that, preparatory to a final settlement of the claims and counter claims between the Governments of the Union of Soviet Socialist Republics and the United States of America and the claims of their nationals, the Government of the Union of Soviet Socialist Republics will not take any steps to enforce any decisions of courts or initiate any new litigations for the amounts admitted to be due or that may be found to be due it as the successor of prior Governments of Russia, or otherwise, from American nationals, including corporations, companies, partnerships, or associations, and also the claim against the United

States of the Russian Volunteer Fleet, now in litigation in the United States Court of Claims, and will not object to such amounts being assigned and does hereby release and assign all such amounts to the Government of the United States, the Government of the Union of Soviet Socialist Republics to be duly notified in each case of any amount realized by the Government of the United States from such release and assignment.

The Government of the Union of Soviet Socialist Republics further agrees, preparatory to the settlement referred to above not to make any claim with respect to:

(a) judgments rendered or that may be rendered by American courts in so far as they relate to property, or rights, or interests therein, in which the Union of Soviet Socialist Republics or its nationals may have had or may claim to have an interest; or,

(b) acts done or settlements made by or with the Government of the United States, or public officials in the United States, or its nationals, relating to property, credits, or obligations of any Government of Russia or nationals thereof.

I am [etc.]

Maxim Litvinoff

Washington, November 16, 1933.

My Dear Mr. Litvinov: I am happy to acknowledge the receipt of your letter of November 16, 1933, in which you state that:

[Here follows quotation of statement made by Mr. Litvinov in his note printed *supra*.]

I am glad to have these undertakings by your Government and I shall be pleased to notify your Government in each case of any amount realized by the Government of the United States from the release and assignment to it of the amounts admitted to be due, or that may be found to be due, the Government of the Union of Soviet Socialist Republics, and of the amount that may be found to be due on the claim of the Russian Volunteer Fleet.

I am [etc.]

Franklin D. Roosevelt

Washington, November 16, 1933.

My Dear Mr. President: I have the honor to inform you that,

following our conversations and following my examination of certain documents of the years 1918 to 1921 relating to the attitude of the American Government toward the expedition into Siberia, the operations there of foreign military forces and the inviolability of the territory of the Union of Soviet Socialist Republics, the Government of the Union of Soviet Socialist Republics agrees that it will waive any and all claims of whatsoever character arising out of activities of military forces of the United States in Siberia, or assistance to military forces in Siberia subsequent to January 1, 1918, and that such claims shall be regarded as finally settled and disposed of by this agreement.

I am [etc.]

Maxim Litvinoff

In addition to the agreements which we have signed today, there has taken place an exchange of views with regard to methods of settling all outstanding questions of indebtedness and claims that permits us to hope for a speedy and satisfactory solution of these questions which both our Governments desire to have out of the way as soon as possible.

Mr. Litvinov will remain in Washington for several days for further discussions.

BIBLIOGRAPHY

PRIVATE PAPERS

The Herbert Hoover Archives. Hoover Institute and Library, Stanford University, California.
The Franklin D. Roosevelt Papers. The Franklin D. Roosevelt Library, Hyde Park, New York.

OFFICIAL PUBLICATIONS

Anglo-sovetskie otnosheniia so dnia podpisaniia torgovogo soglasheniia do razryva (1921-1927 gg.), noty i dokumenty. Narkomindel. Moscow, 1927.
Annuaire diplomatique du Commissariat du Peuple pour les Affaires Etrangères pour l'année 1933. Septième livraison. Narkomindel. Moscow, 1933.
Bullitt, William Christian, *The Establishment of Normal Relations Between the United States and the Union of Soviet Socialist Republics.* Address before the Chamber of Commerce of Philadelphia, January 19, 1934. Department of State. Washington, 1934.
Congressional Record, 68th Congress, 73rd Congress, 74th Congress. Washington, 1924, 1933-1934, 1935-1936.
Documentation Relating to the Foreign Economic Relations of the USSR. Prepared for the World Economic Conference in London June 1933. Moscow, 1933.
Establishment of Diplomatic Relations with the Union of Soviet Socialist Republics. Department of State. Washington, 1933.
xv *let bor'by za monopoliiu vneshnei torgovli.* Institut mirovogo khoziaistva i mirovoi politiki komakademii i nauchno-issledovatel'skii institut monopolii vneshnei torgovli. Moscow, 1932.
Foreign Commerce and Navigation of the United States, 1921-1939. Department of Commerce. Washington, 1922-1940.
"Investigation of Communist Propaganda," *House Reports,* No. 2290, 71st Congress, 3rd Session, January 17, 1931. Washington, 1931.
League of Nations Official Journal. Vol. 3. Geneva, 1933.
Loans to Foreign Governments, Senate Document No. 86, 67th Congress, 2nd Session. Washington, 1921.
Memorandum on Certain Aspects of the Bolshevik Movement in Russia. Department of State. Washington, 1919.

Kliuchnikov, Iu., and Andrei Sabanin, eds., *Mezhdunarodnaia politika noveishego vremeni v dogovorakh, notakh i deklaratsiiakh.* 3 v. Moscow, 1925-1928.

Mezhdunarodnaia Zhizn. Zhurnal narodnogo komissariata po inostrannym delam. Narkomindel. Moscow, 1925-1930.

Moore, Robert Walton, *Recognition of the Union of Soviet Socialist Republics.* Radio address by Robert Walton Moore, Assistant Secretary of State, November 22, 1933. Department of State. Washington, 1934.

Papers Relating to the Foreign Relations of the United States
———— 1918, *Russia.* 3 v. Washington, 1931-1932.
———— 1919, *Russia.* Washington, 1937.
———— 1920. 3 v. Washington, 1935-1936.
———— 1921. 2 v. Washington, 1936.
———— 1923. 2 v. Washington, 1938.
———— 1929. 3 v. Washington, 1943-1944.
———— 1931. 3 v. Washington, 1946.
———— 1932. 5 v. Washington, 1948.
———— 1933. 4 v. published. Washington, 1949-1950.
———— 1934. 4 v. published. Washington, 1950-1951.
———— *The Soviet Union 1933-1939.* Washington, 1952.

Paton, G. P., *The Organization of Foreign Trade of the Union of Soviet Socialist Republics.* Report by the Commercial Counselor to His Majesty's Embassy in Moscow. London, 1931.

Press Releases. Vols. IX-XIII. Department of State. Washington, 1934-1936.

Records of the Conference for the Reduction and Limitation of Armaments. Series C, v. II. League of Nations. Geneva, 1936.

Sbornik deistvuiushchikh dogovorov, soglashenii i konventsii, zakliuchennykh s inostrannymi gosudarstvami. 8 v. Narkomindel. Moscow, 1925-1935.

The Sorge Spy Ring: A Case Study in International Espionage in the Far East. U.S. Department of the Army [?]. Washington, 1948 [?].

Sovetsko-amerikanskie otnosheniia. Sbornik dokumentov po mezhdunarodnoi politike i mezhdunarodnomu pravu, No. 9, Narkomindel. Moscow, 1934.

Sovetsko-kitaiskii konflikt, 1929 g.: sbornik dokumentov. Narkomindel. Moscow, 1930.

Torgovye otnosheniia SSSR s kapitalisticheskimi stranami. Nauchno-issledovatel'skii institut monopolii vneshnei torgovli. Moscow, 1938.

Treasury Decisions. Vols. LVII-LXV. Treasury Department. Washington, 1930-1934.

BIBLIOGRAPHY

Vestnik narodnogo komissariata inostrannykh del. Narkomindel. Moscow, 1921.

Vneshniaia torgovlia SSSR za 20 let, 1918-1937 gg.: statisti- cheskii spravochnik. S. N. Bakulin and D. D. Mishustin, eds. Nauchno-issledovatel'skii institut monopolii vneshnei tor- govli. Moscow, 1939.

Vneshniaia torgovlia sovetskogo soiuza. D. D. Mishustin, ed. Naucho-issledovatel'skii institut monopolii vneshnei torgovli. Moscow, 1938.

Zhirmunskii, M. M., *Organizatsiia i tekhnika sovetskogo eks- porta.* Nauchno-issledovatel'skii institut monopolii vneshnei torgovli. Moscow, 1935.

OFFICIAL COMINTERN RECORDS

VII *Congress of the Communist International: Abridged Steno- graphic Record of the Proceedings.* Moscow, 1939.

Kommunisticheskii internatsional v dokumentakh: resheniia, tezisy, i vozzvanie kongressov kominterna i plenumov IKKI, *1919- 1932.* Bela Kun, ed. Moscow, 1933.

XII *plenum* IKKI: *stenograficheskii otchet.* 3 v. Moscow, 1933.

XIII *plenum* IKKI: *stenograficheskii otchet.* Moscow, 1934.

AUTOBIOGRAPHIES, DIARIES, MEMOIRS AND COLLECTED WORKS

Baker, Ray Stannard, and William E. Dodd, eds., *War and Peace: Presidential Messages, Addresses, and Public Papers (1917-1924) by Woodrow Wilson.* 2 v. New York, 1927.

Bessedovsky, Grigory, *Revelations of a Soviet Diplomat.* London, 1931.

The Bullitt Mission to Russia: Testimony Before the Committee on Foreign Relations United States Senate of William C. Bullitt. New York, 1920.

Davies, Joseph E., *Mission to Moscow.* New York, 1941.

Dodd, William E., Jr., and Martha Dodd, eds., *Ambassador Dodd's Diary, 1933-1938.* New York, 1941.

Farley, James A., *Jim Farley's Story: The Roosevelt Years.* New York, 1948.

Fischer, Louis, *Men and Politics: An Autobiography.* New York, 1941.

Gitlow, Benjamin, *The Whole of Their Lives.* New York, 1948.

Graves, William Sidney, *America's Siberian Adventure, 1918- 1920.* New York, 1931.

Grew, Joseph C., *Ten Years in Japan.* New York, 1944.

Harper, Samuel N., *The Russia I Believe In.* Chicago, 1945.

Hull, Cordell, *The Memoirs of Cordell Hull.* 2 v. New York, 1948.
Lenin, V. I., *Sochineniia.* 2nd edition. Vol. xxvi. Moscow, 1930.
Litvinov, Maxim, *The Soviets Fight for Disarmament.* With Introduction by M. Lunacharsky. New York, 1932.
—————— *Vneshniaia politika SSSR: rechi i zaiavleniia, 1927-1935.* Moscow, 1935.
Molotov, V. M., *Stat'i i rechi, 1935-1936.* Moscow, 1937.
Roosevelt, Eleanor, *This I Remember.* New York, 1949.
Roosevelt, Franklin D., *The Public Papers and Addresses of Franklin D. Roosevelt.* 13 v. New York, 1938-1950.
Stimson, Henry L. and McGeorge Bundy, *On Active Service in Peace and War.* New York, 1947.
The Stalin-Howard Interview. Recorded by K. Umansky. New York, 1936.
Tchernavin, Vladimir, *I Speak for the Silent Prisoners of the Soviets.* Boston, 1935.
Trotskii, L., *Kak vooruzhalas revoliutsiia.* 3 v. in 5 parts. Moscow, 1924.

ARTICLES

Bullitt, William C., "How We Won the War and Lost the Peace," Part i, *Life*, August 30, 1948, 83-97.
Furniss, Edgar S., "Soviet Diplomatic Successes," *Current History*, xxxviii (1933), 757-761.
Girshfeld, A., "O roli SShA v organizatsii antisovetskoi interventsii v Sibiri i na Dalnem Vostoke," *Voprosy Istorii*, No. 8 (August, 1948), 3-22.
Graham, Malbone S., "Russian-American Relations, 1917-1933: An Interpretation," *American Political Science Review*, xxviii (1934), 387-409.
Höffding, W., "German Trade with the Soviet Union," *The Slavonic (and East European) Review*, xiv (1936), 473-494.
Katayama, Sen, "Iaponskii imperializm i voina," *Kommunisticheskii Internatsional*, July 20, 1933, 19-23.
Kedrosta (pseud.), "Vybory v Amerikanskikh Soedinennykh Shtatakh," *Mezhdunarodnaia Zhizn*, No. 1 (1925), 44-57.
Kuusinen, O., "Mezhdunarodnoe polozhenie i zadachi sektsii kominterna," *Bol'shevik*, November 1, 1932, 1-18; November 15, 1932, 28-38; December 31, 1932, 12-34.
Landa, M., "Etapy, itogi i perspektivy vneshne-torgovykh otnoshenii mezhdu SSSR i SASSh," *XV let bor'by za monopliiu vneshnei torgovli.* Institut mirovogo khoziaistva i mirovoi politiki komakademii i nauchno-issledovatel'skii institut monopolii vneshnei torgovli. Moscow, 1932.

Mad'iar, L., "SSSR i kapitalisticheskie strany na ekonomicheskoi konferentsii," *Kommunisticheskii Internatsional*, July 10, 1933, 34-39.

Martin, Charles S., "Some Observations on the Recognition of Russia," *Proceedings of the Institute of World Affairs*, XI (1933), 24-50.

Morgenthau, Henry, Jr., "The Morgenthau Diaries," Part III, *Colliers*, October 11, 1947, 20-21, 72-79.

Mohrenschildt, Dmitri von, "American Intelligentsia and Russia of the N. E. P.," *The Russian Review*, VI, No. 2 (1947), 59-66.

Ostrinsky, D., "Five Billion Dollar Customer," *Forum*, XC (1933), 131-136.

Palme-Dutt, R., "Britanskii imperializm, fashizm i antisovetskaia kampaniia," *Kommunisticheskii Internatsional*, July 20, 1933, 46-54.

Radek, Karl, "Mezhdunarodnye protivorechiia v 1932 godu," *Bol'shevik*, November 30, 1932, 50-64.

————, "The Basis of Soviet Foreign Policy," *Foreign Affairs*, XII (1934), 193-206.

————, "The War in the Far East: A Soviet View," *Foreign Affairs*, X (1932), 541-557.

Ropes, E. C., "American-Soviet Trade Relations," *The Russian Review*, III, No. 1 (1943), 89-94.

Safarov, G., "Bor'ba za novyi razdel Kitaia," *Bol'shevik*, August 31, 1933, 72-83.

Serebrianskii, E., "Prinuditel'nyi trud v istorii SASSh," *Bor'ba Klassov*, No. 2 (1931), 90-95.

Stalin, I., "Gospodin Kempbell priviraet," *Bol'shevik*, November 30, 1932, 10-16.

Turin, S. P., "Foreign Trade of the USSR," *The Slavonic (and East European) Review*, X (1931-1932), 338-343.

Val'ter, D., "Russkii vopros v Amerike," *Mezhdunarodnaia Zhizn*, No. 4-5 (1925), 44-57.

Varga, E., "Chem ob'iasniaetsia, neudachnyi iskhod londonskoi konferentsii," *Bol'shevik*, August 16, 1933, 97-105.

————, "O iapono-amerikanskikh protivorechiiakh," *Bol'shevik*, April 30, 1934, 53-63.

Voitinskii, G., E. Iolk, and N. Nasonov, "Sobytiia na Dalnem Vostoke i opasnost voiny," *Bol'shevik*, March 31, 1932, 42-55.

NEWSPAPERS

Boston Evening Transcript, 1933.
Christian Science Monitor, 1933.

243

BIBLIOGRAPHY

Commercial and Financial Chronicle (New York), 1933.
Daily Worker (New York), 1929-1935.
Ekonomicheskaia Zhizn (Moscow), 1932-1935.
Izvestia (Moscow), 1929-1935.
Japan Times and Mail (Tokyo), 1933.
Journal of Commerce (New York), 1933.
Krasnaia Zvezda (Moscow), November, 1933.
Manchester Guardian Weekly, November, 1933.
New Leader (New York), 1933.
New York Times, 1929-1935.
New York World-Telegram, March 4, 1936.
Pravda (Moscow), April 27, 1926, September 15, 1927, 1929-1935.
San Francisco Chronicle, November, 1933.
Sotsialisticheskoe Zemledelie (Moscow), November, 1933.
Trans-Pacific (Tokyo), November, 1933-January, 1934.
Trud (Moscow), November, 1933.
United States News (Washington, D.C.), 1933.
Wall Street Journal (New York), 1933.
Le Temps (Paris), November, 1933.
Times (London), June-November, 1933.
Za Industrializatsiiu (Moscow), 1932-1935.

PERIODICALS

American Federationist (Washington, D.C.), September, 1930, 1933.
Bol'shevik (Moscow), 1929-1935.
Bor'ba Klassov (Moscow), 1931.
Business Week (New York), 1932-1933.
Catholic World (New York), 1933.
Commonweal (New York), 1933.
The Commonwealth (San Francisco), May, 1932.
Communist International (Moscow), January 5, 1935.
Congressional Digest (Washington, D.C.), October, 1933.
Current History (New York), 1933-1934.
Economic Review of the Soviet Union (New York), 1929-1935.
Forbes (New York), November-December, 1933.
Forum (New York), 1933.
International Press Correspondence (Berlin, Basel), 1932-1933.
Kommunisticheskii Internatsional (Moscow), 1929-1935.
Literary Digest (New York), 1932-1935.
Living Age (New York), 1933.
Magazine of Wall Street (New York), 1933.
National Republic (Washington, D.C.), 1933.
Nation (New York), 1932-1933.

244

New Republic (New York), 1933.
Quarterly Review, USSR Chamber of Commerce (Moscow), 1932.
Russian Review (New York), 1943, 1947.
Slavonic (and East European) Review (London), 1931-1932, 1935-1936.
Sotsialisticheskii Vestnik (Paris), 1933.
Soviet Russia Today (New York), 1932-1935.
Soviet Union Review (Washington, D.C.), 1930-1934.

SECONDARY WORKS

American Foundation, Committee on American-Russian Relations, *The United States and the Soviet Union.* New York, 1933.
Baykov, Alexander, *Soviet Foreign Trade.* Princeton, 1946.
Beloff, Max, *The Foreign Policy of Soviet Russia, 1929-1941.* 2 v. London, 1947-1949.
Borkenau, F., *The Communist International.* London, 1938.
Campbell, Thomas D., *Russia, Market or Menace?* New York, 1932.
Carr, Edward Hallett, *German-Soviet Relations Between Two World Wars, 1919-1939.* Baltimore, 1951.
Chamberlin, William Henry, *The Russian Revolution, 1917-1921.* 2 v. New York, 1935.
Coates, William Payton, and Zelda K. Coates, *A History of Anglo-Soviet Relations.* London, 1943.
Condoide, M. V., *Russian-American Trade.* Ohio State University (Columbus, Ohio), 1946.
Dallin, David J., *Soviet Russia and the Far East.* New Haven, 1948.
Davis, Kathryn Wasserman, *The Soviets at Geneva: The USSR and the League of Nations 1919-1933.* Geneva, 1934.
Dulles, Foster Rhea, *The Road to Teheran: The Story of Russia and America, 1781-1943.* Princeton, 1944.
Fischer, Louis, *The Soviets in World Affairs: A History of Relations Between the Soviet Union and the Rest of the World.* 2 v. London, 1930. (2 v. Princeton, 1951. A reissue with a new introduction.)
————, *Why Recognize Russia?* New York, 1931.
Fisher, Harold H., *The Famine in Soviet Russia, 1919-1923.* Stanford University, California, 1935.
Griswold, Alfred Whitney, *The Far Eastern Policy of the United States.* New York, 1938.
Hoetzsch, Otto, *Le caractère et la situation internationale de l'Union des Soviets.* Genève, 1932.
Huntington, William Chapin, *The Prospects of British and American Trade with the Soviet Union.* Monographs No. 7 and 8,

School of Slavonic and East European Studies in the University of London. London, 1935.

Johnson, Claudius O., *Borah of Idaho*. New York, 1936.

Kantorovich, Anatolii, *Amerika v bor'be za Kitai*. Moscow, 1935.

Kornev, N., *Litvinov*. Moscow, 1936.

Lovenstein, Meno, *American Opinion of Soviet Russia*. Washington, D.C., 1933.

Lovestone, Jay, *Soviet Foreign Policy and the World Revolution*. New York, 1935.

Mahaney, Wilbur Lee, Jr., *The Soviet Union, the League of Nations and Disarmament, 1917-1935*. University of Pennsylvania, 1940.

Milioukov, P., *La politique extérieure des Soviets*. 2nd ed. Paris, 1936.

Moore, Harriet, *Soviet Far Eastern Policy, 1931-1935*. Princeton, 1935.

Moore, John Bassett, *Candor and Common Sense. An Address Before the Association of the Bar of the City of New York, December 4, 1930*. New York, 1930.

Moyer, George Samuel, *Attitude of the United States Toward the Recognition of Soviet Russia*. Philadelphia, 1926.

Myers, William Starr, *The Foreign Policies of Herbert Hoover, 1929-1933*. New York, 1940.

Pavlovich, Mikhail, *Sovetskaia Rossiia i kapitalisticheskaia Amerika*. Moscow, 1922.

Pim, Sir Alan, and Edward Bateson, *Report on Russian Timber Camps*. London, 1931.

Pope, Arthur Upham, *Maxim Litvinoff*. New York, 1943.

Potemkin, V. P., ed., *Istoria diplomatii*. 3 v. Moscow, 1941-1945.

Rozenholtz, A., *Foreign Trade and Economic Independence of the USSR*. Moscow, 1935.

Rubinshtein, N. L., *Sovetskaia diplomatiia v bor'be protiv izoliatsii SSSR i ustanovlenie diplomaticheskikh otnoshenii s kapitalisticheskimi stranami*. Moscow, 1947.

Schuman, Frederick Lewis, *American Policy Toward Russia Since 1917*. New York, 1928.

Shapiro, Leonard, *Soviet Treaty Series: A Collection of Bilateral Treaties, Agreements and Conventions, etc., Concluded Between the Soviet Union and Foreign Powers*. Vol. I, 1917-1928. Washington, D.C., 1950.

Stoupnitzky, A., *Statut international de l'U.R.S.S.: état commerçant*. Paris, 1936.

Tompkins, Pauline, *American-Russian Relations in the Far East*. New York, 1949.

BIBLIOGRAPHY

Walsh, Edmund A., *The Last Stand: An Interpretation of the Soviet Five Year Plan.* Boston, 1931.

White, John Albert, *The Siberian Intervention.* Princeton, 1950.

Williams, Benjamin H., *Foreign Loan Policy of the United States Since 1933.* New York, 1939.

Yanson, J. D., *Foreign Trade in the USSR.* London, 1934.

INDEX

Afghanistan, 143

Alexander I, 4

Amalgamated Clothing Workers, 39n

American Committee on Religious Rights and Minorities, 114n

American Communist party. *See* Communist party of the United States

American Federation of Labor, opposes recognition of Russia, 22, 39, 79, 84, 121, 169-170

American Foundation, Committee on Russian-American Relations, conducts newspaper poll on recognition, 85, 119

American Labor Delegation to Russia, 24

American Legion, opposes Soviet recognition, 84, 121

American Relief Administration, 22; administers famine aid to Russia, 20; Soviet evaluations of, 21, 21n

American-Russian Chamber of Commerce, 37, 152; favors resumption of relations with Russia, 82

American Women's Committee for the Recognition of Russia, 82

Amtorg, 29n, 37, 103; establishment of, 26; propagandizes Soviet market, 42-44; receives RFC loan, 92; and prerecognition negotiations, 101-102

Anderson, Sherwood, 161

Angriff, 167

Archangel. *See* Intervention

Arcos, 25

Arcos-America, 25

Asahi, 125, 167, 199n

Bakhmetev, Boris, 14, 135

Baltimore Sun, 172

Belgium, 35

Berengaria, 128, 129

Bertron, S. L., 40

Bessedovsky, Grigory, 53

Bogdanov, Peter, 43

Bol'shevik, 198

Bolshevik *coup d'état* of November 7, 1917, 3, 135

Bolsheviks. *See* Communist party of Russia, communism, and Third International

Borah, William, 56, 69; advocates Soviet recognition, 21, 39, 78, 82-83

Bor'ba Klassov, 36

Borev, N., 160

Boston Evening Transcript, 121, 170

Brest-Litovsk, Peace of, and Soviet-American relations, 5-7

Bromley, John, 58

Brookhart, Smith W., 171n

Brooklyn Eagle, 31

Brooklyn *Tablet*, 83-84

Browder, Earl, speaks at Seventh Comintern Congress, 205n, 210; attends Thirteenth Plenum of Comintern, 209

Brown, Neil S., Bullitt plagiarizes dispatch of, 212

Brown, Walter L., 20

Budd, Ralph, 37

Buell, Raymond L., 81

Bullitt, William C., 161, 165n, 177, 198; mission to Russia in 1919, 11-12; at London Economic Conference, 90, 92, 105; prerecognition activities of, 100, 102, 104, 113, 115ff, 128; and reasons for recognition, 111, 112n; and the recognition negotiations, 131, 133ff; appointed ambassador to the USSR, 150-151; presents credentials to Kalinin, 162-163; welcomed to Moscow, 163-164; and the debt negotiations, 135ff, 182ff; signs trade agreement with Soviets, 195; voices hope recognition will promote peace, 197; and the suggested Soviet-American nonaggression pact, 200-201; views of on Soviet Far Eastern policy, 202-203, 213; and the Seventh Comintern Congress, 206ff; disillusioned over results of

American opinion on in the 1920's,
21-22; Litvinov urges, 22, 91, 94;
influence of First Five Year Plan
on, 28ff; influence of depression
on, 30ff; and the American press,
31, 57, 80-81, 85-86, 119-122,
169-174; and Congress, 31, 38-
39, 59, 71, 78, 82-83; and the
Communist threat, 32, 39, 73,
78-79, 82-85, 104-106; effect on
of drop in trade after 1931, 37ff,
48, 91, 108; President Hoover's
opposition to, 39-41, 69, 75-76,
79; and the Soviet press, 41-42,
57-59, 80-81, 86, 87-89, 122-123,
148-150, 153-156, 159-161; urged
by Amtorg to facilitate trade, 42-
44; effect of Japanese Far Eastern activities on, 51ff, 65ff, 70-
71, 72-73, 80-81, 87-88, 95-98,
103, 107, 108-110, 118-119, 123-
126, 128, 129, 146-147; rumors
of, 58; and Communist theory and
practice, 60ff; and the resumption
of Sino-Soviet relations, 65ff; and
the election of 1932, 75-81; campaign for gains momentum after
Roosevelt election, 82-83; and Soviet "respectability," 83, 91, 95,
103, 207; acts of Roosevelt which
encouraged advocates of, 86ff,
97-98; and Hitlerism, 111-112;
Roosevelt works toward, 99ff;
reasons for, 108-112; American
public opinion on immediately
preceding, 119-122; procedure
for, 102, 104-106, 112ff, 128, 132,
138, 140-141, 148; preparation
of American public for, 112-113;
and religious guarantees, 113-
114, 128, 131, 132, 144, 230-234;
and legal guarantees, 114, 131,
145, 234-235; and "economic
espionage," 114, 145, 236; invitation to discuss issued and accepted, 117; and debts (*see* debts
and claims); and the foreign
press, 123-125, 165-168; and noninterference guarantees, 128, 131,
132, 142-144, 149-150, 157-158,
174-175, 205ff, 228-229; negotiations leading to, 130ff; granted, 141; terms of, 142ff, 225-238;
treatment of by Soviet information media, 148-150; opposition
to, 12-13, 21-22, 39-40, 68-69,

78-80, 82-85, 92, 101, 104, 121-
122, 144, 170, 190; first reactions to, 153ff; brings hopes of
closer diplomatic collaboration,
197-198; effect of on Far East,
198-199, 200; assessed, 212, 213,
214ff
Reconstruction Finance Corporation,
120; extends loan to USSR, 91-93
Red Army, 55
Reed, John, 52, 165n
Robins, Raymond, 6, 161
Robinson, Arthur, 82
Robinson, Joseph T., 39, 71
Roman Catholic Church, and the
recognition question, 22, 39, 170
Roosevelt, Eleanor, 114
Roosevelt, Franklin D., 74, 75, 86,
97, 163-164, 176, 182, 183, 187,
197-198, 212; and the recognition issue during 1932 campaign,
75ff; presidential acts of encourage recognition hopes, 86ff; attitude of toward recognition, 99,
108-112; begins work toward recognition, 100ff; issues invitation
to Kalinin, 117, 225; receives Litvinov, 139; takes over negotiations with Litvinov, 132ff; signs
recognition correspondence, 141;
praised by Soviet leaders, 163-
164; speaks on recognition, 175;
assessed by Third International,
209n; and the Seventh Comintern Congress, 205n, 212; and
the debt negotiations, 138-140,
186
Root Mission, 40
Rozenholtz, A., 191
Rubinshtein, N. L., 21n
Rumania, 35
Russian Communist party. *See* Communist party of Russia

Sabath, Adolph, 38
Sakhalin Island, 199
San Francisco Chronicle, 120, 173
Schuman, Fredrick L., 58
Second Five Year Plan, 43, 93, 181
Seiberling Rubber Company, 30
Seventh Congress of the Comintern.
See Third International
Shiratori, Toshio, 71, 124-125
Siberia, 8, 9, 19, 50, 54-55, 61, 136,
146-147. *See also* Japan, Inter-
vention, debts and claims